DAYS OF Freedom

Divrei Torah on Pesach, Sefira, and Shavuos from TorahWeb.org
1999 - 2018

With contributions by

RABBI HERSHEL SCHACHTER, RABBI DR. ABRAHAM J. TWERSKI,
RABBI YAKOV HABER, RABBI ELIAKIM KOENIGSBERG
RABBI YAAKOV NEUBURGER, RABBI MICHAEL ROSENSWEIG,
RABBI YONASON SACKS, RABBI ZVI SOBOLOFSKY,
RABBI DANIEL STEIN, RABBI MAYER TWERSKY,
RABBI MORDECHAI WILLIG & RABBI BENJAMIN YUDIN

Copyright © 2019 The TorahWeb Foundation

No part of this publication may be translated, reproduced, stored in a retrieval system, or transmitted in any form or by any means, electronic, mechanical, photocopying, recording, or otherwise, without prior permission in writing from both the copyright holder and the publisher.

Please send any suggestions, comments, or questions to TorahWeb@TorahWeb.org

All rights reserved
ISBN: 978-0-57846-447-3

Hyman & Ann Arbesfeld

Young Israel of Woodmere
IS PROUD TO HONOR

THE
Y.U. ROSHEI YESHIVA

DEDICATED BY

Congregation Bnai Yeshurun

TEANECK, NEW JERSEY

RABBI STEVEN PRUZANSKY

ETHAN KEISER, PRESIDENT

In Appreciation and Recognition of
Rabbi and Rebetzin Mordechai and Feigi Willig
For 45 years of Dedication and Devotion
to the Young Israel of Riverdale
and the Riverdale Community

Young Israel of Riverdale
Raphael Rosenbaum President
Marty Katzenstein Chairman of the Board

לעילוי נשמת
הרב יעקב ב"ר משה הלוי ז"ל ווילינ
מרת עלא בת הרב דוד הכהן ע"ה ווילינ
הרב יעקב אהרון ב"ר אברהם אליעזר ז"ל הייזלער
מרת חיה שרה בת ר' אלימלך ע"ה הייזלער

Congregation Ohr HaTorah
36 Rector Court, Bergenfield, NJ 07621
201-244-5905 • www.ohrhatorah.com

In dedication to our Rav and Rebbetzin

Rav Zvi & Dr. Efrat Sobolofsky

May you continue your wonderful work on behalf of our shul, the greater Teaneck/Bergenfield community, and Klal Yisrael in general, ad meah v'esrim.

Congregation Ohr HaTorah

Rabbi Zvi Sobolofsky
Mara D'asra

Gabe Hanauer
President

Yechiel Stobezki
1st Vice President

Yitz Novak
2nd Vice President

Avrami Tabacznik
Treasurer

Naftali Rothman
Secretary

Judah Eizikovitz
Aaron Kopstick
Josh Rozenberg
Michele Moskowitz
Board of Directors

Tamar Gross
Ricki Kurtz
Sisterhood

Jordan & Eileen Silvestri
Youth Directors

לז"נ

הרב שלמה בן

הרב יהושע וינברגר ז'ל

In Gratitude to TorahWeb
and all the wonderful
Rebbeim who are spreading
and sharing their
inspirational Torah
Rabbi Efrem Goldberg

Boca Raton Synagogue

We proudly recognize the time and effort expended by the authors of the weekly divrei Torah on TorahWeb.org. Their teachings enhance our Shabbos tables and our spiritual growth.

Congregation Shomrei Torah

Fair Lawn, N.J.

In memory of our beloved grandparents:

אברהם יוסף בן גדליה
רוזה בת דניאל
אפרים בן יואל
שבע בת שמואל
אברהם בן דוד זאב הכהן
אסתר בת אביעזרי
יעקב מרדכי בן ישראל הלוי
ליבא בת גבריאל

May the Zechus of learning Torah be an Aliyah for their neshamos.

In loving memory of

Adeena Poknoush a"h

A kind and gentle soul whose unwavering strength and infectious smile impacted all who were privileged to meet her.

Dedicated by her many admirers at Camp Simcha

Table of Contents
Pesach

Rabbi Hershel Schachter
- *Matza*: The Food of *Emuna* 23
- True *Simcha* 24
- It's All One *Matza* 26
- *Davening* on Airplanes 28
- True Freedom 30

Rabbi Yakov Haber
- *Shevi'i shel Pesach*: The Climax of *Geulas Mitzrayim* 35
- *Pesach* and *Techiyas HaMeisim* 38
- *Yetzias Mitzrayim*: The Source of *Kabbalas Ol Malchus Shamayim* 43
- *Matza*: *Mitzva* and Theme of All of *Pesach* 45
- Save Us for Your Sake 49
- History and the Jewish People 52

Rabbi Eliakim Koenigberg
- The Connection between *Yetzias Mitzrayim* and *Kerias Yam Suf* 57

Rabbi Yaakov Neuburger
- From *Birkas HaChama* to *Hallel HaGadol* 63
- Unmasking *Hester Panim*, Hearing Prayer and Pain 66

Rabbi Michael Rosensweig
- *Shevi'i shel Pesach*: The *Yom Tov* of *Shira* 73
- The Special Connection between *Pesach* and *Shabbos* 75
- *Chag HaPesach*: The Ideal Introduction to *Chag HaMatzos* 82
- *Matza* as an Expression of *Hoda'a* 86
- *Pesach Sheini*: A Quest for Spiritual Opportunity and National Identity 89
- *Korban Pesach*: A Symbol of Faith and Commitment 93
- The Triad of *Pesach, Matza, Maror*: *Maror* as a Catalyst for Faith and Redemption 97
- The Conjunction of *Sippur* and *Zechiras Mitzrayim* 101
- *Chag HaCheirus*: Autonomy and Liberation in the Pursuit of Transcendence 105
- *Sippur Yetzias Mitzrayim*'s *Mikra Bikkurim* as a Statement of Faith 109

Rabbi Yonason Sacks
- Perspective on the *Omer* and *Shtei Halechem* 115
- The *Arba Kosos* 116
- *Yachatz* 121
- Suffering and Salvation 124

Rabbi Zvi Sobolofsky

After *Kerias Yam Suf*: Where Do We Go From Here? 131
Time Is of the Essence 132
Kashering Our Utensils and Our Hearts 135
Yetzias Mitzrayim: *Pesach* and Beyond 137

Rabbi Daniel Stein

Making the *Pesach* Story Personal 143

Rabbi Dr. Abraham J. Twerski

Zeman Cheiruseinu: An Independence Day Celebration? 151

Rabbi Mayer Twersky

And It Happened at Midnight 157
Matza and *Maror* 159
Emuna and *Masora* 160
The Gift of Speech 162
Miracles and Wonders 165
A Lesson in Humility 167

Rabbi Mordechai Willig

The *Hallel* of *Purim*, *Pesach*, and the Final Redemption 173
Vehiggadeta Levincha 176
Pesach: The Holiday of Faith 181
Seeing Clearly 185
Above Time and Beyond Time 188
Eating to Live 190

Rabbi Benjamin Yudin

Not Just Lip Service 197
Guess Who's Coming to Dinner? 201
Listen to Your *Matza* 203
The Sacred Ingredient 205
Hashem's Used Vehicle 207

Sefiras HaOmer

Rabbi Hershel Schachter

Aveilus, *Sefira* and *Hallel* 215

Rabbi Yaakov Neuburger

Respect and Appreciation for One Another 219
Maintaining Torah through Healthy Respect 221

Rabbi Michael Rosensweig
- Reflections on *Sefiras HaOmer* 227
- The *Sefiras HaOmer* Period: A Dimension of *Kedushas HaZeman* 232
- *Sefiras HaOmer*: A Process of Individual and National Growth 236

Rabbi Yonason Sacks
- Between *Pesach* and *Atzeres*: Perspectives on *Sefiras HaOmer* 243

Rabbi Zvi Sobolofsky
- *Omer* and *Shtei Halechem*: Two Sides of Man 249

Rabbi Mayer Twersky
- *Kabbalas HaTorah* 253
- Reassuring Rabbi Shimon bar Yochai 254

Rabbi Mordechai Willig
- *VeAhavta LeReiacha Kamocha* 259

Rabbi Benjamin Yudin
- A Reaction Speaks Louder Than Words 265
- When Is Every Day a *Mon*-day? 268
- The *Omer*: Grateful Beyond Measure 270
- Love Is Blind, but Respect Can't Be 272

Shavuos

Rabbi Hershel Schachter
- Why Was the Torah Forced upon Us? 281
- Is God Still Talking to Us? 283
- The "Giving" of the Torah 288
- "*Anochi*" 290

Rabbi Eliakim Koenigsberg
- The Individual and the Community 295

Rabbi Yaakov Neuburger
- From Censure to Sinai: A Fresh Look at *Shavuos* 299

Rabbi Michael Rosensweig
- *Shavuos*: Celebrating Human Responsibility and Involvement in the Giving and Receiving of the Torah 305

Rabbi Yonason Sacks

Anticipating *Kabbalas HaTorah* 311

Rabbi Zvi Sobolofsky

Our Master and Our Beloved: A Dual Approach to *Avodas Hashem* 315
You Can Be a *Kohein* and a King 316
Guarding the Ultimate Treasure 319
Days and Weeks: Two Worlds, Yet One Goal 320
Shavuos: Do Not Forget, for Ourselves and Our Children 322

Rabbi Dr. Abraham J. Twerski

Shavuos: Dawn of Intellectual Emotion 327
Shavuos: A Recall Phenomenon 330

Rabbi Mayer Twersky

As One Person with One Heart 335
The Dangers of Drinking; Consolidating Spiritual Gains 338
Eat, Drink and Be Merry... For Today We Accept the Torah 340
Ratza HaKadosh Baruch Hu LeZakkos Es Yisrael 341

Rabbi Mordechai Willig

Bamidbar and *Shavuos* 345
Modesty: A Timeless Principle 346

Rabbi Benjamin Yudin

A Healthy Tension before *Matan Torah* 355
Torah: Spiritual CPR 357
Na'aseh VeNishma: Faith and Intellect 360

Introduction

The *yomim tovim* are not merely "holidays", i.e. times to break from the routine of daily life and celebrate some past event, group of people, or societal institution. Rather, each *yom tov* is distinctively, intrinsically holy, and it is the unique *kedushas ha-yom* of each *yom tov* which generates the *mitzvos* which *Hakadosh Baruch Hu* commands us to keep that day. Each *yom tov*, if properly appreciated and taken advantage of, can be a time of unique spiritual growth.

Our annual spiritual journey which begins with סיפור יציאת ממצרים on *Pesach* and culminates with *kabbalas haTorah* on *Shavuos* is replete with opportunities for one to achieve new levels of freedom. סיפור יציאת מצרים is not primarily a story of achieving political freedom, rather it is the story of our spiritual transformation from an enslaved, formerly idolatrous, people into *Hashem*'s chosen people. Even something as essential as freedom has no inherent significance if not translated into spiritual attainment[1].

> Superficially, freedom entails liberation from control and demands of some person or power…In truth, however, genuine freedom depends not only upon political liberation, but primarily upon <u>internal</u> liberation. Genuine freedom entails liberation from unrefined instincts and unredeemed passions. One who is hostage to his own anger, or can not curb his desire for physical pleasure or is forever driven to seek honor and riches may be politically free, but leads a brutal, <u>slavish</u> existence.

---

[1] Paraphrased from "Miracles and Wonders", by Rav Mayer Twersky, found later in this volume

By contrast, one who refines his instincts and redeems his passions, and, thus ennobled, commits himself to doing *ratzon Hashem*, is truly free.

Talmud Torah leads to such genuine, existential freedom[2]...

This volume collects twenty years (1999-2018) of *divrei* Torah that provide insight and guidance regarding the obligations and opportunities that we each have during this season of spiritual freedom. We hope that making them available in a *sefer* will, *b'ezras Hashem*, help each of us take maximal advantage of the unique opportunities intrinsic to *Pesach*, *Sefira*, and *Shavuos*.

The *divrei* Torah contained herein were originally written by our *rebbeim* for publication on TorahWeb.org. The realities of the time pressures with which these Torah leaders function on a daily basis result in the *divrei* Torah on the web site often not being sufficiently edited, missing *mareh mekomos*, etc. These shortcomings were addressed for the version of the *divrei* Torah included in this volume.

The TorahWeb Foundation, a 501(c)(3) not-for-profit organization, was founded in 1999 at the initiative of members of our community. Its goal is to disseminate *divrei* Torah and *hashkafa*, with special attention to contemporary religious and social issues. TorahWeb's board consists of Rav Hershel Schachter, Rav Michael Rosensweig, Rav Mayer Twersky, and Rav Mordechai Willig. TorahWeb's primary projects have been publishing weekly divrei Torah written by our *rebbeim* on TorahWeb.org as well as on our email list, and arranging for *leilei iyun* a number of times a year in various communities, the audio and video of which is available on TorahWeb.org as

---

[2] "Learning to be Free", by Rav Mayer Twersky, *parshas Ki Sisa*, 2005, TorahWeb.org

well. Neither the *rebbeim* nor other individuals involved in TorahWeb receive any financial compensation. In addition, shuls receive the *leil iyun* programming free of charge.

Please send suggestions, comments, and questions to TorahWeb@TorahWeb.org.

Pesach

Rabbi Hershel Schachter

Matza: The Food of *Emuna*

The Torah mentions several times that the purpose of all the miracles connected with *yetzias Mitzrayim* was to demonstrate the existence of God, His power, and all the principles of our faith to the Jewish people. *Pesach* was designated as the *yom tov* of *emuna*, and *matza* is called "the food of *emuna*" by the *Zohar*. The theme of *Pesach* is *emuna* in *Hashem*. *Shavuos*, by contrast, has a different theme. *Shavuos* is the *yom tov* of receiving the Torah.

The *Kedushas Levi* points out two contrasts between the two *yamim tovim*: (1) On *Pesach* we may not even possess any *chametz*, as opposed to *Shavuos* which is the one and only time in the year that a *korban* is brought from *chametz*. The Talmud considers the *shtei halechem* brought on *Shavuos* as a more elegant *korban* because it consists of *chametz*. (2) The *minchas ha'omer* brought on *Pesach* is most unusual as it consists of barley grain, as opposed to almost all other *minachos*, including the *shtei halechem*, which all come from wheat. Barley is usually used to feed animals, as opposed to wheat, which is traditionally used for human consumption.

It may well be that these contrasts are due to the differences between the themes of the two *yamim tovim*. *Pesach* represents *emuna*, and regarding our understanding of God we must all have the attitude that, "if I really understood Him, I would be Him" (*Kuzari*). None of us can really understand any aspect of *Elokus*. Our understanding is compared to that of the animals (see *Tehillim* 42:2 and 73:22, and see *Tanya* chapter 18). The *omer korban* on *Pesach* must consist of *ma'achal beheima* to emphasize this idea. No *chametz* is permitted at all, since *matza* represents elementary simplicity, whereas *chametz* represents sophistication. On *Shavuos*, when

---

"*Matza*: The Food of *Emuna*" was originally published in 2000 on TorahWeb.org

we celebrate Torah learning, the *shtei halechem korban* should be *ma'achal adam*, representing the idea that we were commanded to use our human intelligence to the best of our ability to delve into the study of the Torah. That *korban* must be made into *chametz*, representing the sophistication one should attain in Torah learning.

Sophistication is not necessarily a trait that we want to develop in regards to *emuna*. The Chasid Yavetz (who was among the Jews who were expelled from Spain in 1492) wrote that he noticed that the percentage of Jews who converted to Christianity to save their lives was much higher among those who were philosophers than among the *peshutei ha'am* who adhered to an *emuna peshuta*.

If one delves deeply into Torah learning, his faith will remain neither simplistic nor primitive. Our tradition teaches us that the Torah is a description of *Elokus*. (This is the meaning of the concept of "משל הקדמוני"; see Rashi on *Shemos* 21:13.) Moshe *Rabbeinu* was the only prophet to whom the Torah was revealed, and this is referred to by the Torah as his having had a glimpse of "the image of God" (*Bamidbar* 12:8). The best way to develop a love of God is by learning His Torah (see *Rashi* on *Devarim* 6:6). By gaining Torah knowledge and developing a sophisticated approach to Torah, which is a description of *Elokus*, we come to understand Him better and our *emuna* is enhanced.

True *Simcha*

Many misunderstand the *minhag* (custom) of reciting *Yizkor* as representing a few solemn moments of sadness. There is a universal *minhag* that one who has both parents alive leaves before *Yizkor*. This too is misunderstood as representing the idea of "אל תפתח פה לשטן." Since those

---

"True Simcha" was originally published in 2006 on TorahWeb.org

reciting *Yizkor* are participating in an act of *aveilus* (mourning), we do not want those whose parents are alive even to be present, so as not to imply that they too are in mourning. It is the practice in many shuls to make an appeal for charity whenever *Yizkor* is recited. This *minhag* too is usually misunderstood. Many assume that since many more people come to shul for *Yizkor* than on other days of the year, we have a captive audience which presents a better opportunity for an appeal.

All three assumptions are incorrect! *Yizkor* is always recited on *yom tov*, when there is a *mitzva* of *simcha*. *Aveilus* and *simcha* are mutually exclusive. One may not observe any forms of mourning on *yom tov*.

In the times of the *Ba'alei haTosafos*, when the *tefilla* of *Yizkor* was instituted, the same number of people would be present in shul on the weekdays as on *Shabbos* and *yom tov*.[1]

The *Yizkor* appeal was not instituted "after the fact" because so many people were reciting the *Yizkor* prayer. Rather, as an expression of שמחת יום טוב, an appeal for the poor was introduced on *yamim tovim*. Rambam writes (*Hilchos Yom Tov* 6:18) that one who eats and drinks on *yom tov* and does not share with the poor is merely engaging in "שמחת כרסו – the rejoicing of his stomach." The Torah defines *simcha* as being *mesameach* others who are less fortunate, such as orphans, widows and converts. The *yom tov* appeal was always for the poor and needy. Once people were pledging for *tzedaka*, as a method of fulfilling שמחת יום טוב, the *Yizkor* prayer was introduced: let this pledge be considered as a *zechus* (merit) for one's parent(s) who raised a child with proper attitudes and values regarding the sharing of their assets with others. And the reason those who do not recite *Yizkor* leave the *shul* is that the Talmud mentions[2] http://www.torahweb.org/torah/2006/moadim/rsch_pesach.html - _edn2

---

[1] This fact even affected observance of *halacha*. See *Tosafos Gittin* 59b, s.v. *aval*.
[2] *Berachos* 20b. See *Nefesh HaRav* p. 153.

that it does not look right when everyone in shul is praying and one individual abstains. The mistaken impression conveyed is that perhaps that individual does not believe in the power of *tefilla*.

We just celebrated *Purim*. Two of the special *mitzvos* of that holiday are *mishloach manos* and *matanos la'evyonim*. Rambam writes (*Hilchos Megilla* 2:17) that if one can afford to go above and beyond the basic obligation of these two *mitzvos*, it is preferable to give extra *matanos la'evyonim* as opposed to placing the extra emphasis on the *mishloach manos*. He writes: "There is no more glorified form of *simcha* than to cheer up the hearts of the orphans, widows, and converts; the one who cheers up the hearts of these unfortunate individuals is to be compared to God Himself."

In recent years, some have started a new and most meaningful and beautiful *minhag*: when spending lots of money here in America on *bar mitzvas* or weddings, in order to enhance the *simcha*, they will sponsor a *bar mitzva* or wedding on behalf of those who can not afford to make one on their own[3] (or, alternatively, contribute in another way to *tzedaka*). This is the most glorious method of engaging in *simcha*.

It's All One *Matza*

On the *seder* night we do *yachatz* before we begin *maggid*, i.e., we break the middle *matza* in half, and put away the larger half for the *afikoman*, before we tell the story of *yetzias Mitzrayim*. The Talmud understood that the *matza* on *Pesach* night is called "*lechem oni*" for two reasons: (1) the *matzos* should be on the table while we tell the story of *yetzias Mitzrayim* ("לחם שעונין עליו דברים הרבה"), and (2) the *matza* should

---

[3] One of the organizations that facilitates such sponsorships is Yad Eliezer.

"**It's All One *Matza***" was originally published in 2008 on TorahWeb.org

be a *perusa* (broken and not whole). These two reasons combined cause us to have the broken *matza* (*perusa*) on the table before *maggid* ("לחם שעונין...").

We find that the same *matza* is symbolic of both the slavery of our ancestors as well as their being freed (the *geula*). Immediately following *yachatz*, we declare "הא לחמא עניא," that this type of *matza* was eaten by our forefathers in Egypt, and is therefore referred to by the Torah as "*lechem oni*." Later on in the *Haggada* we quote the statement of Rabban Gamliel that the *matza* we eat is reminiscent of the fact that at the time of the *geula* the Jews left Egypt in such haste that there was not enough time for their dough to rise. Why have the *matza* symbolize two opposite concepts?

The *Mishna* (*Berachos* 54a) tells us that just as one recites a *beracha* to praise *Hashem* when something wonderful occurs, so too we ought to recite a *beracha* praising *Hashem* when a tragedy occurs. The wording of the *mishna* ("just like…so too") seems to equate the two *berachos*. The Talmud (*Berachos* 60b) finds this equation difficult, since in fact the *beracha* we recite on good tidings (הטוב והמטיב) is different from the *beracha* we recite when a tragedy occurs (דין האמת). This equation seems no more valid than saying that just as one recites a *beracha* upon eating potato chips (*ha'adama*), so too one should recite a *beracha* upon putting on *tefillin* (*lehaniach tefillin*) – the two *berachos* recited on the two occasions have nothing to do with each other!

The *Gemara* answers the question by explaining that while the wording of the two *berachos* is different, they do in fact share something common: both should be recited in a state of joy (*simcha*). Why should both be recited *besimcha*? The *Shulchan Aruch* quotes from *Rabbeinu Yonah* that we ought to have *emuna* (faith) that everything that God does is really for the good. While the wording (*nussach*) of the *berachos* for good tidings and tragedy cannot be the same, since according to our perception we experience a tragedy, at the same time we are expected to believe that an awful tragedy is really *letova* and that God would never allow anything that is objectively bad to occur. Therefore, we recite the *beracha* of דין האמת in a state of *simcha*.

At *yachatz* one *matza* is broken into two parts. The impression at first is that the *matza* represents the pain and suffering that our forefathers experienced while in slavery. But we refer to the *afikoman* as *tzafun* (the hidden piece). What was concealed from us during all the years of slavery was that all of the suffering was really *letova*. The two pieces are from the same *matza*! Just as the second half-*matza* representing *geula* was clearly *letova*, so too the first half-*matza* representing the years of pain and suffering was also *letova*.

Davening on Airplanes

Several times a year I visit *Eretz Yisrael*. When I take a night flight, I notice that many men sleep for five or six hours, and then recite *Shema* and *daven Shacharis* after waking up, just as if they were at a seven o'clock *minyan* back in the United States. However, because the airplane is flying from west to east and traversing several time zones, the זמן קריאת שמע keeps getting earlier and earlier, following the זמן קריאת שמע on the ground over which the airplane is flying.[4] Often, by the time many of the passengers wake up and get ready to start *Shacharis*, the *zeman* on the ground below is already after *chatzos* and well into the *zeman* of *mincha*.

Another common mistake people make is regarding *davening* with a *minyan*. The Talmud emphasizes the importance of *tefilla betzibbur*, and

---

[4] Editor's note: Chaitables.com calculates the *zemanei tefilla* for your flight given your departure and arrival locations and times.

"Davening on Airplanes" was originally published in 2010 on TorahWeb.org

one who *davens* with a *minyan* stands a much better chance of having his prayers answered than one who lacks a *minyan*. However, it is highly improper for the *chazzan* of a *minyan* on an airplane to shout at the top of his lungs to enable the other *mispallelim* to hear him over the airplane noise, and thereby wake up all the passengers around him. It is true that there is a halachic principle of כופין על המצוות, i.e., that *beis din* has an obligation to force people to observe the *mitzvos* even when they are not interested in doing so, but this only applies when pressuring an individual will result in his becoming observant. However, when Orthodox Jews disturb non-observant Jewish passengers with their *davening*, the non-observant passengers remain non-observant, and just have another point about which to be upset with the Orthodox. The practice of the Orthodox passengers under such circumstances appears simply as an act of harassment. Rather than having accomplished the *hiddur mitzva* of *davening tefilla betzibbur*, they have violated *lifnei iver* by causing the non-observant passengers to become more antagonistic toward *shemiras hamitzvos*. The shouting tone of voice employed by the *shaliach tzibbur* to overcome the noise on the airplane clearly does not constitute a *kavod hatefilla*.

The *halacha* states that when traveling, if it is too difficult to stand for *Shemoneh Esrei*, even the "*Amida*" may be recited while seated. On a short flight of an hour and a half to Canada, it is more correct to *daven* the entire *tefilla* while still buckled in, in a sitting position. On the long flight to *Eretz Yisrael* it is healthier to not sit the entire time; walking around somewhat helps the blood circulation in one's legs. As such, there is nothing wrong with standing for *Shemoneh Esrei*, provided that there's no turbulence at that time. However, it is still not proper to gather a *minyan* together near the washrooms, disturbing all the other passengers and the flight attendants. As much as various Torah giants of our generation have expressed their opposition to such *minyanim* on airplanes,[5] their message has not yet been

---

[5] Rav Shlomo Wahrman (*She'eiris Yosef* vol. 7, *siman* 3) quotes Rav Shlomo Zalman Auerbach (*Halichos Shlomo*, p. 75), Rav Moshe Feinstein (*Iggeros Moshe Orach Chayyim*

accepted. We wish everyone a חג כשר ושמח, and all those traveling to *Eretz Yisrael* should have a safe trip, but keep in mind – these airplane *minyanim* are שלא ברוצן חכמים!

True Freedom

During intersession I participated in a special tour of *Eretz Yisrael* together with a group of Yeshiva students. The purpose of the tour was to study various aspects of Israeli society. Among many other places, we visited a *chareidi* yeshiva high school in Haifa. The *rosh yeshiva* spoke with us and said, among other things, that if 90 percent of his graduates do not end up learning long-term in a *kollel*, he considers himself a failure. We were all stunned!

Certainly learning Torah is most important! Every morning, right after reciting *birchos haTorah*, we all recite the passage from the Talmud stating that "תלמוד תורה כנגד כולם". But can it be that anyone who does not go into full-time learning is wasting his life? *HaKadosh Baruch Hu* calls upon all people to be His slaves. The message that Moshe *Rabbeinu* was to deliver to Pharaoh was, "שלח את עמי ויעבדני – let My people go and they will serve Me." Until *Pesach* evening, the Jews were slaves to Pharaoh, and then, when he freed them, they became slaves to *Hashem*.

The Jews in every generation were always at the forefront of fighting for freedom. Our tradition teaches, however, that true freedom does not mean that one is free to do whatever he pleases. Only one who is a slave to *Hashem* and follows the Torah is considered truly free. In *Hallel* we recite, "אני עבדך בן אמתך פתחת למוסרי," i.e., that only by becoming a complete slave to *HaKadosh Baruch Hu* do we feel that "our shackles have

---

vol. 4, *siman* 20), Rav Ovadiah Yosef, and Rav Shmuel Wosner all objecting to *minyanim* on airplanes that disturb other passengers.

"True Freedom" was originally published in 2012 on TorahWeb.org

been broken" and that we have become free!

Moshe *Rabbeinu* was described by the Torah as an "*eved Hashem* – a slave of *Hashem*." Radak explains the use of this expression to describe Moshe based on the Talmudic principle of "כל מה שקנה עבד קנה רבו – everything a slave acquires is automatically transferred to his master." Just as all that a slave does belongs to his master, so too everything Moshe *Rabbeinu* did, all day long, was in the service of his Master, *Hashem*. Similarly, when commenting on the *pasuk*, "וירד משה מן ההר אל העם" (*Shemos* 19:14), *Chazal* highlight the fact that even though Moshe was returning from being on *Har Sinai* for 40 days, he did nothing for his own purposes when he came down; rather he went straight back to serving *Hashem*'s people.

The Torah calls upon all of us to serve as *avadim* to *Hashem*, "כי־לי בני־ישראל עבדים" (*Vayikra* 25:55). Rambam (*Hilchos De'os* 3:2-3), citing the *pasuk* "בכל דרכיך דעהו – know Him in all your ways" (*Mishlei* 3:6), writes that all of our daily activities – getting dressed, eating, working, spending time with our spouses and our children, sleeping, etc. – should be done *lesheim Shamayim*. Rambam goes on to say that one who follows this path is in constant service of *Hashem*! The Torah dictates not only how we must deal in business but even how we should put on our shoes and tie them, how we should shower, and how we should go to sleep at night. A Jew can not divide his activities between the holy and the secular. **All** day long we are *avdei Hashem*, and "כל מה שקנה עבד קנה רבו." **All** of our activities are expected to be done in the service of our Master.

Our love for *Hashem* is expected to be **all-encompassing**. We are called upon to love him "with **all** of our hearts." Our love for our spouses and family members is expected to be part of our love for *Hashem*. He wants us to raise families.

After receiving *semicha* from Rav Yaakov Kamenetsky at Torah Vodaath, many of the students would go into secular fields. Rav Kamenetsky would not rebuke them for the decision not to enter the rabbinate or *chinuch*. He would simply tell them that whatever they choose to do for a living they must do honestly, and they must always act and deal with others in a proper fashion to make a *kiddush Hashem*.

The Torah tells us (*Bereishis* 5:22) that Chanoch was a holy *tzaddik* who "walked with *Hashem*." According to the *Zohar*, Chanoch was an honest and hard-working shoemaker who did all of his work *lesheim Shamayim*. Chanoch's life was one of great success; he acted as an *eved* to *Hashem* by dedicating all of his daily activities to His service.

Rabbi Yakov Haber

Shevi'i shel Pesach:
The Climax of *Geulas Mitzrayim*

The last days of *Pesach* commemorate the miraculous splitting of the sea, leading to the rescue of the Jewish people from the hands of their Egyptian pursuers and Pharaoh's last stand against his erstwhile slaves ending in ignominious failure, defeat and powerlessness before the Almighty. The *kerias haTorah* for the day is appropriately taken from *Parashas Beshalach* which recounts precisely this story. The *halacha* indicates that, unlike its counterpart, *Shemini Atzeres*, the last day of *Sukkos, shevi'i shel Pesach* forms an integral part of the *Pesach* holiday itself. Hence, whereas the former is a "רגל בפני עמצו," an independent festival regarding several *halachos* (including the number of *korbanos* brought, the reciting of the *shehecheyanu* blessing and the recital of the full *Hallel*), the latter has none of these characteristics, thus blending in with the rest of the Passover festival.

On a simple plane, the reason for this is obvious. The first day of *Pesach* commemorates the initial exodus, the 15th day of *Nisan* being the day when the Jews left Egypt after the last of the ten *makkos*, the plague of the firstborn. The last day commemorates the final step of the exodus, when the pursuing Egyptian forces were destroyed. In the words of Moshe *Rabbeinu*, "כי אשר ראיתם את־מצרים היום לא תסיפו לראתם עוד עד־עולם" – for as you see Egypt (or the Egyptians) today, you will no longer see them forever more!" (*Shemos* 14:13).

The Slonimer Rebbe, R. Berzovsky *zt"l*, in his *Nesivos Shalom* (*Shevi'i shel Pesach, ma'amar* 4) offers a deeper insight into the connection between the two parts of the *chag* and the respective events which they commemorate. The first step of the *geula* was an act of utter Divine

---

"*Shevi'i shel Pesach*" was originally published in 2003 on TorahWeb.org

rachamim (mercy). Lacking the requisite merit to be redeemed and in imminent danger of becoming utterly assimilated in the Egyptian culture, the Jewish people were rushed out by *Hashem* (hence the need for *chipazon*, according to many commentaries). In the language of Yechezkel *haNavi* (16:7) cited in the *Haggada*: "ואת ערום ועריה– you were unclothed as a newborn," utterly dependent on the mercy of our Heavenly Father. However, such a redemption could not last. A *yeshua* brought about solely by Divine mercy will eventually cease when *Hashem*'s attribute of justice demands that the redeemed deserve their redemption. Hence, *Hashem*, in His mercy, brought about an event that necessitated *Klal Yisrael*'s earning precisely the necessary merit to retroactively earn their redemption. This was the episode of *kerias Yam Suf*. In the famous words of *Hashem* to Moshe occasioned by his and *Bnei Yisrael*'s heartfelt prayer for salvation from the rapidly approaching Egyptian hordes, "דבר אל־בני־ישראל ויסעו! – tell the Jews they should travel [into the Sea]!" (*Shemos* 14:15). Rashi comments that *Hashem* was telling Moshe that now is not the time for prayer; now they must travel into the sea. The supercommentaries to Rashi raise the obvious question: is not this time of *tzara* precisely the time for prayer?! R. Berzovsky's approach answers this question as well. *Tefilla* is a request for *rachamim*. (Indeed, the *Gemara* in *Berachos* 20b even refers to *tefilla* as "*rachamei*.") Now, though, such a request would be ineffective. *Klal Yisrael* needed the merit of demonstrating their utter faith and trust in God by hurling themselves into the sea even before it split, showing their confidence that no body of water, indeed nothing in the entire universe, can withstand the power of the Almighty, and that in all situations, however bleak, however hopeless, the *Go'eil Yisrael* can and does deliver salvation. Following the lead of Nachshon ben Aminadav, our ancestors rose to the task and did exactly what was required of them. This *mesirus nefesh* (wholehearted sacrifice), then, allowed them to earn the prior *geula*. Hence, the events of the last day of *Pesach* served to solidify and make permanent the events of the first day.

Perhaps we can suggest an alternative approach. The *makkos* in *Mitzrayim* and, indeed, the entire process of the exodus punctuated by Moshe's coming to Pharaoh demanding the Jews' freedom and Pharaoh's many acts of defiance served a twofold purpose: first, to free the Jews and to demonstrate unquestioningly to them *Hashem*'s omnipotence and omnipresence in the world; second, to inform, instruct, and demonstrate to the arrogant Pharaoh who had deified himself and to his nation, and through them to the entire world, that the only true power in the world is God Himself. Hence, the constant refrain resounds throughout the *makkos*: "And you shall know that I am God." (See also "On *Makkos* and Scientific Endeavors," TorahWeb.org, *Parashas Bo*, 2000.) This would also explain why *Hashem* didn't simply incapacitate all of the Egyptians, thus easily allowing the Jews to exit to freedom. To accomplish the second goal of publicizing the Name of God to the entire Egyptian people, it was necessary for **Pharaoh** to bow to God's will and to free the Jews. Therefore, it was necessary for Moshe to insist constantly that **Pharaoh** release the Jews. Pharaoh only did this after the last *makka*, when he ran through the streets of the capital city, demanding that the Jews leave. However, therein lay a danger. The first goal, to demonstrate *Hashem*'s total mastery over the world to His chosen people, necessitated that no other power be involved in the exodus. Hence, the emphasis, as related in the *Haggada*, that the final *makka* was brought about by *Hashem bichvodo uve'atzmo*: "'אני ולא מלאך וגו'" In order to resolve the inherent conflict between these two goals, it would appear that *Hashem* brought about the *geula* in two stages. The first, although orchestrated ultimately by *Hashem*'s power, perforce ended with Pharaoh formally freeing the Jews. The Torah therefore writes "ויהי בשלח פרעה את העם" – when *Pharaoh* freed the Jews" to introduce the *kerias Yam Suf* episode. Then Pharaoh has a change of heart. True, he was forced to consent to free the Jews, but now he reneges on his decision and pursues *Bnei Yisrael* to return them to Egypt. God then reenters the scene, nullifying Pharaoh's plot and serving as the **only** source of salvation for the Jews. As a result, the Jewish people would in no way be beholden to Pharaoh for their freedom, only to *Hashem* Himself, and recognize Him alone as the Master of the world and of history. As the *Haggada* states, "And if *Hashem* had not taken us out of *Mitzrayim*, we and our children and our children's children would have been enslaved to Pharaoh in *Mitzrayim*." Many commentaries note that the physical slavery might have ended a different way in the course of history, but we would still be enslaved, in the sense of indebtedness, if Pharaoh alone had been the one to free us. God's intervention at the sea assured that *Bnei Yisrael* were indebted to no other power but *Hashem* Himself.

Only after the drowning of the Egyptians at the sea does the Torah proclaim: "And they believed in *Hashem* and Moshe his servant" (*Shemos* 14:31). Only then do *Bnei Yisrael* sing to *Hashem* as their only source of salvation: "עזי וזמרת קה ויהי לי לישועה" and "ה' איש מלחמה" (*Shemos* 15:3, 2). What was explicit at the time of the original exodus, and will again be apparent at the time of the ultimate redemption (see "Parallels between the Exodus from Egypt and the Final Redemption," TorahWeb.org, *Shabbos HaGadol*, 2002), is true throughout history. Although *Hashem*'s hand is often hidden, and He works through many agents, He is always the One solely arranging the events behind the scenes. May we merit always seeing the guiding hand of *Hashem* in our private lives and the events affecting *Klal Yisrael*.

Pesach and Techiyas HaMeisim

The *haftara* for שבת חול המועד פסח concerns the famous "dry bones" prophecy of Yechezkel. Upon being shown a vision of piles of bones, Yechezkel is told by God to tell the lifeless heaps, "Behold, I shall bring a soul into you and you shall live!" (37:5). The sages of the Talmud (*Sanhedrin* 92b) debate whether an actual resurrection took place in the time of

---

"***Pesach*** and *Techiyas HaMeisim*" was originally published in 2004 on TorahWeb.org

Yechezkel, or whether the vision was an allegory for the "resurrection" of the downtrodden Jewish people, then in the Babylonian exile. According to Avudraham, quoting R. Hai Gaon, the reading of this passage on *chol hamoed* apparently favors the literal interpretation. Since an ancient tradition states that the awaited *techiyas hameisim* will take place in *Nisan*, we read this *haftara* on *Pesach*. The past resurrection in the days of Yechezkel serves to establish confidence in the future resurrection.

Much mystery and debate surrounds the event of the final resurrection. While the *mishna* in *Sanhedrin* 90a states unequivocally that one who denies the ultimate literal resurrection is in the category of a heretic and is denied a share in the world to come, the *rishonim* debate the exact nature of the physical resurrection. Although considerable controversy arose concerning Rambam's interpretation, he too, as expounded upon in his *Iggeres Techiyas HaMeisim*, fully believed in a physical resurrection. The debate ultimately revolves around the definition of the world to come. Although commonly it is assumed that the world to come is the world of the souls after death, it is also commonly assumed that after the resurrection, those revived will live forever. A moment's thought shows that these two ideas are wholly incompatible, since if the world of reward, *olam haba*, is identical with the soul-world, then the resurrection cannot possibly be for all eternity, for then those resurrected would be denied the subsequent eternal bliss in *olam haba*! What emerges from study of Rambam's *Hilchos Teshuva* (chap. 8) and his aforementioned *Iggeres* is that for Rambam, since *olam haba* is the world of the soul – because only the soul, unfettered and restricted by the corporeal body, is capable of receiving true Divine pleasure (which is the comprehension of *Hashem* to the extent possible for a created being) – the resurrection will be followed again by the death of those resurrected so that their souls can return to *olam haba* (see *Iggeres*).

However, many other *rishonim*, including R. Saadia Gaon (*Emunos veDe'os*), Ramban (*Sha'ar HaGemul*), Ritva (*Nidda* 61b), and *chachmei hakabbala* (see *Derech Hashem* of Ramchal), maintain that existence in the world to come consists of both body and soul, even though the body will no longer need sustenance to survive (see statement of Rav, *Berachos* 17a). Since the body will have to be recreated in order to allow for this new reality and to be capable of existing for all eternity, the body has to be resurrected. Therefore, there are even sources which indicate that those alive at the time of *techiyas hameisim* will momentarily experience death, so that their bodies can be reformed to accommodate their new existence (see *Derech Hashem*). According to this approach, which appears to be the mainstream one, albeit not the one most commonly known, the resurrection serves as the prelude to *olam haba*. The many statements of *Chazal* linking resurrection and the world to come seem to verify this approach. An example is the *mishna* in *Sanhedrin* quoted earlier which states that he who denies *techiyas hameisim* does not receive a share of the world to come. The *Gemara* explains that this is מידה כנגד מידה: since the person denied *olam haba*, therefore he has no share in it. The most straightforward reading of this passage is that the resurrection is the gateway into the world to come. (According to this approach, souls after death before the resurrection enter a temporary world of reward, the world of the souls, or גן עדן של מעלה, awaiting the final *techiya*. Those undeserving may still merit *techiyas hameisim* as a result of the purfication of *Gehinom* in the soul-world [see *Tosafos, Rosh HaShana* 16b, s.v. *leyom hadin*].)

The above dispute serves as the foundation of the discussion of another central eschatological topic, namely, the role of *mitzvos* in the future. It is a fundamental principle of faith that the Torah does not change. However, all agree that in the world of reward, *mitzvos* no longer apply, for *mitzvos* are the means to achieve that reward. Hence, souls do not perform *mitzvos*. According to Rambam's approach, this is straightforward. *Olam haba* is the soul-world; hence, there are no *mitzvos* there. A passage in *Masseches Nidda* 61b, which indicates that the dead may be buried in *sha'atnez* (a wool and linen mixture) since "מצוות בטלות לעתיד לבוא – *mitzvos* will be nullified in the future," is not readily understood according to Rambam since the **soul** is not being buried in *sha'atnez*! Rambam presumably would read this passage as does Rashba (commentary to *Nidda*, erroneously accredited to Ritva) that the thrust of the *Gemara* is that dead **bodies** are exempt from *mitzvos*. However, the simpler reading of this passage is that after *techiyas hameisim*, *mitzvos* no longer apply, and, therefore, we need not be concerned that when the body is resurrected, the person will be in temporary violation of the prohibition of *sha'atnez*. Ramban and Ritva interpret this *Gemara* in exactly this way, that the *Gemara* refers to the resurrection preceding *olam haba*, the world of reward of body and soul, and hence, commandments no longer apply. (All of the above discussion only relates to the world to come. The world of redemption according to all is part of this world, and hence, *mitzvos* certainly apply. As a matter of fact, one of the main features of the redemption is the ability to fulfill **all** of the Torah's commandments, even those which do not apply in the exile in the absence of the *Beis HaMikdash* or in the absence of the majority of the Jewish people dwelling in the land of Israel [see Rambam, *Hilchos Melachim* 11:1].)

However, there are several Torah sources which indicate that *mitzvos* will apply after the resurrection. Although the fact of the future resurrection is primarily recorded in the *Nevi'im* and *Ketuvim*, there are several allusions to it in the Torah itself (see *Sanhedrin* 90b, ff.). One of them is the Torah's statement that we should give *teruma* to Aharon *haKohein*. This is something that was never fulfilled, since Aharon died in the desert before the Jewish people entered the Land of Israel. Perforce, then, Aharon will be resurrected in the future, and we will then give him *teruma*. This indicates the applicability of *mitzvos* after the *techiya*. Furthermore, one opinion (*Sanhedrin* 92b) is that the resurrected dead of Yechezkel's prophecy married and lived full lives, and one *tanna* even states that he has a pair of *tefillin* from them! The simple implication is that they were obligated in *mitzvos* (see also *Kovetz Shiurim*, vol. 2, *siman* 29). In resolution of these contradictory sources, Radvaz (*Responsa*) and Ritva (*Rosh HaShana* 16b, s.v. *sheneʾemar*) state that there will be two resurrections. One will be at the time of the redemption when *mitzvos* will most definitely apply. This is reserved for the exceptionally righteous, giving them an opportunity to see the end of world history play out, the wicked destroyed, and the righteous rewarded. It will also give them a second chance at performing *mitzvos*, to allow them even greater reward in *olam haba* (see *Shaʾar HaGemul*). The second *techiya* will be for all those who merit eternity (both those alive then and those not) and will usher in the new world of *olam haba*, the world of reward, some time **after** the redemption, and hence, *mitzvos* will no longer apply.

According to Ramban and his supporters, who identify *techiyas hameisim* with *olam haba*, belief in this principle expresses belief in reward and punishment, and hence, it is readily understandable why belief in it is so central. According to Rambam, though, that the resurrection is only temporary and is not identified with the world of reward, the centrality of belief in this concept, which, based on the above-mentioned *mishna* in *Sanhedrin*, Rambam includes in the list of the Thirteen Principles of Faith and in *Hilchos Teshuva*, is somewhat difficult. It would appear that the Rambam himself in his *Iggeres* provides an answer to this question. One denying the resurrection ultimately denies God's infinite power. Clearly, the One capable of creating man in the first place out of "dust from the ground" is clearly able to re-create him in the future. Indeed, the natural world itself demonstrates many parallels of life from lifelessness. Human life is produced from drops of liquid; plant life is rejuvenated every springtime; the planting of "dead" seeds produces abundant floral growth even after the seeds lie dormant for hundreds of years; a caterpillar is transformed into a majestic butterfly after "dying" in the cocoon. Only one who does not realize that this is all the hand of God and only sees "mother nature" would deny the eventual miraculous resurrection, miraculous only in the sense that such an event does not regularly occur, but not in the sense that many parallels do not already exist in nature. (See also *Sanhedrin* 90b, where R. Meir uses a similar argument from the vegetable kingdom to prove that the dead will be resurrected in their clothing.) Hence, denial of the resurrection denies God as Creator; affirmation of it confirms God's role in creation and as Master of His world. It is for this reason that *techiyas hameisim* serves as the central theme (it is repeated five times) of the second blessing of *Shemoneh Esrei*, referred to as *Gevuros*, the blessing concerning Divine power.

Based on the above, perhaps we can gain an additional insight as to the reason we read the prophecy concerning the resurrection on the *Shabbos* of *Pesach*. The holiday of *Pesach* commemorates the exodus with all of its manifestations of Divine, miraculous intervention on the world stage, which demonstrated to *Bnei Yisrael* and the whole world *Hashem*'s role as Creator and as Master of the world (see Ramban, end of *Bo*). May we merit to be participants in the ultimate redemption as well as *olam haba*, ushered in by *techiyas hameisim*!

Yetzias Mitzrayim: The Source of *Kabbalas Ol Malchus Shamayim*

Usually we introduce all מצוות בין אדם למקום with a *birkas hamitzva*. The *mitzva* of סיפור יציאת מצרים, as fulfilled through the recital and exposition of the *Haggada*, seems to be a notable exception. Both the *rishonim* and *acharonim* offer a variety of fascinating solutions to this question, each one with ramifications beyond the *Haggada* itself. Among the answers: there is no *beracha* on a *mitzva* without a defined limit (Rashba); no blessing is recited on a *mitzva* whose primary *kiyyum*

"*Yetzias Mitzrayim*..." was originally published in 2005 on TorahWeb.org

(fulfillment) is in the mind or heart (Maharal); the *Haggada* itself is structured in a *beracha* format ending with "ברוך אתה ה' גאל ישראל," and we do not recite a *beracha* on a *beracha* (*Ma'aseh Nissim*, Chida).

Perhaps we can suggest another answer based on concepts developed by Avudraham and Rav Yosef Dov Soloveitchik *zt"l*. Avudraham questions why there is no blessing on *Kerias Shema*. He answers that the purpose of a *beracha* is to be *mekabeil ol malchus Shamayim* upon us before we perform the *mitzva*. We perform Divine commandments as instantiations of accepting *Hashem*'s sovereignty over the entire cosmos, the world, our nation, and our individual selves. *Klal Yisrael* first had to accept the whole package of Torah through the declaration of "נעשה ונשמע" before actually dedicating their lives to Divine service. In the language of *Beis HaLeivi* (*Mishpatim*), only after we offered ourselves as servants of *Hakadosh Baruch Hu* did we become bound by the totality of Torah for all generations. The prospective convert to Judaism must reenact the same process by first accepting the totality of Torah and *mitzvos*; only then can his conversion be valid and meaningful. According to Avudraham, we reaffirm this broader commitment each time we perform a *mitzva*. Hence, before reading *Kerias Shema*, whose very essence expresses a commitment to the dual themes of קבלת עול מלכות שמים and קבלת עול מצוות, no blessing is necessary. We need not accept Divine sovereignty in order to accept Divine sovereignty.

The same approach can be applied to the *Haggada*. The third section of *Kerias Shema* contains זכירת יציאת מצרים, the command to remember the exodus. Rav Soloveitchik (see *Haggadas Siach HaGrid*) notes that Rambam (*Hilchos Kerias Shema*) seems to include all three sections of the *Shema* in the biblical commandment of reading the *Shema*. Rav Soloveitchik explains that the exodus is integrally linked to the theme of קבלת עול מלכות. Throughout the entire experience of *yetzias Mitzrayim* – beginning with Moshe's demand of Pharaoh in the name of *Hashem* to release His nation, moving through the cataclysmic overturning of the rules of nature by means of the ten *makkos*, and culminating with *kerias Yam Suf* with the attendant Divine revelation enabling the Jewish people to prophetically utter the *Az Yashir* in unison – *Hashem* demonstrated His existence, His creation of the world (as evidenced by demonstrating His utter mastery over nature which He created and manages), His omniscience, and His providence (see *Ramban*, end of *Bo*). These majestic events serve as the foundation of our acceptance of *Hashem*'s rule over the world and our obligation of loyalty toward Him. Hence, remembering the exodus brings to the fore the source of our acceptance of Divine rule and therefore His *mitzvos*.

In light of this, no blessing need be recited before the retelling of the exodus, for through its detailed and elaborate recounting on the night of the *seder*, we are reaffirming our loyalty to *Hashem Yisbarach*. Therefore, there is no need to precede the *Haggada* with the same theme through a blessing. Through our reacceptance of Divine sovereignty in the darkness of the world of *hesteir* (concealment), may we merit the open revelation of *Hashem*'s presence in the Third *Beis HaMikdash* – ונאכל שם מן הזבחים ומן הפסחים!

Matza:
Mitzva and Theme of All of *Pesach*

I

Chazal (*Mechilta*, quoted by Rashi, *Shemos* 12:15) teach us that although the Torah states: "You shall eat *matzos* for seven days" (*Shemos* 12:15, *Vayikra* 23:6), the obligatory commandment to eat *matza* only applies on the first night of *Pesach*, the *seder* night. This is based on another *pasuk*: "In the evening [after the 14th of *Nisan*] you shall eat *matzos*" (*Shemos* 12:18). On a simple plane, according to this interpretation, the

---

"*Matza: Mitzva* and Theme..." was originally published in 2010 on TorahWeb.org

first verse, stating we should eat *matza* for seven days, is not commanding us to eat *matza* for seven days, but rather to eat *matza* instead of *chametz* for the rest of *Pesach*, but we can also choose not to eat any "bread-like" foods at all (see *Shulchan Aruch HaRav* 475:32).

The Gaon R. Eliyahu of Vilna, (*Ma'aseh Rav*, 185) famously maintains that this *derasha* does not negate the *mitzva* of eating *matza* on the other days of *Pesach* entirely. Rather, whereas on the first night, the *mitzva* is *chiyyuvis*, obligatory, on the other nights, it is *kiyyumis*, optional. In the *Sefer Achilas Matzos BeYisrael* by R. Shalom Yehuda Gross *shlita*, many other views both in *rishonim* and *acharonim* are presented agreeing with the approach of the *Gra*. Among them are: the view of the *Geonim* that *tefillin* are not worn on *chol hamoed Pesach* since *tefillin* are an *os* (a sign), and *Pesach* already has an *os*, the eating of *matza*. This strongly implies that the eating of *matza* even on the rest of *Pesach* is a *mitzva* act and is consequently considered an *os*. Even the Rosh, who disagrees and maintains that *tefillin* are worn on *chol hamoed*, does not necessarily reject the premise that *matza* on the rest of *Pesach* is a *mitzva* act.[6] The *Aruch HaShulchan* (475) also agrees with the view of the Vilna Gaon. (See the above *sefer* for many other supporters of this view.)[7]

II

What is unique about the *matza* which, unlike the other *mitzvos* of the *seder* night, permeates the entire *yom tov* of *Pesach*?

Many commentaries on the *Haggada* note that *matza* is the only food at the *seder* which incorporates within it symbolism of both slavery[8]

---

[6] Just as the Rosh surely does not reject the premise that *lulav* and *sukka* are *mitzvos* for the entire *Sukkos*, based on which the Geonim maintain that we do not put on *tefillin* on *chol hamoed Sukkos* since they are an *os*.

[7] One ramification of these views is that one should have *kavana* to fulfill a *mitzva* when eating *matza* even during the rest of *Pesach*.

[8] Although see Maharal, quoted below, who strongly disputes this notion.

and freedom. On the one hand, we introduce the *seder* with: "This is the bread of poverty [or: affliction] which our ancestors ate in Egypt." On the other hand, we conclude the first part of the *seder* with: "Why do we eat this *matza*? Because their dough did not have a chance to rise when they left Egypt..."[9] Perhaps this duality might also explain why the *mitzva* of *matza* applies throughout *Pesach*. Throughout this central holiday, we commemorate, relive and attempt to incorporate into our year-round lives the enormous lessons to be gleaned from both the servitude in Egypt[10] and the subsequent freedom forming our nation and preparing us to receive the Torah at Sinai.

On another level,[11] R. Moshe Chaim Luzzato (Ramchal) (*Derech Hashem* 4:8) and Maharal (*Gevuros Hashem* 36, 51, 60) both note that eating *matza*, which through its constitution and its being baked quickly, not only **commemorates** the haste with which we left Egypt, but also **prepared** us spiritually for that exodus and the subsequent receiving of the Torah. In the words of Ramchal:

> The concept of *chametz* and *matza* is that until the exodus from Egypt, the Jewish people were mixed into the other nations, a nation among another nation. Through their exodus, they were redeemed and separated. Until that time, the bodies of mankind were clouded with (spiritual) darkness and defilement which was very prominent in

---

[9] See "It's All One *Matza*" in this volume by *mori verabi* Rav Hershel Schachter *shlita* for a further elaboration of this theme.

[10] One lesson is based on the statement of our Sages (*Megilla* 14a): "'הללו עבדי ה' - ולא עבדי פרעה; 'Praise, O you servants of God' – and not the servants of Pharaoh!" The slavery in Egypt taught *Klal Yisrael* how to be "slaves," that is, to be fully committed day and night to the service of someone or something. This ability, while of little value when for the purpose of serving man, is of infinite value, reflecting our true selves, when utilized to attach ourselves to the Source of all.

[11] This section of this article is based on a *devar Torah* delivered orally by Rav Gedalya Meir Hochberg *shlita* on *Shabbos HaGadol* at *Beis Midrash Nachal Nachshon*, and printed in *Korei Oneg* (*alon* 5) of *Kehilas Bnei HaYeshivos - Mishkenos Yaakov*.

them. At the point of the exodus, the Jewish people were separated. As a result, their bodies were fit to become purified and prepared for [a life of] Torah and Divine service. Because of this, they were commanded to eliminate *chametz* and to eat *matza*. [Regular] bread designed for man was appropriate for man's necessary state. Leaven, which is natural in bread, since it is easily digestible and of good taste, is also in accordance with that which is appropriate for man, for it is necessary that the evil inclination be within him and have a propensity for physicality.[12] However, for a defined period of time, Israel was required to desist from *chametz* and be sustained through *matza*, to lessen within themselves the power of the evil inclination and the propensity toward physicality, and they thus strengthened within themselves the connection toward spirituality. To always be sustained in such a manner is impossible, for this is not what is desired in *olam hazeh*, this world.[13] But during the appropriate days, it is fitting that they should keep this concept, for through this they will remain on the level which is appropriate for them. This is the main theme of "*chag hamatzos*."

Maharal gives several additional approaches why *matza*, devoid of any other flavor or fluff (the leavening), is a food uniquely suited to allow the Jewish people to attach to *Hashem* and to be redeemed in a supernatural manner. It is not dependent on time, meaning that no specific time is required to make it as it need not rise, just as God, Who redeemed them Himself, is not dependent on time. It is unattached to anything else; hence,

---

[12] See *Berachos* (17a) where the *yeitzer hara* is compared to leaven.

[13] See "*VaYeishev* and *Chanuka*: A Different Outlook on the World," TorahWeb.org, for an elaboration on the theme of channeling the evil inclination for good purposes.

it is "poor man's bread" (unlike the wealthy who are "attached" to their assets), symbolizing freedom from all other influences. It is the ultimate of simplicity, symbolizing the upper world, the world through which the redemption supernaturally took place, unencumbered by the misleading "razzle-dazzle" of this world, a necessary component to provide motivation for Divine service, but unnecessary in the world of Divine bliss.[14]

The *Zohar* asks why *matza* is not eaten the whole year. This question is readily understandable in light of all of the spiritual benefits of *matza*. The *Zohar* answers that once one is sanctified and healed with "the food of healing" one time, he no longer needs it. *Tiferes Shlomo* (by R. Shlomo of Radomsk) explains the following passage based on this concept: "*Matzos* should be eaten for seven days, and *chametz* should not be seen… in all of your boundaries" (*Shemos* 13:7). This can be homiletically read as: as a result of your eating *matza* for the seven days of *Pesach*, you will merit that *chametz*, symbolic of the *yeitzer hara*, will not be attractive to you the rest of year.[15]

In the merit of fulfilling the *mitzva* of *matza* the entire *Pesach*, may *Hashem* grant that we absorb all of its spiritual messages throughout the year and see the final redemption speedily.

Save Us for Your Sake

The *Haggada* begins with the words: "We were slaves to Pharaoh in Egypt, and God took us out from there. If the Holy One Blessed Be He had not taken out our ancestors from Egypt, we and our children and

---

[14] Based on Rav Hochberg's interpretation of the words of Maharal.
[15] Quoted in *Sefer Achilas Matzos BeYisrael*. See there for many other spiritual benefits of eating *matza*.

"**Save Us for Your Sake**" was originally published in 2011 on TorahWeb.org

our children's children would [still be] enslaved to Pharaoh in Egypt." A famous question is raised by many of the commentaries in slightly different ways. Would not the vicissitudes of history, the rise and fall of nations, and the change of rulers and government models have eventually led to the freedom of the Jewish people, much as they have led to the freedom of other enslaved peoples? How can we say that the Jews would still be slaves in Egypt? Why was it crucial that *Hashem* directly take us out, as emphasized by this paragraph; would not Pharaoh's releasing us through his own free will, not forced by the *makkos*, have led to the same result? Here, we present an answer by one of the classic commentaries with some elaboration.

Rav Yaakov Loberbaum of Lisa, famous for his *Nesivos HaMishpat*, in his commentary *Ma'aseh Nissim* to the *Haggada* on this opening paragraph, develops a major theme permeating the entire *Haggada*. When *Hashem* took us out of Egypt with great miracles transcending of all of the known rules of nature, he "threw His lot in," so to speak, with the Jewish people. He linked "His image" in the world to the fate of His beloved nation. If the Jews subsequently, due to their sins, would be threatened with severe punishment, or God forbid, elimination, *Hashem* automatically would consider the fact that the downtrodden state or worse, *chas veshalom*, of His nation would be interpreted as a lack of Divine power to save His nation. This of course was the basis of Moshe's powerful prayers which saved the Jewish people from destruction after the disastrous sin of the Golden Calf and, later, the sin of the spies. We continue to utilize this theme of prayer throughout the centuries by reciting in *Shemoneh Esrei*, *Hallel*, *Selichos* and many other places: "עשה למענך אם לא למעננו! – Act for Your sake, if not for ours!" This theme also serves as the means for the ultimate redemption of the Jewish people as stated by Yechezkel (36:22-23): "Say to the Children of Israel, 'So says *Hashem Elokim*: not for your sake do I act, O House of Israel, but for [the sake of] My holy Name which you desecrated among the nations to which you came. And I shall sanctify My great Name which is desecrated among the nations, which you desecrated among them, and the nations will know that I am God – the word of *Hashem Elokim* – when I am sanctified through you before their eyes." Even if the merits of the Jewish people are insufficient, God will redeem them in order to avoid further desecration of His name.

At first glance, this is a result of God having redeemed us from Egypt. In other words, since He chose to form a nation to carry His word to the world, God chooses to save us at subsequent points in history in order to uphold this mission. However, explains the *Nesivos*, God could have redeemed us in another way. He could have orchestrated the redemption in a much more natural way, similar to the *Purim* salvation, so that His "reputation" would not be at stake, since the nations of the world would not necessarily attribute the redemption to God's actions. He specifically chose a direct, openly miraculous redemption. Even Pharaoh's consent, under the duress of the plagues, was rescinded when he and his armies chased after the Jews. Only another miraculous Divine intervention led to the utter destruction of the Egyptian forces and the deliverance, once again, of the Jewish people. God chose to redeem us precisely in this way so that His image in the world should be linked to ours.

This act of Divine love which assured eternal Jewish survival is one of many themes motivating us to truly feel gratitude toward the One Who created us twice, first as people and then as members of the Jewish nation (see *Bereishis* 1:27 and *Yeshayahu* 43:21). Gratitude and recognition of the multi-faceted acts of Divine kindness are major themes of the night of the *seder*. As pointed out by the *Nesivos*, knowledge of the eternal ramifications of the exodus further motivates us to investigate and analyze how every detail concerning this event was not just for our immediate benefit but for our eternal advantage. The *Nesivos* calls this: "the absolute greatest of kindnesses with none greater!"

May we merit to absorb all of the deep, eternal messages of the first exodus and see the fulfillment of the promise of the prophets (*Micha* 7:15), "As when you went out of Egypt, I shall perform miracles for you" in the final redemption.

History and the Jewish People

The main part of the *Haggada* begins with the paragraph "עבדים היינו." There it is stated that had *Hashem* not taken us out of Egypt, we and all of our descendants would still be enslaved to Pharaoh in Egypt. The commentaries note the obvious question. The pattern of history is one of constant change on the world scene. Who is to say that some subsequent Pharaoh would not have freed the Jews? Furthermore, Pharaoh and the Egyptian kingdom are long gone. How can the *Haggada* claim that we still would be enslaved to Pharaoh? Many answers have been presented over the centuries of studying the *Haggada*, with some commentators giving conceptual explanations and some allegorical ones.[16] Netziv in his *Haggada* commentary, *Imrei Shefer*, presents a far-reaching answer, interpreting this statement of the *Haggada* quite literally.

The *Gemara* (*Yevamos* 63a) records the statement of R. Elazar b. R. Avina: "אין פורענות באה לעולם אלא בשביל ישראל – all punishments come to the world because of Israel." At first glance, this means that all tragedies such as wars or natural disasters are meant to awaken *Klal Yisrael* to return to their Father in Heaven. Indeed the *Gemara* quotes as a proof text: "I have cut off nations, their edifices have been laid waste …. I said [hoped] that you would fear Me, and take chastisement!" (*Tzefania* 3:6-7). Netziv interprets this passage in a more extensive manner. Ever since *Klal Yisrael*

---

[16] Elsewhere (see "Save Us for Your Sake," above), we explored a different answer from the one we present here.

"History and the Jewish People" was originally published in 2013 on TorahWeb.org

received the Torah at *Har Sinai*, Divine providence, managing not only Jewish history but world history, has revolved around the Jewish people. The rise and fall of nations, persecutions, emancipations, scientific discoveries and all aspects of world history and its advances and setbacks are forever bound to the preservation of the Jewish people and bringing them to their ultimate destiny, based in turn on their behavior. In turn, *Am Yisrael* serves as the *kohanim* of the world, bringing all the nations to their perfection as well. I have read that Rav Kook (a student of Netziv) expressed a similar idea describing wars as *Hashem*'s way of making massive changes on the world scene in a relatively short period of time, in order to advance Jewish history.[17] Had *Hashem* not redeemed the Jews from Egypt and brought them to receive the Torah at *Har Sinai*, this specialized Divine providence guiding history would not have operated. The world would have stagnated and would not have progressed toward its ultimate destiny, for its main actors would be missing from its stage. The Egyptian empire would still exist, since the pattern of the rise and fall of nations would not have been operative and the Jews quite literally would still be slaves there!

Mori verabi Rav Hershel Schachter *shlita* presented a related idea. The first *mishna* in *Masseches Rosh HaShana* relates that the reign of Jewish kings is reckoned from *Rosh Chodesh Nisan*. By contrast, the reign of non-Jewish kings is counted from *Rosh Chodesh Tishrei*, *Rosh HaShana*. Elaborating on the comments of the Ran, Rav Schachter explained why this should be so. *Nisan*, the month of the exodus, represents the miraculous,

---

[17] Specifically, I believe he noted that it was in the context of World War I that the Balfour Declaration, the first international breakthrough in the foundation of what was to become the State of Israel, was issued. The war also led to the fall of the Ottoman Empire and Great Britain's seizing control of then-Palestine. Ultimately, it was under the latter's rule that the land was returned to the Jewish people. Others have added that it was in the aftermath of World War II and the awesome havoc it wreaked on the Jewish nation that the State of Israel was born, serving as the framework for the massive rebuilding of the land both physically and spiritually, to the extent that currently almost six million Jews (*kein yirbu!*) have been enabled to return to their ancestral homeland and re-establish Torah observance, including the *mitzvos hateluyos ba'aretz* there.

providential intervention of *Hakadosh Baruch Hu* on the world scene. *Tishrei*, the month during which the world was created, represents the "natural order." The nations of the world follow the natural patterns of history. Jewish history follows a supernatural pattern. Consequently, the corresponding kingdoms count the years of their reign from the month that best represents the mode of their history. For the other nations of the world, this is *Tishrei*, the "natural month"; for the Jewish people, this is *Nisan*, the supernatural month. According to Netziv, although it seems that the history of the *ummos ha'olam* is following a natural pattern, the reality is that it is linked to the supernatural history of the Jews.

The Netziv's words demonstrate to us the intensity of the love *Hashem* has for His nation. He not only tends to us lovingly throughout history but machinates the entire world for our benefit and ultimate mission. His words should also awaken within us a sense of awesome responsibility, indicating the enormous effects our actions have not only on our immediate selves and communities but, indeed, on the entire world. Perhaps, then, *Pesach* can be described as the holiday celebrating not only the birth of the Jewish nation, but as the holiday commemorating the beginning of Jewish and world history!

Rabbi Eliakim Koenigsberg

The Connection between *Yetzias Mitzrayim* and *Kerias Yam Suf* (2018)

Toward the end of the *maggid* section of the *Haggada*, we mention a dispute among the *tannaim* as to how many plagues the *Mitzrim* suffered at the *Yam Suf*. What does this have to do with the *mitzva* of retelling the story of *yetzias Mitzrayim*? In fact, Rambam omits this section in his version of the *Haggada*. Rav Soloveitchik explains that this follows the Rambam's opinion (*Hilchos Chametz uMatza* 7:1) that on the night of the *seder* we are commanded to recount only the miracles that *Klal Yisrael* experienced in *Mitzrayim* and while leaving *Mitzrayim*, but not the miracles that occurred after *yetzias Mitzrayim*. Apparently, the author of the *Haggada* disagrees. He understands that even the miracles at the splitting of the sea are relevant to סיפור יציאת מצרים.

The *Magen Avraham* (67:1) takes this idea even further. He claims that one can fulfill the daily obligation to remember *yetzias Mitzrayim* by reciting the *Shiras HaYam*, the song that *Klal Yisrael* sang after the splitting of the sea. Both the *Chasam Sofer* and Rav Akiva Eiger (in their glosses to the *Shulchan Aruch* there) are troubled by this statement. After all, the *pasuk* explicitly states that one is required to remember "the day that you left *Mitzrayim*" (*Devarim* 16:3), which implies that simply reciting the *Shiras HaYam* is insufficient. How can the *Magen Avraham* claim that just by mentioning the splitting of the sea one can fulfill the daily *mitzva* of זכירת יציאת מצרים?

The Talmud *Yerushalmi* (*Pesachim* 10:6) comments that although there is an obligation to sing *shira* whenever *HaKadosh Baruch Hu* performs miracles for *Klal Yisrael*, nevertheless *Klal Yisrael* did not sing *shira* when they left *Mitzrayim* because that was still only the beginning

---

"The Connection between..." was originally published in 2018 on TorahWeb.org

of their redemption. They did not experience a complete redemption until the splitting of the sea. Similarly, *Rabbeinu* Bachya (*Shemos* 6:6) writes that the phrase, "And I will redeem you with an outstretched arm and with great judgments" is a reference to *kerias Yam Suf*, since that is when *Klal Yisrael* achieved a complete redemption.

This idea is also hinted to in the fact that we do not recite a full *Hallel*, nor do we say the *beracha* of *shehecheyanu*, on the seventh day of *Pesach*. It is quite different from *Shemini Atzeres*, the last day of *Sukkos*, which is "a holiday of its own" (*Sukka* 47a). Some explain that we do not recite a full *Hallel* on the seventh day of *Pesach* because it would be inappropriate to sing a complete *shira* for the splitting of the sea, since that miracle also caused the drowning of the *Mitzrim*, and the *pasuk* says, "When your enemy falls, do not rejoice" (*Mishlei* 24:17). But the *Gemara* (*Arachin* 10a) suggests a different reason why we do not recite a full *Hallel* on the last day of *Pesach*, and that is because it has no special *korban musaf*. Since its *korban* is the same as that of the first day of *Pesach*, the seventh day is not considered an independent *yom tov*, so it does not get a full *Hallel* of its own, and for the same reason we do not say the *beracha* of *shehecheyanu*. These *halachos* highlight the idea that the seventh day of *Pesach*, which commemorates the splitting of the sea, is not considered a separate celebration. Rather, it is viewed as the culmination of the celebration of *yetzias Mitzrayim*, since *kerias Yam Suf* was the time when *Klal Yisrael* achieved a full redemption.

What happened at the *Yam Suf* that made the redemption of *Klal Yisrael* complete? *Rabbeinu* Bachya explains that until the *Mitzrim* were drowned at the sea, *Klal Yisrael* were concerned that their former masters would chase after them and enslave them once again. But after the *Mitzrim* were eliminated at the *Yam Suf*, *Klal Yisrael* finally felt a complete sense of freedom since they no longer feared that they would be forced to return to *Mitzrayim*.

The Vilna Gaon (quoted in *Kol Eliyahu, Parashas Bo*) adds that the *geula* was not complete until *kerias Yam Suf* when the *Mitzrim* were punished in the water, מידה כנגד מידה, in return for the evil they perpetrated against *Klal Yisrael* when they decreed that every Jewish newborn male child should be thrown into the river. Netziv (*Ha'amek Davar, Shemos* 14:31) suggests that a similar idea is alluded to by the *pasuk*, "And *Klal Yisrael* saw the great hand that *Hashem* used against *Mitzrayim*, and the people feared *Hashem*." This refers to how *HaKadosh Baruch Hu* meted out precise punishments for each and every Egyptian, corresponding to the pain and suffering that each one inflicted on the Jewish people in *Mitzrayim*. Rashi (*Shemos* 15:5) quotes the Midrash that the most wicked of the Egyptians were tossed around in the *Yam Suf* like straw, the average ones fell like stones, and the relatively decent ones sank immediately like lead. Each one received a punishment that was commensurate to his actions against *Klal Yisrael*.

After *kerias Yam Suf* the Torah says, "And they believed in *Hashem* and Moshe his servant" (*Shemos* 14:31). Until then, the people could have deluded themselves into thinking that Moshe *Rabbeinu* had magically orchestrated the ten plagues and *yetzias Mitzrayim*. But when the people saw how precise the Divine punishment was, they had complete *emuna* in *Hashem*, and they realized that Moshe was only *Hashem's* agent in bringing about *yetzias Mitzrayim*.

That is why the redemption was incomplete until *kerias Yam Suf*, because one of the purposes of *yetzias Mitzrayim* was to instill in the hearts of *Klal Yisrael* a strong sense of *emuna* in the *Ribbono Shel Olam*. The ten plagues were designed to strengthen *Klal Yisrael's* belief in the existence of *Hashem*, Divine providence and omnipotence, and the concept of reward and punishment (see *Maharal, Gur Aryeh, Shemos* 9:14). At the *Yam Suf*, this process reached its climax when *Klal Yisrael* saw the element of מידה כנגד מידה in the punishment of the *Mitzrim*. At that moment, they totally believed in *Hashem* and His power, and they appreciated His sense of justice. That was when *Klal Yisrael* achieved a complete redemption. (See *Yareiach LaMoadim* 67, for further elaboration.)

It is no wonder that the author of our version of the *Haggada* includes the miracles of *kerias Yam Suf* in the text of the *Haggada*, because it was only at the *Yam Suf* that one of the primary goals of *yetzias Mitzrayim*, namely, developing a complete trust in the *Ribbono Shel Olam*, was finally achieved. This perhaps is also why the *Magen Avraham* rules that if one recites the *Shiras HaYam*, he has fulfilled his daily obligation to remember *yetzias Mitzrayim*, because the miracles of *kerias Yam Suf*, which are described in the *shira*, were the catalyst that completed the process of *yetzias Mitzrayim*.

Rabbi Yaakov Neuburger

From *Birkas HaChama* to *Hallel HaGadol*

For many, the vivid memories of where we were and with whom we stood the last time we recited the *birkas hachama* challenge us to create a meaningful recollection for our children as well. Even the giant *Chasam Sofer*, in his landmark responsum on the topic (#56), recalls the towering figure of his life, Rav Noson Adler, leaning heavily on the young student's shoulder, waiting for the sun to clear the clouds. From this experience and from a powerful argument from the language of Rambam, Rabbi Moshe Shreiber would, many years later, insist that one must actually see some semblance of the sun before reciting the *beracha*. He was refuting the argument that was proposed, though never acted upon, by an earlier decisor, the renowned *Panim Meiros*. The latter had argued that the *beracha* could be recited once we simply became aware that the sunrise had occurred. Different from other *berachos*, the refuted argument ran, this *beracha* was not responding to a visible event but rather to the recognition of the completion of the 28-year cycle of the earth's orbit.

In fact, some would argue that given that we view *Rosh Hashana* as the world's birthday and given that the twenty eight-year cycle was not used by the Rabbis in their calculations, we are in fact not marking any significant event at all. Nevertheless, the long-standing custom that the *Chasam Sofer* established, and the precise language of Rambam, argue that we remind ourselves of our Creator and His act of creation only after sighting the sun. If no sun would appear from behind a cloudy sky, one would delete *Hashem*'s name from the *beracha*, thus reciting the form of the *beracha* but not its essence.

What in fact are we to "see" when we view the sun on Wednesday morning? What is going to merit a blessing? Though we are hoping for a

---

"**From *Birkas HaChama* to *Hallel...*"** was originally published in 2009 on TorahWeb.org brilliant cloud-free horizon, we nevertheless wish for a sunrise, more or less, like any other. Of course there are different kinds of *berachos*. Yet, other than *berachos* that prepare us for procuring pleasure or performing *mitzvos*, *berachos* are usually a part of our response to an impressive if not overwhelming event, or a discovery that at least catches our attention. The text of the *birkas hachama*, "עושה מעשה בראשית" is first introduced to us as the response to the amazement generated by the sights of untouched mountains and canyons or by the expanse of an impenetrable desert. Every sunrise, to be sure, is fascinating for the introspective and "unjaded" soul, but routine events do not earn the blessing "עושה מעשה בראשית". No doubt, the knowledge of the completion of the 28-year cycle is remarkable, but why must we wait to see the sun as the *Chasam Sofer* concluded?

It seems to me that the 28-year cycle, inaccuracy aside and the *Nisan/Tishrei* inconsistency notwithstanding, should bring to mind the constancy of the orbits and the seasons, and indeed the predictability, for the most part, of *Hashem*'s world. It does not take great imagination to conjure a world whose days, seasons and climates vary wildly from year to year and whose unpredictability stymies productivity for starters, and generates great anxiety as well. The moments of *birkas hachama* will allow us to dwell on the blessings and values of "laws" in nature. Moreover, the sun will represent the many parts of creation given to us, from which we can learn those laws.

Still sounds like much ado about nothing? Not according to a comment of the second Rebbe of Ger, the celebrated *Sefas Emes*, that is recorded in his *Pesach* discourses. He establishes that the laws of nature are the "*penimiyus*" of *Hashem*, the "inner" or deeper revelation of *Hashem*. I imagine that this means that the ongoing laws of nature reveal to us, to the best of our abilities to absorb, some insights into *Hashem*'s governance. Thus, while the miraculous reveals the omnipresence, omniscience, and providence of *Hashem*, the laws of nature reveal to us some ideas that are dear to our Creator. The ideas of discipline, constancy and loyalty are revealed through the very existence of laws of nature; the concept of spontaneity is relayed through random mutations; the notion of carefully prepared gradual growth is the stuff of evolving forms of nature; and the natural interdependence of so much of the natural world creates, when appreciated, a "culture" that prizes working interaction amongst humans.

Is it not profoundly remarkable that as we complete the last-minute preparations of the 5769 holiday set to mark the miraculous aberrations of nature, that we take time to mark the laws of nature as well? It is Ramban in his final comments on *Parashas Bo*, who explains that for us, the routine and the fantastic are inextricably bound. He teaches us how the miraculous plagues in *Mitzrayim* form the basis of our beliefs, proving the existence of *Hashem*, His involvement in our world and the veracity of prophecy. However, opines Ramban, *Hashem* continues to relate to all of us throughout time via the less discernible. According to Ramban, a heart and mind trained to celebrate the miraculous will format life through them and continue to be sensitive to *Hashem* through the laws of nature as well.

If not for these insights of Ramban and *Sefas Emes*, we should all be taken aback that the *seder* night does not culminate with the *Hallel haMitzri*. After all, *Hallel haMitzri* seems to be Dovid *haMelech*'s song for the generation that was redeemed from Egypt. Rather, the evening continues with great force to include the *Hallel HaGadol* and the weekly *Nishmas*. The *Hallel HaGadol* does include the redemption from Egypt, but it must share company with the stability of dry land and the expanse of the sky and the presence of the sun and the moon. Rather surprisingly, this chapter of *Tehillim* which includes all that we have grown accustomed to, is called nothing less than the "Great *Hallel*." In *Pesachim* 118a, the Rabbis explain that the reason that this list of 26 events is referred to as the "Great *Hallel*" is that it includes the daily bread that *Hashem* provides for all.

Apparently, *Chazal* saw that the personal ongoing appreciation of the "little miracles," the ones so much within our grasp, even the miracle of being able to feed our families, may give us great insight when they stand on the shoulders of the miracles of redemption and *Har Sinai*. Through this miracle we stand to learn at the very least, about *Hashem*'s compassion, concern and commitment to all of His creations. To us, a nation of believers, gaining greater insight into *Hashem*'s "conduct" is of immeasurable value in and of itself, even without underscoring the impact it will have on those instructed to emulate His conduct.

Thus the *seder* night becomes complete in similar fashion to the character of this year's *erev yom tov*, shaped by the 206th blessing of the sun. We pray that we will be blessed with a renewed sense of wonder over the ongoing routine laws of nature, and that in turn will generate greater depth in our relationship with *Hashem* and a greater understanding of His expectations of all of us. חג כשר ושמח.

Unmasking *Hester Panim*, Hearing Prayer and Pain

The turning point in the diaspora of *Mitzrayim*, the first crack in the *hester panim*, the hiddenness of *Hashem* and the distance from Him that we felt, came in response to the prayers that consumed our hearts at that time: "[After the Egyptian king died] the Jews sighed due to the labor, they yelled (*vayizaku*), and their screams (*shavasam*) rose up to *Hashem* from their labor. *Hashem* heard their groans (*na'akasam*) and He recalled His covenant with Avraham, with Yitzchak, and with Yaakov" (*Shemos* 2:23-24).

Indeed, as we have pointed out in this space in the past (see "The Prayers Within," TorahWeb.org, 2013), it is unclear from the text whether

---

"**Unmmasking *Hester Panim*...**" was originally published in 2015 on TorahWeb.org

we were in fact shouting out to *Hashem* altogether. *Or HaChayyim* points this out and interprets that whereas our shrieks were pure expressions of our torment and despondency, *Hashem* received them and responded to them as if we were indeed *davening*. Accentuating this ambiguity is that *Hashem* hears "*na'akasam*" even as the Jews offered up "*shava*" and "*ze'aka*." Thus *Hashem* records for us that long before He revealed to us His absolute and responsive mastery over all matters, He was for us a *shomea tefilla*.

The Rav *zt"l*, who left this world on *Pesach*, and who often discussed the absurdity of the individual bringing his personal requirements to the attention of the Almighty, suggested that this phrase catches the attribute of *Hashem* that encourages what would otherwise defy all logic. In other words, being a listener is a defining characteristic of *Hashem*, much as "*rachum vechannun*" and other descriptions that *Hashem* has provided for us. This is how the Rav explained a seeming incongruity in our *Shemoneh Esrei*. It makes ample sense to request wisdom from the One who provides wisdom to all and to request cures from the One who heals. Does it make sense, in the penultimate *beracha* of request, i.e., the *beracha* of "*shomea tefilla*," to ask for anything other than empathy from a "great listener"?

Thus the Rav explained that *Hashem*, as a *shomea tefilla*, invites us to request even that which would seem to be insignificant from *Hashem*'s perspective. This attribute allows us to *daven* from our perspective, to ask what is meaningful to us, even though we could not ask for it would we consider *Hashem*'s perspective.

The significance of this part of our relationship with *Hashem* is underscored by a Rashi on the *Aseres HaDibros*. Rashi (*Shemos* 20:2) teaches us to grapple with the formulation prohibiting the service of "other gods." Rashi argues that it cannot be read literally without giving a measure of credibility to some aspect of divinity of a pagan system, and that would be offensive to the *Ribbono Shel Olam*. At first Rashi explains that "others" (presumably unworthy humans) appointed these idols as gods for themselves. The second interpretation explains the falseness and deceptiveness of these gods, as they are "others" to those who serve them, i.e., they do not answer when they appeal to them and act as if they don't recognize the supplicant at all.

Therefore it is clear that the placement of this comment at the head of the Decalogue, as monotheism is being described, instructs us to appreciate that *Hashem*'s responsiveness to us is not only a license for one particular *beracha* and request, but distinguishes our core beliefs in a most meaningful manner. It follows, quite counterintuitively, that it is because God presented Himself as the ultimate *shomea tefilla* that almost every prayer is meaningful, and that allows otherwise insignificant concerns to connect us to our Creator.

Hashem introduced us to His trait of *shomea tefilla* as He opened to us the phases of His revelation and the steps of our redemption. Interestingly, He described Himself as listening to our *ne'akos* (groans) rather than our *tefillos*. Moreover, according to Rabbi Yochonon (*Midrash Rabba*, beginning of *Parashas Va'eschanan*) it is in this moment that *Hashem* begins to describe to us the many and varied dimensions of prayer, for it is from the previously cited *pesukim* that we learn that "*ze'aka*," "*shava*" and "*ne'aka*" are types of prayer. Each of the ten formulae of prayer listed by Rabbi Yochanan (ibid.) presumably reveals new facets of prayer. Both Malbim and Rav Hirsch, through different parallel studies, explain *ne'aka* as a despairing prayer, one final gasping shot, if you will. Rav Hirsch continues to observe that the text teaches that *Hashem* accepted prayers that were not yet mouthed and responded to dangers with an urgency that we had not yet felt.

Rav Shimshon Pincus *zt"l*, in his classic work *Shearim BeTefilla*, explains that we present *bakashos* – requests – in our prayers, but behind every request is a *ne'aka*. For example, in our *Shemoneh Esrei* we list our *bakashos* for wisdom, health, *parnasa*, the ingathering of our people and our return to *Yerushalayim*, and we do not readily give expression to the *ne'aka*.

We may simply ask for *parnasa*, and that comprises our *bakasha*. Yet the underlying *ne'aka* is the fear of foreclosure, the anxiety of having to borrow again, the embarrassment of meeting one's creditors, the fear that the next phone call is one of them, etc. Our *bakashos* may ask to be blessed with family, while the unstated *ne'aka* is the month-by-month disappointment, the tug every time one sees a friend's baby carriage, hears of a *shalom zachar*, or is part of a conversation about carpools. Our *bakasha* asks for a complete recovery and a life free of a nagging ailment, while the latent *ne'aka* is to never have to see the young suffer and to be full of faith and free of questions and doubts.

In *Mitzrayim*, we cried out from suffering that defied words, and that was our *bakasha* and *ze'aka*. Nevertheless, *Hashem* saw that anguish and heard as well the cry of a people whose lives had become seemingly meaningless, whose glorious legacy had been driven down to misery and emptiness. Whereas we, for the most part, were focused on surviving the day and could hardly feel pained by lost opportunities, *Hashem* saw the hollowness of an unfulfilled destiny and the crushing disappointment of the vacant dreams of His beloved Avraham, Yitzchak and Yaakov.

Thus, not only do we learn the fullness and uniqueness of *Hashem*'s *midda* of *shomea tefilla* from His response to *Bnei Yisrael*, but we also can try to enrich our own *davening* (whether we are the subject of the *tefilla* or others are) by focusing on the *ne'aka* latent within every *bakasha*.

Rabbi Michael Rosensweig

Shevi'i shel Pesach: The *Yom Tov* of *Shira*

Shevi'i shel Pesach is an unusual *yom tov*. Though it commemorates the extraordinary miracle of *kerias Yam Suf*, this theme is omitted in *Emor* and the other relevant *parshiyos* in the Torah. Notwithstanding the significance of the miracle, this is the only *yom tov* in which the complete *Hallel* is not recited, as it does not differ from the days of *chol hamoed* with respect to its *korbanos* (*Arachin* 10b). Indeed, this *yom tov* is completely subsumed under the broad rubric of *chag hamatzos* in the *parshiyos of Bo, Mishpatim, Emor, Pinchas* and *Re'eh*. While the *Drisha* (*Tur, Orach Chayyim* no. 490) cites Maharil's view that one should formulate this *yom tov* in *tefilla, kiddush*, and *birkas hamazon* as "*yom simchaseinu*" due to *kerias Yam Suf*, this position is almost uniformly rejected in favor of the continued emphasis on the exodus from Egypt and "*zeman cheiruseinu*."

There are also some indications that the *shira* that followed the miracle may be as central to this *yom tov* as the event that inspired it. Indeed, the selection of a *haftara* reading for this *yom tov* entirely ignores the specific occurrence of this day. Instead, the portion (Samuel II, 22) reflects the broader themes of *shira*, faith, and gratitude. Perhaps a brief examination of the phenomenon of *Shiras HaYam* may further illuminate these emphases.

Shiras HaYam is written in a special formation in the Torah, underscoring its uniqueness. At the same time, its relevance is attested to by its inclusion in the daily prayers. While it seeks to commemorate a singular event, there are indications that its significance transcends its origins. The fact that a *shira* did not follow immediately in the aftermath of the *makkos* or even of *yetzias Mitzrayim* seems to underscore that it was not just a response to a supernatural experience. Moreover, the double

---

"**Shevi'i shel Pesach...**" was originally published in 2002 on TorahWeb.org

introduction to the *shira*: "ויראו העם... ויאמינו – and the people feared... and they believed" (*Shemos* 14:31), requires clarification. The mention of Moshe *Rabbeinu* in conjunction with *Hashem* is puzzling, as well. Having articulated their faith in *Hashem*, is it not superfluous or even inappropriate to affirm their belief in Moshe? The term "*az*" ("then"), implying a transition from, as well as a connection to, what preceded it suggests that the inspiration to express *shira* constitutes an important juncture in the fledgling development of *Klal Yisrael*. Commenting on the future tense of "*yashir*" ("will sing"), *Chazal* view this moment also as a foundation for faith in the future destiny of the nation: "שר לא נאמר אלא ישיר. מכאן לתחית המתים מן התורה – it did not state 'sang,' but rather 'will sing'... from here we have a source in the Torah for the future resurrection of the dead." Furthermore, there is an interesting debate as to when the *shira* begins: *Tosafos* in *Sota* see "אז ישיר" as an introductory sentence, while Rambam, *Hilchos Sefer Torah*, perceives it as the first verse of the *shira* itself. Rambam's intriguing perspective implies that *Klal Yisrael's* state of awareness is an integral aspect of the *shira* itself!

Perhaps what differentiates this miracle and the response of *shira* that it engendered was precisely the timing, as well as the order and emphasis delineated in the Torah that reflected a moment of spiritual clarity for *Am Yisrael*. The fact that the nation did not previously respond with *shira* although they had frequently encountered supernatural manifestations, demonstrates that the *shira* was more than a reaction to a superficial stimulus. The double introduction in which the theme of *yira* (fear) preceded that of *emuna* (faith), after a period of deliberation and reflection implied by this series of *pesukim*, projects, at least momentarily, the spiritual maturity of *Klal Yisrael*. It was indeed "*az*," a moment of import, with implications for the application of the concept of *emuna* for the future – "שר לא נאמר." Thus, according to Rambam, the verse of "אז ישיר" constitutes not only the introduction but the beginning of the *shira*! Moreover, it is consistent with this newly discovered broader perspective that at that moment, the nation finally fully comprehended the subtle critical role of Moshe *Rabbeinu*. An understanding of the relationship between observing the *mitzvos* "זה קלי ואנוהו," especially as expressed in *Chazal*'s doctrine of הידור מצוה, and acknowledging Divine intervention – "אשירה לה׳ כי גאה גאה" was critical at that special moment of *kerias Yam Suf*, but is no less pivotal in daily prayer.

The Torah chose not to formulate a separate *yom tov* commemorating *kerias Yam Suf*, since the primary significance of this miracle was its impact on the concept of *emuna* and *yiras Hashem* that well transcended the event. The *shira* that it engendered was possibly not less important than the physical salvation of *Klal Yisrael*. It is appropriate, indeed, that the last day of *chag hamatzos*, the anniversary of *kerias hayam* and the *shira*, be fully integrated into the celebration of *yetzias Mitzrayim* and "*zeman cheiruseinu*," as both the miracle of *kerias hayam* and the *shira* that it inspired magnificently highlight the theme of *emuna* and *hashgacha* that stand at the core of the significance of the exodus from Egypt (see Ramban, end of *Parashas Bo*) and the integrated holiday of *chag hamatzos*.

The Special Connection between *Pesach* and *Shabbos*

Rambam (*Hilchos Chametz uMatza* 7:1) begins his discussion of the *mitzva* of סיפור יציאת מצרים on the night of *Pesach* by invoking a parallel obligation to remember and recognize the sanctity of *Shabbos* (כמו שנאמר זכור את יום השבת) that is the basis for reciting *kiddush* on *Shabbos*. Why does Rambam feel the need to link סיפור יציאת מצרים with *kiddush* on *Shabbos*, and how does this intriguing link enhance our appreciation and understanding of the *mitzva* of סיפור יציאת מצרים?

"The Special Connection between..." was originally published in 2003 on TorahWeb.org

The *Gemara* in *Pesachim* (117b) does connect the זכור's of *Shabbos* and *Pesach*, albeit in the opposite direction. It establishes the need to refer to the exodus in *Shabbos kiddush* on this basis. It is possible that Rambam viewed the very fact that *yetzias Mitzrayim* is incorporated into the *kiddush* of *Shabbos* as indicative of its wide scope and great prominence, which in turn adds greater urgency and accentuates its centrality on *Pesach* itself. Perhaps, absent its defining role on *Pesach*, this theme would not have impacted on *Shabbos* either. Moreover, it is conceivable that Rambam perceived the bond between *Shabbos* and *Pesach*, reflected in the concept of "*zachor*" that ties them together, as necessarily reciprocal. Thus, the *Gemara* in *Pesachim*, establishing the incorporation of *yetzias Mitzrayim* on *Shabbos*, dictates the relevance of *kedushas Shabbos* as a theme that enhances סיפור יציאת מצרים as well. In order to better comprehend these ideas, it is necessary to further explore the bond between *Shabbos* and *Pesach*.

The Torah itself links *Shabbos* and *avdus Mitzrayim* in the second rendition of the *Aseres HaDibros* (*Devarim* 5:14): "וזכרת כי־עבד היית בארץ מצרים ויצאך ה' א-לקיך משם ביד חזקה ובזרע נטויה על־כן צוך ה' א-לקיך לעשות את־יום השבת – You shall remember that you were a slave in Egypt, and *Hashem* your God took you out from there with a mighty hand and an outstretched arm, therefore *Hashem* your God has commanded you to observe *Shabbos*." Indeed, Maharsha (*Pesachim* 117b) questions why the insertion of the exodus into *Shabbos kiddush* isn't simply rooted in this *pasuk*. While Ibn Ezra limits the role of *yetzias Mitzrayim* to the inclusion of *shevisas eved*, and Rashi explains that it serves only to underscore why we are obligated to adhere to any Divine obligation, Rambam and Ramban do assign greater prominence to this link, which further strengthens Maharsha's question. Ramban (ad loc.) argues that *yetzias Mitzrayim* strongly reinforces the primary theme of זכר למעשה בראשית that conveys our recognition of *Hashem*'s unique role and status as the omnipotent Creator, Who also intervenes and exercises *hashgacha* in the real world.

(See also his comments on *Shemos* 20:2 and at the end of *Parashas Bo*.) Rambam (*Moreh Nevuchim* 2:31) attaches even greater significance to *yetzias Mitzrayim*'s contribution to *Shabbos*. He argues that while the significance and stature of the day is due to the theological and philosophical affirmation of *Hashem*'s role as Creator, the reason that we observe it is an expression of our recognition and appreciation of His overwhelming kindness reflected in the redemption from Egypt.

An analysis of the *Gemara* in *Pesachim* reveals other difficulties. Rashbam asserts that the reference to "זכר ליציאת מצרים" in the *kiddush* and *tefilla* of other holidays is derived directly (*binyan av*) from *Pesach*. Maharsha wonders why a similar mechanism could not have sufficed for *Shabbos*. Is there some greater resistance to this theme on *Shabbos*, which would also help explain why the *pasuk* in the *Aseres HaDibros* was not a sufficient reason to accent this theme on *Pesach*? It is also noteworthy that, notwithstanding Rashbam's comment to the contrary, we do not refer to *yetzias Mitzrayim* in *tefillas Shabbos* (see Rashash, *Pesachim* 117b). Other *rishonim* (*Behag*, Ran) assume that other holidays refer to the exodus because of their link with *Shabbos*! It seems that *Shabbos*, rather than *Pesach*, is the gateway for this theme in the broader scheme of the *moadim*, as only its role in *Shabbos* demonstrates its broader significance beyond *Pesach*. The *Tosfos Rid* (*Pesachim*, ad loc., *mahadura telita*) is disturbed by the irony that *Shabbos*, which is the foundation for זכירת יציאת מצרים of other festivals in *tefilla* as well as *kiddush*, limits its own reference to the exodus to the *kiddush*. Apparently, while the impact of the exodus on *Shabbos* is a model for other *moadim*, its own singular focus on זכר למעשה בראשית limits a fuller expression. Apparently, the themes of *Shabbos* and *Pesach*, reflected by their motifs – the exodus and the creation – are both competing and complementary.

It is unsurprising that these two pivotal episodes compete for prominence in several contexts. *Chazal* and the *mefarshim* question why the Torah didn't begin with a discussion of Jewish history and *Pesach* –

"החודש הזה לכם ראש חדשים" (*Shemos* 12:2), instead of the account of creation. While Rashi (*Bereishis* 1:1) needs to justify this reality, Ramban asserts that creation is the most appropriate foundation for the Torah. When *Hashem* introduces Himself in the revelation of *matan Torah* by referring to His role in the exodus, *mefarshim* debate whether ideally it would have been more appropriate to make reference to the apparently more impressive and universally significant act of creation. Again, different perspectives emerge in the assessment of the Torah's choice (see Ibn Ezra and Ramban, *Shemos* 20:2). When the Torah delineates the festivals, it formulates two different beginnings, one associated with *Shabbos* (*Vayikra* 23:2: "מועדי ה' אשר־תק־ראו אתם מקראי קדש אלה הם מועדי"), and the other with *Pesach* (*Vayikra* 23:4: "אלה מועדי ה' מקראי קדש אשר־תקראו אתם במועדם"). (For a different perspective on this point, see TorahWeb.org, *Parashas Emor* 5760.) *Shabbos* provides the model of *issur melacha* for all of the *moadim*, though that theme is primary and intrinsic to *Shabbos*. At the same time, the characteristic התר אוכל נפש that applies to all *moadim* (excluding *Yom Kippur*), has its origin in the model of *Pesach*, which is first formulated in the image of *Shabbos* (*Shemos* 12:16): "כל מלאכה לא יעשה בהם" – no manner of work shall be done," (as opposed to the "מלאכת עבודה" formulations of *Emor*; see Ramban, *Shemos* 23:7), and only then qualified: "אך אשר יאכל לכל נפש הוא לבדו יעשה לכם – only that which every person is to eat, that alone may be done by you." The *rishonim* (see Ramach, *Hilchos Yom Tov* 1:1) question why *Pesach* should serve as the model for this *halacha*. The parallel influences of *yetzias Mitzrayim* and creation, of *Pesach* and *Shabbos*, are striking. *Chazal* indicate that the entire week revolves around *Shabbos* (*Beitza* 16a) and the cycle of festivals and months takes its cue from *Pesach-Nisan*, the time of past and future redemption. Ramban develops the idea that numbers, rather than names, are used to designate days and months because *Shabbos* and *Pesach* are the double foci of Jewish life. The use of numbers is a mechanism to maintain constant awareness of the centrality and inspirational quality of these episodes.

While the integrity of each event and theme requires a predominant focus in its own context, perhaps reflected in the omission of "זכר ליציאת מצרים" in the *tefilla* of *Shabbos*, the relationship of these values is mutually enhancing and complementary. An expansion of Rambam's perspective, cited previously, which accentuates the differences between the two themes within the context of *Shabbos*, can be used to illustrate how each theme can enhance the other. Creation can be perceived predominantly as conveying a theological axiom that reflects *Hashem*'s existence and omnipotence, even as it underscores that seemingly insuperable gap between Infinite Creator and impotent creation. Man did not even exist until the final stages of the creation process. On the surface, the truth of creation is relevant not only to the covenantal community of *Klal Yisrael*, but to universal mankind as well. At first glance, it is puzzling that *Halacha* views *Shabbos* as the special *os* of *Klal Yisrael*, like *mila* etc., and even prohibits non-Jews from partaking in this day – "גוי ששבת חייב מיתה." On the other hand, *yetzias Mitzrayim* constitutes an acknowledgement of the close, personal bond between *Hashem* and *Klal Yisrael*, attesting to a special *hashgacha*. It was a concrete experience, affecting and transforming a desperate people. *Hashem*'s protection and intimate involvement seems almost inconsistent with His transcendence.

The fusion of *Shabbos* and *Pesach*, of creation and the exodus, projects a more ambitious and nuanced perspective. In light of the exodus, *Hashem*'s personal involvement ("אני ולא מלאך...") and *Klal Yisrael*'s special status and destiny as "*am segula*," one needs to reassess the nature and purpose of "*bereishis*" – creation. The apparent objective is, indeed, to create an environment conducive to the ideals of Torah and *mitzvos* – "בשביל תורה (וישראל) שנקרא ראשית" – for the sake of the Torah (and *Yisrael*) which are called 'the first'" (Rashi, *Midrash Bereishis Rabba* 1:1). Man surfaces only at the end of the process, not as an afterthought, but as the telos. The implication of insuperable distance is to be replaced by the quite different emphasis of *imitatio Dei* – "*lehidamos laHashem*" – which demands that man, *betzelem Elokim*, refrain from *melacha*. Observing *Shabbos* by means of *issur melacha* conveys both man's greatness and approximation to *Hashem*, as well as his recognition of absolute distance and obvious inadequacy in His presence. *Shabbos*, when viewed properly, is a singular and exclusive *os* between *Klal Yisrael* and *Hashem*, because it is crucial to the multifaceted, ambitious agenda of the *am segula*. At the same time, our assessment of *yetzias Mitzrayim* undergoes serious revision when we contemplate *Hashem*'s transcendence. The intimate participation and the mutuality-reciprocity of the relationship to *Klal Yisrael* built on *Hashem*'s *chesed*, but also *Klal Yisrael*'s *emuna* and *mesirus nefesh* (reflected in "משכו וקחו לכם – draw out, and take for yourselves" [*Shemos* 12:21] – שישחטו אלוהיהם לעיניהם, slaughter the Egyptian deity openly) is more surprising and therefore more impressive, certainly more fully appreciated, and also assumes greater religious significance in light of the awesome omnipotence implicit in creation. If *yetzias Mitzrayim* projects greater sensitivity to the personal, experiential aspects of religion and to the role of human destiny and potential, *ma'asei bereishis* insures that man more fully appreciate and be humbled by that greater religious scope and opportunity inherent in serving *Hashem*, both in His immanence and in His transcendence.

    The integration of the two themes is expressed through the insertion of זכר ליציאת מצרים in the *kiddush* of *Shabbos*, although primarily as a way of enhancing זכר למעשה בראשית. Its impact on *Shabbos*, notwithstanding a different primary emphasis, demonstrates its centrality to all of the *moadim*, where it is conveyed even in the *tefilla*. Perhaps the *Gemara* in its presentation of the source of this conclusion seeks to underscore that the insertion of זכר ליציאת מצרי into *Shabbos kiddush* draws not upon the second rendition of the *dibros* where the link is internal to *Shabbos*, disentangled from *Pesach*, and in a context that de-emphasizes

זכר למעשה בראשית, but upon the full concrete experience of the actual exodus in the *Pesach* context designed to be most memorable (*Devarim* 16:3) – "למען תזכר את יום צאתך מארץ מצרים כל ימי חייך" – so that you may remember the day that you left Egypt all the days of your life." Thus, it is intentionally derived specifically from the first rendition of *Aseres HaDibros*, in which the commemoration of creation is the exclusive focus (*Shemos* 20:7-11) in order to demonstrate that its contribution is not a dilution, but an enhancement of that theme.

Rambam (*Hilchos Chametz uMatza* 7:1) stresses this reciprocal link in the other direction, as well. In addressing the central theme of סיפור יציאת מצרים, he finds it meaningful to invoke the *kiddush* of *Shabbos*. By doing so, he reminds us of the overwhelming impact of this experience, and perhaps also hints at the reciprocal impact of זכר למעשה בראשית on our precise evaluation of סיפור יציאת מצרים. The reciprocal link intentionally focuses not on the more abstract and generally didactic *mitzva* of זכירת יציאת מצרים (which according to Rambam is a dimension of the קבלת עול מלכות שמים of *Kerias Shema*, as the Rav *zt"l* noted), but the more concrete, vivid, detailed and even visceral experience of the *sippur*.

The tie between *Shabbos* and *Pesach* may be reflected in other issues as well. In one *pasuk*, *Pesach* itself is designated as "*Shabbos*" (*Vayikra* 23:11, regarding the *korban omer*). Conceivably, only *Pesach* [and *Yom Kippur*, by virtue of its special bond with *Shabbos*] might qualify for this designation. The *poskim* are perplexed about the origins and status of *Shabbos HaGadol*. Many argue that this special *Shabbos* commemorates the extraordinary standard of *emuna* exhibited by *Klal Yisrael* in responding on *Shabbos*, the 10th of *Nisan*, to the challenge to ready "שה לבית אבות שה לבית – a lamb according to their fathers' houses, a lamb for each household" (*Shemos* 12:3), publicizing their intent to sacrifice the Egyptian deity. The *poskim* note that rarely do we commemorate events by the day of the week rather than the calendar day of the month. Why, then, do we always observe this important step in the process of *yetzias Mitzrayim* on the *Shabbos* before *Pesach*? R. Levi ibn Haviv (*Chiddushei Hagahos, Tur*, 430) suggests that the process began on *Shabbos* because *yetzias Mitzrayim* was destined to play a crucial role in *Shabbos*! One might add that the reciprocal relationship of *Shabbos* and *Pesach*, and the mutually enhancing themes that are so strongly identified with them, made this truly a *Shabbos HaGadol*.

Chag HaPesach: The Ideal Introduction to *Chag HaMatzos*

In *Parashas Emor* (*Vayikra* 23:4), the Torah introduces all of the festivals, designating them as days of "*mikraei kodesh*." Expecting to encounter the first of the *moadim*, we are instead initially surprised to be told of the *korban pesach* that is brought on the afternoon of the 14th day of *Nisan*. Only in the next verse do we read of "*chag hamatzos*" which commences on the 15th of the month. Why does the Torah present the preparation of the *korban pesach*, which seemingly takes place before the festival, as the first of the Torah's festivals?

Chizkuni suggests that the period in which the *pesach* is offered and eaten, from the afternoon of the 14th of *Nisan* through the evening of the 15th, is halachically designated as "*Pesach*," while "*chag hamatzos*," which briefly overlaps that first night, extends seven days. Netziv, in his commentary on the Torah, suggests that the bringing of the *pesach* constituted a *moed* in its own right. In his *Haggada*, Netziv explains that our yearning to experience other "*moadim*" refers to the offering of the *pesach* which has the status of a festival, as reflected by its inclusion in the list of *moadim* in *Parashas Emor*.

This perspective is projected by the Gaon of Vilna as well. The

---

"Chag HaPesach: The Ideal..." was originally published in 2004 on TorahWeb.org

Rama (*Yoreh De'ah* 399:3) rules that while a mourner in the midst of the *shiva* period should continue adhering to the mourning prohibitions until late in the day before other festivals, he concludes his mourning period at noon before the onset of *Pesach*. The Gaon explains that this distinction is based upon the fact that the *korban pesach*, which was prepared in the afternoon prior to *chag hamatzos*, constitutes a *moed*, *chag hapesach*, as indicated by its inclusion in *Parashas Emor*.

The status of this period as a *moed* resonates in other *halachos*. Rambam (*Hilchos Yom Tov* 8:17-19) formulates the prohibition to engage in "*melacha*" during this period as comparable to a "*chol hamoed*" (See *Pesachim* 50a-b, and Rashi, *Tosafos*, *Ba'al haMaor*, Ramban and Ravad op. cit.). *Rabbeinu* Chananel (*Pesachim* 98a) describes the *Hallel* that accompanied the slaughtering of the *korban pesach* as a *yom tov Hallel* (see *Pesachim* 64a, 95a, 117a, and *Griz al haRambam, Hilchos Korban Pesach*). Rambam (*Hilchos Chametz uMatza* 1:8) rules according to R. Yehuda's view (*Pesachim* 28b) that *chametz* eaten in the afternoon of the 14th is subject to a *lav* and *malkos* because it is the period of the *pesach* offering. Perhaps this link between *korban pesach* and the prohibition of *chametz* can be explained on the basis that *chag hapesach* has commenced, although *chag hamatzos* has yet to have begun.

Why should this sacrifice generate a quasi-festival in its own right? R. Gamliel (*Pesachim* 116b) established that there are three indispensable components in the *Haggada-seder* experience: *pesach*, *matza* and *maror*. Yet, the *pesach* appears to have a disproportionate impact upon the other two. The *maror* constitutes a biblical obligation only in conjunction with the *pesach*. Many aspects of *matza* are defined by the timing of the *pesach*. Netziv argues that in the ideal circumstances in which there is a *korban pesach*, that theme dominates our focus during the *seder*, relegating *matza* and *maror* to a supporting role (*Imrei Shefer*, regarding different formulations of *matza*'s role in R. Gamliel's triad. See also Maharsha,

Pesachim 116b). Furthermore, Netziv notes in his introduction to the *Haggada* that many unique practices at the *seder* can be traced to the effort to sustain the centrality of the *korban pesach* even in our post-*churban* era.

Indeed, the *korban pesach*'s singular character and its pivotal role in Judaism is attested to in other halachic contexts. It is inextricably linked to the only other *mitzvas asei* whose neglect triggers a punishment of *kareis*, i.e., *bris mila*. *Chazal* note that the phrase "בדמיך חיי, by your blood you shall live" refers to the blood of *mila* and *korban pesach*. Circumcision is a prerequisite for participation in the *korban pesach*. Just as the *mila* is an indispensable component in Jewish commitment, so too *korban pesach* is perceived as crucial to Jewish destiny. *Chazal* (see *Mechilta* cited by Rashi, *Shemos* 12:48) even found it necessary to preclude the notion that one who converts to Judaism any time during the year would have to bring a *korban pesach*, just as a male convert would have to undergo circumcision in the process of joining *Klal Yisrael*!

The Torah consistently describes the *korban pesach* as "*pesach laHashem*," implying a special expression of devotion and recognition of *Hashem*'s role. The *parasha* of *pesach sheini* (*Bamidbar*, chapter 9) records the urgency with which *Klal Yisrael* regarded *korban pesach* as a spiritual opportunity to forge a relationship with *Hashem*. It was inconceivable to the nation that there would not be another opportunity to experience this *korban*. The requirement that this sacrifice be undertaken strictly *lishma* (see the *mishna* on *Zevachim* 2a), that it alone follow rather than precede the afternoon *tamid*, and other anomalies associated with this *korban* (its *minui*, its *nosar*, its *yotzei* etc.) attest to its *sui generis* character. The fact is that this *korban* is not developed in the Torah in the context of other sacrifices (*Vayikra*, *Tzav*, *Pinchas*, etc.), just as it is not sacrificed within the traditional time frame bracketed by the two *temidim*. Unlike other *korbanos*, there is no focus even on *ritzui*, no hint of the otherwise ubiquitous concept of "אשה ריח ניחוח," (see *Chasam Sofer*, Netziv and other *poskim* regarding the possibility of its sacrifice in the aftermath of the *churban haBayis*), and no special portion for the *kohanim*. *Korban pesach* is sometimes formulated as a *korban tzibbur*, though the *mitzva* devolves upon each individual and is achieved by means of voluntary groupings. This *korban* defies classification because its role is unique.

The *Noda BeYehuda*, in his commentary to the *Haggada*, explains that R. Gamliel's three components correspond to three tenets of our faith. *Pesach* symbolizes *Hashem*'s personal providence (השגחה פרטית). *Hashem*'s special supervision and devotion to *Klal Yisrael* was manifested in the personal intervention on the night of the 15th of *Nisan*. In his view, *matza* accents the nation's faith, and *maror* is associated with the concept of reward and punishment. But the fact is that *pesach* also integrates *Hashem*'s *hashgacha* on the night of the 15th with *Klal Yisrael*'s remarkable faith initiative in following the command to publicly slaughter the symbol of Egyptian divinity on the afternoon of the 14th of *Nisan*. The significance of this remarkable interaction between *Klal Yisrael* and *Hashem* establishes the *korban pesach* as a singular symbol and vehicle of *avodas Hashem*, and even generates a period of *kedushas hazeman*.

R. Levi Yitzchak of Berdichev posits that the Torah formulates the holiday as *chag hamatzos* because *Hashem* chooses to credit *Klal Yisrael*'s extraordinary commitment evidenced by their rush to follow His norm notwithstanding the uncertainty of their situation, while *Klal Yisrael* traditionally refers to the same holiday as *chag hapesach*, underscoring *Hashem*'s extraordinary devotion to *Klal Yisrael* reflected by His personal intervention on their behalf ("לא על ידי מלאך" etc.). In fact, both themes also find expression in the preparation and eating of the *pesach* itself during the quasi-*moed* of *chag hapesach* that actually commences in the afternoon of the 14th, as recorded in *Parashas Emor*, preceding, overlapping, setting the tone for, and ultimately enhancing the entire experience of *chag hamatzos*.

Matza as an Expression of Hoda'a

The *Mishna* (*Pesachim* 35a) excludes the use of *tevel* (produce that has not been tithed and is therefore forbidden food) for the fulfillment of the *mitzva* of *matza* on *Pesach* night. The *Gemara* (35b-36a) justifies this disqualification based on the rule of אין איסור חל על איסור (an existing prohibition is not subject to an additional injunction). Thus, the status of *tevel* would preclude the further prohibition of *chametz* that applies on *Pesach*. Consequently, *tevel* cannot produce *matza*, based on the rule invoked by the *Gemara* that only that which is subject to the *issur* of *chametz* may qualify for the *mitzva* of *matza*.

Ramban (*Pesachim* 35b) rejects the *Mishna*'s ruling because he concludes that a more expansive and inclusive *issur* such as *chametz* (*issur mosif*) would apply even to *tevel*. In his view, *tevel matza* would accomplish the *mitzva* since *tevel* could conceivably violate *chametz*, although one would also violate the injunction against *tevel*. Ramban notes an apparent inconsistency in Rambam's position on this matter. Rambam (*Hilchos Chametz uMatza* 6:7) excludes *tevel matza*, like the *Mishna*, even though he does not accept the *Gemara*'s rationale regarding אין איסור חל על איסור!

In fact, Rambam projects a different justification for the exclusion of *tevel matza*, asserting that any substance that does not warrant a *birkas hamazon* will not qualify for the *mitzva* of *matza*. The commentators struggle with the source and logic of this principle. Perhaps a better understanding of the objective of סיפור יציאת מצרים generally and of the role of *matza* specifically may clarify Rambam's thinking.

It is particularly Rambam (*Sefer HaMitzvos*, *asei* 157) who develops the idea that סיפור יציאת מצרים transcends relating the detailed events of the exodus and acknowledging their theological and spiritual significance. He

---

"*Matza* **as an Expression of Hoda'a**" was originally published in 2006 on TorahWeb.org

articulates that personal *hoda'a* (thanksgiving) is an essential component as well. This concept is reflected in the *Gemara*'s report (*Pesachim* 116a) that one who comprehends that liberation coupled with self-sufficiency must stimulate personal gratitude and praise is exempt from formulating the *ma nishtana* passage, as the principles of the passage have already been internalized. Indeed, more than any halachic authority, Rambam (*Hilchos Chametz uMatza* 7:6) accentuates the need to personalize the experience of the exodus and to express it demonstratively. (See *Pesachim* 116a and *Hilchos Chametz uMatza* 7:6-7, and compare 8:5.) Rambam also intensifies the link between the *Haggada* experience and the chapter of "ארמי אבד אבי"/*mikra bikkurim* (see *Pesachim* 116a and *Hilchos Chamtez uMatza* 7:4), which underscores the theme of personal thanksgiving.

The *seder* revolves around the four cups of wine, each representing a different motif of redemption, and סיפור יציאת מצרים. Three of the four cups are linked with themes that have evident significance on this night. The *kiddush* of the *seder* (the first cup) is perceived by some halachists as the actual *beracha* of סיפור יציאת מצרים. The second cup focuses on the actual story of the exodus (*maggid*), culminating with the sections of *Hallel* that are devoted to the events of this night. The fourth cup (*birkas hashir*) completes the *Hallel* by applying, expanding and universalizing the implications of the exodus experience. Only the third cup, *birkas hamazon*, appears to be generic and routine, disconnected from the specific themes of the night. However, in light of the essential role of personal *hoda'a*, this conclusion should be reassessed. *Birkas hamazon* is, after all, the quintessential blessing for thanksgiving. According to many authorities, it may be the only biblically mandated *beracha*!

The *mitzva* of *matza* is particularly related to this theme of thanksgiving. The Gaon of Vilna explains that the beginning section of the *Haggada*, "הא לחמא עניא," establishes *matza* as *lechem oni* (poor bread) and as the paradigm for the four categories who are obligated to give thanksgiving (*arba'a tzerichim lehodos*; *Berachos* 54b). The Gaon explains that the four questions, four sons, four formulations of redemption etc. all reflect the theme that is encapsulated in *matza*!

Maharsha (*Pesachim* 116a-b) questions why the *mitzva* of *matza* requires an accompanying formula (R. Gamliel) beyond the routine *beracha*, why one formulation in the *Mishna* links it to redemption ("על שם שנגאלו, because they were redeemed" vs. "על שם שלא הספיק בצקם להחמיץ, because their dough did not have a chance to rise"), and why the nation was involved in this *mitzva* even before they actually departed from Egypt. He concludes that *matza* also constituted a form of *korban*, like *menachos* which were made of *matza*. It appears that he is referring to the model of the *korban toda*.

Although the *korban toda* actually contained a component of *chametz* (*Vayikra* 7:12-14), it is noteworthy, as Ramban indicates, that the Torah defines that *korban* primarily in terms of the *matza* loaves, while the *chametz* is mostly an adjunct to the *korban*. (See also Ramban's remarks on 7:14, on the difference between *toda* and *shtei halechem*.) Seforno argues that the *chametz*'s function in the *toda* is to insure that in our euphoria we do not ignore the catalyst to our initial distress and become complacent regarding future challenges to our spiritual and physical wellbeing. It is possible that the *mitzva* of *matza* on the *seder* night represents a more pristine form of *toda*, one which does not allow any *chametz*, one in which all the ingredients are worthy of the *mizbeach*. Moreover, the formula of "מתחילין בגנות ומסיימין בשבח," in the context of *mitzvas* סיפור יציאת מצרים and *matza* guarantees a balanced assessment of the past that helps to secure a proper perspective in the present. The *Chasam Sofer* (commentary on the *Haggada*) suggests that the first question of the *ma nishtana* focuses on why *chametz* could not be eaten as a prelude to the *matza* of *Pesach* just as *chametz* can be eaten before any *korban mincha*. The response provided in the section of

"עבדים היינו" conveys the idea that *Klal Yisrael* emerging from Egypt required a more radical rejection of *chametz* and an absolute immersion in the symbol of *matza*.

We may now return to the innovative and apparently enigmatic formula of Rambam. Rambam postulated that one cannot fulfill the *mitzva* of *matza* with any substance that is disqualified for a *birkas hamazon*. We can now better appreciate that a *matza* that does not stimulate the blessing of thanksgiving contravenes the very objective of *mitzvas matza*. In this principle, Rambam succinctly and profoundly formalized the central function of personal and national thanksgiving on this singular evening.

Pesach Sheini: A Quest for Spiritual Opportunity and National Identity

Parashas Behalosecha records the extraordinary petition of a group that had been excluded from the *mitzva* of *korban pesach* due to ritual impurity (*tuma*) that they be afforded the opportunity to participate in this singular experience. The impassioned plea moves Moshe *Rabbeinu* to consult with *Hashem*, ultimately leading to the formulation of a new halachic institution, *pesach sheini*.

Why did the Torah choose to reveal these important *halachos* in this unusual manner? The *Sifrei* (cited also in Rashi *Bamidbar* 9:7) indicates that *pesach sheini* was part of the original halachic structure and might have been conveyed by Moshe along with the rest of the Torah, but was articulated as a response to the demands of this group to credit them for their halachic initiative and commend them for their spiritual ambition (מגלגלין זכות על ידי זכאי). Indeed, Seforno cites the view that the eager quest for *pesach sheini* was one of four pivotal attainments that would have

---

"*Pesach Sheini*: A Quest for Spiritual...." was originally published in 2006 on TorahWeb.org

merited *Klal Yisrael*'s immediate entry into *Eretz Yisrael* if not for the transgression of the *meraglim*.

However, the urgency of the demand for participation in the *pesach* is puzzling, as is the significance attached to this initiative. Undoubtedly, this was not the first group to be excluded from halachic performance when minimum standards could not be met. Moreover, the *Or HaChayyim, Kli Yakar*, and other commentators note that it is difficult to comprehend the argument of the *temei'im*, as they acknowledged the requirement of ritual purity as a *sine qua non* of *pesach* participation. Several suggestions are offered to explain their argument. Some posit that they were objecting to the fact that they could not be passively included in the *pesach* of a *tahor*. Others theorize that they were offended by the irony that their disqualification resulted from an act of *chesed* such as the carrying of Yosef's remains or the burial of a *meis mitzva*. None of these explanations satisfactorily justify the tone or content of their argument. The dramatic, forceful, insistent language associated with their plea (*Bamidbar* 9:7) – "למה נגרע לבלתי הקרב את קרבן ה' במעדו בתוך בני ישראל, why are we to lose out by not bringing *Hashem*'s sacrifice at its set time among *Bnei Yisrael*" – suggests a sense of frustration, loss and alienation that transcends the lost opportunity to perform even a notable *mitzva*.

Perhaps it is precisely the wording and tone of this very powerful petition that provides a solution to the puzzle. The phrase "בתוך בני ישראל", apparently superfluous, conveys an awareness that *korban pesach* binds individual Jews together as an integrated community and forges a special bond between *Klal Yisrael* and *Hashem*. The *korban pesach* is a unique *korban* that defies easy classification. Ideally it is shared by a group (*chabura*) appointed (*minui*) at the time of the *shechita*. The *pesach* is sometimes referred to as a *korban tzibbur*, although it is not a single *korban* of collective *Klal Yisrael* because it is offered en masse ("*bekinufya*"; *Yoma* 51a). There are compelling indications that *pesach* reflects the communal covenant between *Hashem* and *Klal Yisrael* in a way that parallels the function of *bris mila* on an individual plane. In fact, *mila* is a prerequisite for *korban pesach*. Among the positive commandments (*esin*), only the neglect of *mila* and *korban pesach* are punished with *kareis*.

Thus, the excluded group lamented not only their having forfeited an important *mitzva*, but their inability to express their identification as members of the covenantal community of *Klal Yisrael* by means of this singular halachic vehicle. Their anguish was not meant as a legal argument, as they were aware of the prerequisite of purity. The group simply could not abide the implications of their exclusion from the *tzibbur* even if there was no logical foundation to their plea. They turned to Moshe *Rabbeinu* to respectfully explore whether there was a halachic basis for their inclusion in *korban pesach*. Indeed, it is possible that Moshe *Rabbeinu* found their passion and persistence to be more compelling than logic. He addressed the query to *Hashem*, confident that an answer would be forthcoming given the sincerity and piety of the questioners. According to the *Sifrei*, the institution of *pesach sheini* was always intended to enable an additional opportunity to participate in the *korban pesach*, but it was only revealed in response to the initiative of the *temei'im*.

We may now appreciate that this *parasha* of *pesach sheini* was credited to the *temei'im* whose sensitivity to the importance of *korban pesach* constitutes an important contribution to the substance of the *mitzva*. Furthermore, it is appropriate that the passion and idealism reflected by this group would have enabled an early entrance into *Eretz Yisrael*. The commitment to the notion of a covenant of community ("בתוך בני ישראל") is particularly central to Jewish life in the national homeland. Rash, Ramban (9:1) and other *mefarshim* discuss whether it was appropriate to offer a *korban pesach* yearly in the desert. They note that in *Sefer Shemos* it appears that *korban pesach* was specifically designed for *Eretz Yisrael*, a condition that is consistent with its communal character.

Or HaChayyim is puzzled by the use of the singular form (9:6) – "ויהי אנשים אשר היו טמאים, it was that there were some men who were impure" – that introduces the group that was the catalyst for *pesach sheini*. Possibly the Torah already provides a clue as to the source of the group's frustration and their unwillingness to accept their halachic fate without at least exploring the alternatives with Moshe *Rabbeinu*. Absent the spiritual opportunity to bond as a *chabura-tzibbur* by means of the *korban pesach*, their sense of alienation precluded a group self-image. (Ironically, they could not bond even as a group that shared this sense of lost opportunity!)

The *Or HaChayyim* also questions why the *kareis* punishment for intentionally bypassing the *mitzva* of *pesach* is mentioned only after *pesach sheini* is introduced. Perhaps the theme of a covenant of community that parallels the individual covenant of the *bris mila* and warrants the punishment of *kareis* is particularly accentuated by the quest of the *temei'im* to participate in this pivotal *mitzva*. The Torah's establishment of *pesach sheini*, affording a second opportunity to attain this crucial *bris*, constitutes the perfect context to introduce the *kareis* penalty. (There is an additional important dimension to this perspective according to Rambam's view [*Hilchos Korban Pesach* ch. 5] that the *temei'im* themselves could never actually incur *kareis* even if they intentionally neglected the opportunity of *pesach sheini*.)

Finally, it is noteworthy that the *pesach sheini* section culminates (*Bamidbar* 9:14) with a *pasuk* that includes the convert in the obligation of *pesach*. It is conceivable that with this conclusion, the Torah again subtly but effectively conveys that *korban pesach* reflects the *bris* between *Hashem* and *Klal Yisrael*. Although the convert as an individual cannot trace his personal history to the exodus from Egypt and the first *korban pesach*, as a completely integrated member of *Klal Yisrael* he partakes fully in the historical memory and national *bris* of *pesach*. Indeed, the *Sifrei* (see Rashi 9:14) finds it necessary to preclude a potential misconception based on this *pasuk* that a convert would have to bring a *korban pesach* as part of his conversion process at any time during the year! The fact that *korban pesach* reflects the singular bond between collective *Klal Yisrael* and *Hashem* justifies this perspective.

Korban Pesach: A Symbol of Faith and Commitment

The Torah in *Parashas Bo* delineates the events of the exodus from Egypt (*yetzias Mitzrayim*), including the pivotal role of *korban pesach* in the unfolding of that momentous evening of redemption. The Torah details the procedure of this *korban* (*Shemos* 12:21-28), beginning with the charge of " משכו וקחו לכם צאן למשפחתיכם ושחטו הפסח – draw out and take for your selves a lamb for your families, and slaughter the *pesach*." It subsequently, records the enduring legacy of this *korban* as well (12:24-27): " ושמרתם את־הדבר הזה לחק־לך ולבניך עד־עולם –you shall keep this as institution for you and your children forever והיה כי־תבאו אל־הארץ ... – when you come to the land אליכם בניכם והיה כי־יאמרו ... – when your children say to you... 'זבח־פסח הוא לה ואמרתם – you shall say that it is a *pesach* offering to *Hashem*..." After interspersing present and future motifs of the *korban*, the Torah returns to an account of the events of that night, culminating with the actual redemption and exodus itself (12:41-42).

It is striking that the Torah then revisits the laws of *korban pesach* (*Shemos* 12:43-50), with the suggestive introduction (12:43) of "זאת חוקת הפסח – this is the *pesach* statute," immediately followed by the law ("כל בן נכר לא יאכל בו") that prohibits idolaters or even Jewish apostates (*yisrael meshumad*; *Mechilta* op. cit.) from partaking in the *korban*. Why did the Torah add this postscript at this juncture when it previously specified many of the *korban*'s regulations and already alluded to its enduring normative

---

"*Korban Pesach*: A Symbol of Faith... " was originally published in 2010 on TorahWeb.org

status (12:24) as a "חק־לך ולבניך עד־עולם"? What accounts for the interruption of the narrative at a critical moment in its unfolding with allusions to the continuing relevance of this *korban*? It is also significant that subsequent to formulating further principles of *korban pesach*, the Torah reformulates the climax of the narrative (12:51): "ויהי בעצם היום הזה הוציא ה' את־בני ישראל מארץ מצרים על־צבאתם – that very day *Hashem* took *Bnei Yisrael* out of Egypt with their legions," as if to convey that this rendition of enduring *pesach* laws, too, is intimately connected with the actual experience of the exodus and redemption.

We may better understand the double juxtaposition of *korban pesach* laws and *yetzias Mitzrayim* if we recognize that undoubtedly this later section is not merely a random supplement of *pesach* laws, but is meant to highlight a crucial dimension of the exodus experience and legacy. Moreover, it seems evident that "כל בן נכר לא יאכל בו," the exclusion of idolators and apostates, was carefully chosen to characterize the *korban pesach*, and by extension, the important perspective it contributes to *yetzias Mitzrayim*.

The exclusion of Jewish apostates from the consumption of a *korban* is unique to *korban pesach*. The *Sefer HaChinuch* (no. 13) explains that the rationale for this unusual law is self-evident since *korban pesach* embodies the ideal of faith in *Hashem* and an unreserved commitment to leading a Torah life, principles that are absolutely incompatible with the figure of an apostate. *Minchas Chinuch* and others debate some of the nuances of this prohibition that may defy the routine regulations of *korbanos*. They examine the possibility that apostasy in this particular context may be restricted to idolatry (as opposed to *Shabbos* desecration, for example), or that an apostate may be excluded from *pesach* even if he is not technically subject to the death penalty because he was never properly warned (*hasra'a*). If the exclusion of apostates derives from the nature of *korban pesach* as an offering of faith and commitment, it might be expected that the application of this principle may not conform to other *korbanos* norms.

Elsewhere ("*Pesach Sheini*: A Quest for Spiritual Opportunity and National Identity"; "*Chag HaPesach*: The Ideal Introduction to *Chag HaMatzos*") we have elaborated other unique facets of *korban pesach*, suggesting that it constitutes an expression of national identification in a manner that is parallel to *bris mila* on the individual plane. The fact that both *mila* and *pesach* constitute the only positive commandments whose neglect triggers a punishment of *kareis* and that *mila* is a prerequisite for *pesach* reinforces this notion. (The mixing of *dam mila* and *dam pesach* in the context of *Pesach Mitzrayim*, referred to by the *Midrash* and *Targum Yonason*, may be explained on this basis, as well. See also *Chiddushei HaGrim*, *Shemos* 12:13. Furthermore, it should be noted that the disqualification of *arel* in *pesach* follows the exclusion of the apostate. It too, is a singular law that may reflect the theme of faith and absolute commitment, as well as of the distinctiveness of *Klal Yisrael*. See the *Minchas Chinuch*'s comments on the prohibition of *arel*. See also *Chiddushei HaGrim*, *Shemos* 12:43.) Moreover, *Klal Yisrael*'s initiative to establish a *pesach sheini* ("*lama nigara...*") attests to the understanding that *korban pesach* affords a singular spiritual opportunity to identify emphatically with the national destiny and spiritual aspirations of *Klal Yisrael*.

The charge of *korban pesach* challenged the very faith and commitment of *Bnei Yisrael*, testing their qualifications for nationhood and the ambitious destiny of being an *am Hashem* and a *goy kadosh*. It demanded political courage, a massive leap of faith and a total abandonment of political correctness for an enslaved, embattled people to defy the most basic cultural norms of the host country. "עד שישחטו אלוהיהם לעיניהם" (slaughtering the Egyptian deity openly) was an incredibly ambitious feat which exemplified *Klal Yisrael*'s vast potential, qualifying them not only for physical exodus and redemption but for the ultimate telos of that exodus, the revelation at Sinai. The *korban pesach*, then, encapsulated the goal of the exodus, even as it also facilitated that process.

We may now appreciate the double juxtaposition of the experience of the exodus and the renditions of the laws of the *korban pesach*, as well as the emphasis on its enduring binding character. The *pesach* conveyed the need to surrender one's will and even one's sensibilities to *Hashem* as a *sine qua non* to achieving authentic freedom and redemption. True liberty consists of internalizing Torah values and embracing belief and faith in *Hashem*, even in trying times and circumstances, even rejecting accepted cultural norms. The experience of exodus and redemption absent the *pesach* is shallow, hollow, even meaningless. The detailed *pesach* process, then, is not really an interruption of the exodus narrative. The Torah considered it particularly crucial to underscore that this *pesach* legacy is not confined to a given era and location, but transcends place, time and circumstances. Hence the initial allusion to the relevance and binding character of the *pesach* laws. Moreover, in the aftermath of the full narrative, it was important to revisit the principle motifs underlying the *pesach*. The laws delineated in this second context (exemplified by *ben neichar lo yochal bo*) normalized the motifs of faith, sacrifice and commitment that were viscerally experienced in the actual event of the exodus. By reiterating and integrating these themes in the structure of *hilchos korban pesach*, the Torah provided a clear perspective on the ultimate spiritual objective of the exodus and redemption. This prompted a reiteration, really a reformulation, of the experience itself: "ויהי בעצם היום הזה הוציא ה' את־בני ישראל מארץ מצרים על־ צבאתם – that very day *Hashem* took *Bnei Yisrael* out of Egypt with their legions" (*Shemos* 12:51).

The spiritual challenge of *yetzias Mitzrayim* endures throughout history. Every generation invariably confronts its own crises. Sometimes halachic commitment entails physical hardship or financial sacrifice; other circumstances may demand a policy of political isolation, or may impose a posture of social disengagement and cultural alienation.

Irrespective of the particulars, it is incumbent upon us to respond in a principled manner, embracing the model of *Pesach Mitzrayim* in all of its spiritual ambition so that we will truly be worthy of our status as *am Hashem* and *goy kadosh*.

The Triad of *Pesach, Matza, Maror*: *Maror* as a Catalyst for Faith and Redemption (2010)

The *Mishna* in *Pesachim* (116b) and the *Haggada* text record R. Gamliel's ruling that one is obligated to articulate and explicate the role of *pesach*, *matza* and *maror* as a prerequisite to discharging one's obligations during the *seder*. The fact that *pesach* and *matza* occupy such a preeminent role on this night is self-evident. Each accentuates a pivotal theme in the history of the redemption and encapsulates the values, respectively of faith and of focused liberation, that characterize the singular quality of the exodus and that establish its critical significance in Jewish thought and life. However, the inclusion of *maror*, corresponding to the bitter experience of the unpleasant servitude of Egypt, is somewhat puzzling. While the *Mishna* and *Haggada* convey the order of *pesach, matza, maror*, it is noteworthy that Rambam (*Hilchos Chametz uMatza* 7:5, 8:4) reorders the triad: *pesach, maror, matza*. The placement of *maror* between the two positive motifs of *pesach* and *matza* also demands attention. Certainly, this bridging location excludes the idea that *maror* simply represents the historical background from which the faith and freedom of the exodus issued. By briefly examining some aspects of the halachic status of *maror*, we may glean some insight into the contribution of *maror* to this triad, and, generally, to the celebration of *yetzias Mitzrayim*.

The *Gemara* (*Pesachim* 120a) concludes that while *matza* remains an independent biblical obligation even when there is no *korban pesach*,

---

"The Triad of *Pesach, Matza, Maror*..." was originally published in 2010 on TorahWeb.org

maror's status as a Torah commandment is dependent upon the sacrifice of the *pesach*. Rambam (*Hilchos Chametz uMatza* 7:12; *Korban Pesach* 8:2) perceives this linkage to *pesach* as an indication that *maror* is merely an adjunct to *pesach*, never an independent obligation. Consequently, he does not count *maror* in the count of 613 *mitzvos*, a decision that he defends at great length (*Sefer HaMitzvos, asei* 56). (For a discussion of the dissenting positions of the *Yerei'im* and R. Daniel *haBavli*, see *Sefer HaMitzvos* of R. Saadia Gaon, no. 47.) On this surface, the dependence of *maror* on *pesach* deepens the mystery of its prominence in R. Gamliel's formulation of the essential focus of the evening.

Upon further reflection *maror*'s adjunct status may illuminate its special role. *Maror* as an independent theme contravenes the joyous spirit of the *seder* night. At best, it might serve as historical background and as a striking contrast to the redemption that ensued. This role should hardly qualify *maror* as a primary theme of סיפור יציאת מצרים, and certainly not as an equal to *pesach* and *matza*. Moreover, R. Gamliel's order precludes against this limited, comparative perspective, as previously noted. However, *maror* in the context of and as an enhancement to the *korban pesach* proves to be a profound and, indeed, a pivotal perspective on *yetzias Mitzrayim*. Elsewhere ("*Korban Pesach*: A Symbol of Faith and Commitment"), we have suggested that the *korban pesach*, consisting of a public sacrifice of the Egyptian deity, exemplifies the concept of faith and commitment. The capacity to attain this level is infinitely more impressive in light of the harsh physical and especially psychological conditions symbolized by the *maror*. Ibn Ezra, in particular, documents the enduring impact of the slave mentality on the Jewish people. He attributes the nation's panic prior to *kerias Yam Suf*, and ultimately the need for the generation of the exodus to die in the desert, to this condition. The fact that an afflicted, embittered nation could, even momentarily, set aside the trauma of suffering to embrace a leap of faith and idealism entailed by the *korban pesach* dramatically redefines the profundity of that faith gesture. Moreover, the capacity to overcome the *maror* experience demonstrates *Klal Yisrael*'s organic connection to *Hashem* and their innate thirst for *avodas Hashem*.

On another plane, it is conceivable that the *maror* experience of slavery and suffering was actually a catalyst for faith, as it served accentuate quality of life issues, underscoring the futility of servitude to finite beings (עבדים לעבדים), thereby facilitating the refocusing of *Klal Yisrael*'s priorities. In this sense, the Egyptian *maror* experience was truly a "*kur habarzel*" which refined the Jewish taste for an authentic spiritual life and true, purposive liberty. *Chazal* emphasize this transition when they emphasize that the opening words of the *Hallel* that is so prominent on the *seder* night- "הללוקה הללו עבדי ה'" is intended to contrast to their previous status as "*avdei Pharaoh*."

There is equally persuasive evidence that *maror*, juxtaposed in R. Gamliel's declaration between *pesach* and *matza*, constitutes an important enhancement of *matza* and its theme of redemption and thanksgiving, as well. The *pasuk* that establishes *maror*'s role (*Shemos* 12:8) specifically ties it to *matza*: "ומצות על מררים יאכלהו." According to Hillel (*Pesachim* 116a) the *matza* and *maror* are to be consumed in an integrated fashion. Rambam (*Hilchos Chametz uMatza* 8:6, 8; see *Lechem Mishneh*) apparently rules that even the Rabbis ideally preferred this integrated approach which focused (in Rambam's view) specifically on *matza* and *maror*. (See also Rambam, *Hilchos Chametz uMatza* 6:2, where he indicates that the *maror* is an adjunct to the *matza*!) Rashi (*Pesachim* 91b) explains that women were mandated to eat *maror* because of their obligation to eat *matza*, even according to those authorities who ruled that they were exempt from the *korban pesach*! Items disqualified for *matza* use, such as *tevel*, were evidently generally also excluded for *maror* simply by virtue of this link between *matza* and *maror* (see the *Mishna*, *Pesachim* 39a, and Rashi, and see the *Gemara* 39b regarding *ma'aser sheini*)! Furthermore, there are strong indications that the *Halacha* intended that the *maror* be consumed only in the context of the eating of the *matza* (see the discussions regarding a situation where the *maror* is the lone vegetable and has to be eaten as *karpas*; *Pesachim* 114b-115a, *Tosafos*, Ramban, etc.)

This connection, too, requires some clarification. *Matza* and *maror* constitute antithetical motifs. *Matza* signifies redemption (*Pesachim* 116b: על שם שנגאלו), inspires the recitaiton of *Hallel* (*Pesachim* 36a: עונין עליו דברים הרבה; see Rashi), requires *heseiba* (leaning) as an expression of liberty, and symbolizes the theme of thanksgiving (see "*Matza* as an Expression of *Hoda'a*"). *Maror*, which symbolizes oppression and suffering, is not consumed in a reclining position, but is dipped in *charoses*.

Yet the link between *matza* and *maror*, as documented, is undeniable. The connection between *maror* and *matza* reflects the *Halacha*'s ambitious, if complex, perspective on freedom and suffering. The themes of "כור הברזל - the iron furnace" and "עבדי ה' ולא עבדי פרעה – servants of God and not of Pharaoh" apply to the motif of freedom, as well as to the principle of faith. The *Halacha* advocates a liberty which is spiritually constructive and in which self-imposed limits direct man to submit to *Hashem*'s will, as the ultimate expression of true freedom. The *maror* epic in Egypt sensitized the nation to the cruelty and moral bankruptcy of the unbridled and undirected freedom exercised by Pharaoh. Moreover, the *Chasam Sofer* (*peirush* on the *Haggada*) shares an important insight. He notes that the *maror* follows the *matza* because only one who is truly liberated can fully appreciate the bitterness of oppression and servitude. In this respect, the retrospective *maror* experience highlights the genuine achievements of the exodus. The *Aruch HaShulchan* (in his *peirush* on the *Haggada* entitled "*Leil Shimmurim*") emphasizes another contribution of the *maror*. He posits that it was necessary for *Klal Yisrael* to undergo a measure of servitude and self-restraint so that the experience could then be channeled constructively into an ambitious, idealistic *avodas*

Hashem. The *matza* motif of *geula* then redeems the *maror* motif, even as it is transformed by it. (Rambam rules [*Hilchos Chametz uMatza* 8:8] that *matza*, like *maror*, requires *charoses*. R. Manoach queries how *matza* and *charoses*, a symbol of slavery, may integrate. However, in light of our analysis generally, and our survey of Rambam's perspective in particular, this poses no difficulty.)

Maror's capacity to redefine and refine both major themes of the exodus qualifies it with equal status in the triad and justifies its position as the bridge between both themes.

The Conjunction of *Sippur* and *Zechiras Mitzrayim*

The *mitzva* of סיפור יציאת מצרים, to publicize the story of the exodus on the first night of *Pesach*, constitutes an independent *mitzva*, and is a central component in the *Pesach* experience. Rambam devotes a full chapter (chapter seven) of his *Hilchos Chametz uMatza* to the details of this *mitzva*. This focus is particularly noteworthy when contrasted with his treatment of the parallel obligation of זכירת יציאת מצרים, to remember the exodus, which applies daily. Rambam omits that continuous obligation from the list of the 613 commandments, as many *mefarshim* note; he subtly integrates that theme with the daily *mitzva* of *Kerias Shema* (see *Shiurim LeZeicher Abba Mari* on this topic). Rambam's formulation of סיפור יציאת מצרים is especially intriguing in light of this stark contrast. In the beginning of chapter 7, he introduces the theme of סיפור יציאת מצרים by invoking a verse (*Shemos* 13:3) that specifically articulates the obligation of זכירת יציאת מצרים. He states as follows: "מצות עשה של תורה לספר בנסים ונפלאות שנעשו לאבותנו במצרים בליל חמשה עשר בניסן שנאמר (שמות יג:ג) זכור את היום הזה אשר יצאתם ממצרים כמו שנאמר (שמות כ:ז) זכור את יום השבת – it is a

---

"*The Conjunction of Sippur...*" was originally published in 2011 on TorahWeb.org

positive biblical commandment to recount the miracles and wonders that were performed for our forefathers in Egypt on the night of the 15th of Nisan, as it says, 'Remember this day you went out from Egypt' (*Shemos* 13:3) just like it says, 'Remember the *Shabbos* day' (*Shemos* 20:7)...."

Indeed, Rashi, citing the *Mechilta*, explicitly links that verse to the daily obligation to remember the exodus. Rambam's emphasis of *zechiras Mitzrayim* in the *sippur* context is especially puzzling when one considers that in the very next line he cites "והגדת לבנך ביום ההוא לאמר, and you shall tell your son on that day, saying" (*Shemos* 13:8), a proof text that does refer to סיפור יציאת מצרים. The reference in Rambam's סיפור יציאת מצרים presentation of "זכור את יום השבת" – the fact that we usher in the *Shabbos* by means of the *kiddush* – as an apparent parallel also commands our attention. What did Rambam seek to convey about סיפור יציאת מצרים with these seemingly gratuitous references?

Perhaps Rambam's linkage to daily זכירת יציאת מצרים and weekly *kiddush* conveys an important perspective on how the *Halacha* perceives and projects even (and, perhaps, especially) singular themes and unique experiences. Rather than innovate an entirely novel structure to celebrate and commemorate the inimitable event of the exodus, the *Halacha* invariably invokes and applies, and in some cases adapts, broader existing categories, albeit in singular fashion. This approach accomplishes the dual yet complementary objectives of sharpening the contrast to highlight particularly novel dimensions, while simultaneously integrating the novel components into the totality of halachic life, also demonstrating its wider relevance and coherence vis-a-vis total halachic commitment. By invoking the *pasuk* of זכירת יציאת מצרים and by alluding to the parallel role of *kiddush*, Rambam provides a wider halachic context, framework, and perspective for the singular manifestation of סיפור יציאת מצרים. By reminding us of זכירת יציאת מצרים, Rambam subtly underscores that the obligation of *sippur* does not arise in a vacuum, nor is its scope and impact restricted to a single night. Moreover, the coordinating and tone-setting effect of סיפור יציאת מצרים on the total commemoration and celebration of the *seder* night is not unprecedented; the ubiquitous *kiddush* every *Shabbos* effectively serves that very function.

Rambam's carefully crafted articulation of the *mitzva* of סיפור יציאת מצרים subtly yet artfully conveys that the singular focus of the actual night of *Pesach* is further enhanced by its wide and pervasive impact, as expressed in daily *zechiras Mitzrayim*. Moreover, while the emphasis on details, the need to verbalize, perhaps the requirement to engage in a dialectic, and various other components differentiate the *sippur* of the *seder* night from the daily *zechira*, it is the ubiquitous *zechira*, which according to Rambam is integrated with the tenet of קבלת עול מלכות שמים in the context of *Kerias Shema*, that determines *sippur*'s ultimate significance even as a concrete commemoration of the historical event of the exodus. Thus, זכירת יציאת מצרים and סיפור יציאת מצרים are mutually enhancing, even mutually dependent. Without the detailed, intense and more concrete *sippur* practiced once a year, the more amorphous and abstract *zechira* would be compromised; absent the continuous outlet and impact provided by daily *zechira*, the anniversary of the exodus would be nothing more than a nostalgic memory.

This halachic formula for structuring singular motifs, particularly regarding the *Pesach* holiday, is typical, as demonstrated by other aspects of the *seder* night. The *korban pesach* constitutes an extraordinary, rule-breaking *korban* in many respects, reflecting the singular dimensions of סיפור יציאת מצרים and the actual experience of *pesach Mitzrayim*. It is brought outside of the confines of the regular *temidim* structure ("*aleha hashleim*"). Moreover, the function of *shechita* and the eating of the *korban*, the institution of the *minui* and *chabura*, the application of *yotzei*, and numerous other novelties differentiate *pesach* from typical *korbanos* as well. Yet, with all of its novelty, *korban pesach* retains the fundamental form, structure and status of a *korban* and is rightly perceived by the *Mishna* and Talmud in that context. The adaptations of various principles as they are applied to *korban pesach* accommodate its special themes, yet retain the core of the classical *korban* structure.

The four *kosos* of the *seder* certainly represent a novelty. Yet surely the utilization of existing halachic structures of *kiddush*, *birkas hamazon* and *Hallel* is significant. This method accentuates the singular facet of the *seder* night by highlighting sharp contrasts, even as it also establishes a sense of continuity, relevance and coherence with the totality of halachic life. Rambam ruled (*Hilchos Chametz uMatza* 8:6) that the typical *yom tov* requirement of *lechem mishneh* should include a broken *matza* (*perusa*) on the night of the *seder*. He explains that while the generic requirement of *lechem mishneh* is retained, its application on this unique night should reflect the singular motif of *Pesach*. Refashioning the existing structure subtly further underscores the novel aspects of סיפור יציאת מצרים; retaining the classical structures of halachic conduct accentuates the themes of continuity and integration with the totality of halachic life.

While this perspective reflects a general tendency, it is of particular importance and relevance with respect to the celebration of *yetzias Mitzrayim*. This unique experience literally transformed the Jewish people, paving the way for *matan Torah* and a singular relationship with *Hashem*, reflected by the reference to *yetzias Mitzrayim* in the introduction of the *Aseres HaDibros*. At the same time, as Ramban (end of *Parashas Bo*) notes, this singular event confirmed and reinforced the very purpose of Creation and Jewish destiny, and became the ultimate expression of the theological tenets of *Hashem*'s existence and special providence that underpin every important dimension of halachic life. (Hence also the link between זכירת יציאת מצרים and קריאת שמע.) Everything we do on the *seder* night, including some of the general routines of *yom tov*, cannot help but be refashioned and reformulated to reflect the profound impact of that singular evening and experience. The innovative application of the traditional halachic structures on the *seder* night highlights this reality, even as the continuity afforded by typical and conventional halachic structure conveys the equally powerful motifs of the general indispensability of halachic structure, as well as of the dual status of *yetzias Mitzrayim* as a singular event on the one hand, and as a transformative experience that profoundly impacted on and integrated into the totality of halachic life, on the other.

Rambam's subtle yet elegant articulation and integration of *zechiras* and *sippur yetzias Mitzrayim* truly captures this central theme as the focal point of our national celebration.

Chag HaCheirus: Autonomy and Liberation in the Pursuit of Transcendence

Chag hamatzos is a holiday that joyously celebrates personal freedom and national liberation as it commemorates the exodus from Egypt and *Klal Yisrael*'s extrication from bondage and servitude. Indeed, the *ya'aleh veyavo* insertion in *birkas hamazon* and *Shemoneh Esrei* identifies the *chag* as "*zeman cheiruseinu*." The themes of *geula* and the methodology of "*derech cheirus*" (*heseiba*, four *kosos* etc.) pervade the *Pesach seder*. However, a narrow focus on the motifs of political autonomy and personal freedom, while more universally appealing and certainly spiritually significant as well, does not accurately capture the true character of the celebration.

Many *mefarshim* note that the experience of *yetzias Mitzrayim* was transformative and its impact enduring. The Torah repeatedly revisits the theme of the exodus, projecting it as a linchpin of Jewish identity,

---

"*Chag HaCheirus*: **Autonomy...**" was originally published in 2016 on TorahWeb.org

and the foundation and anchor of many *mitzvos* (see Ramban, end of *Parashas Bo*). Undoubtedly, this perspective explains why the impact of *Pesach*, the festival of freedom, was never perceived to have been diluted or compromised by the too-numerous subsequent persecutions that plagued the Jewish people. Evidently, the redemption from Egypt transcended mere liberation; it reflected and stimulated a profound recognition of *Hashem*'s transcendence, as well as His singular providential relationship with the Jewish people.

In this vein, Rambam (*Hilchos Chametz uMatza* 7:1; *Sefer HaMitzvos, asei* 157) emphasizes the obligation to elaborate the miracles and Divine intercession that occurred on the night of 15 *Nisan*, rather than focusing on the liberation of the exodus per se. Only when he conveys (7:2) the appropriate message for a child or simpleton, exemplifying the flexible character of the educational obligation of "והגדת לבנך," does Ramban accentuate the experience of liberation itself! (See also 7:5-7.)

Indeed, Rambam's depiction of "מתחילין בגנות ומסיימין בשבח" (7:4, expounding and expanding the *Mishna Pesachim* 116a and *Gemara* op. cit.) further illustrates his more expansive posture on this *mitzva*. The Talmud records a debate between Rav and Shmuel whether one focuses on the theme of servitude-redemption by reciting עבדים היינו, or that of the spiritual impoverishment-advancement of our ancestors, embodied in the passage of "מתחלה עובדי עבודה זרה, our ancestors were idol worshippers." The very suggestion that we would emphasize the religious component reflects a more complex perspective on the significance of the exodus. Our practice (as noted already by R. Chananel, and reflected in the standard text of the *Haggada*) is to refer to both passages, beginning with "עבדים היינו." However, Rambam intriguingly formulates the recitation of these two sections as if each one is a parallel "beginning": "כיצד? מתחיל ומספר שבתחלה היו אבותינו בימי תרח ומלפניו כופרים... ומסיים בדת האמת... וכן מתחיל ומודיע שעבדים היינו... ומסיים בנסים ובנפלאות שנעשו לנו ובחרותינו – How? He begins and recounts that originally our ancestors, in the days of Terach and those before him, denied [*Hashem*'s existence]… and concludes with the true faith… and also begins and states that we were slaves… and concludes with the miracles and with the wonders that were done for us, and with our freedom." Moreover, he implies that the religious motif is prior (though in his *Haggada*, as in all standard *Haggados*, it is not), and depicts the liberation almost as an afterthought ("ובחרותינו").

Rambam's presentation conveys that the עבדים היינו liberation experience, which we in fact celebrate, requires the spiritual quality-of-life context and perspective supplied by the "מתחלה עובדי עבודה זרה" account. The *Gemara* (*Pesachim* 116a) records that Daru, a slave who was liberated and supported in his effort to enter into a new plane of existence, was ready to appreciate the passage of עבדים היינו only if he first internalized the profound concepts of praise and thanksgiving. These notions, which lie at the foundation of סיפור יציאת מצרים (see *Sefer HaMitzvos*, *asei* 157, and the links to *mikra bikkurim* etc.) are not merely superficial acknowledgements, but constitute core recognition of Divine providence and the priority of seeking transcendence and spiritual meaning.

Chazal relate that authentic freedom entails living a purposeful, spiritual life that is dedicated to *Hashem* and directed by His Torah ("אין לך בן חורין אלא מי שעוסק בתורה"). *Hallel* during the *seder* is introduced by a fervent declaration of our obligation to express *hoda'a* and *shevach* ("לפיכך אנחנו חייבים להודות…"). It begins by proclaiming "'הללו עבדי ה" which is rabbinically understood to contrast to "עבדי פרעה"! The emphasis on the opportunity to surrender to transcendence and authentic meaning is unmistakable. The *Aruch HaShulchan* suggests that *maror* remains a central motif during the *seder* because despite its evident unpleasant associations, it served a constructive function in cultivating the quality of discipline that could, upon liberation, be channeled into meaningful spiritual life as *avdei Hashem*. The central prohibition against *chametz*, symbolic of unrestricted growth, particularly unpredictable and even dangerous in an unconstrained state, underscores the inadequacy of directionless liberation. Only in the context of *kabbalas haTorah* at *matan Torah* on *Shavuos* was it possible to celebrate *chametz* in the form of the *korban shtei halechem*.

Maharal (*Gevuros Hashem*) and others note that the challenges that tested the fledgling Jewish nation under Pharaoh's tyranny far exceeded physical servitude, the absence of autonomy, and even cruelty. The *derashos* of פרשת ארמי אבד אבי reflect a range of dehumanizing and desensitizing tactics that severely eroded and undermined the very basic quality of *Klal Yisrael*'s personal and national identity. The litany included in the *Hallel* introduction – "מעבודת לחרות, מיגון לשמחה, ומאבל ליום טוב, ומאפלה לאור גדול, ומשעבוד לגאולה – from slavery to freedom, from grief to joy, from mourning to festivity, from darkness to great light and from slavery to redemption"– are not synonymous, but register the multiple dimensions in which this liberation was a singular and profoundly transformative national experience that infused spiritual purpose and a fundamental identity to *Hashem*'s chosen nation.

Maharal explains that subsequent exiles and persecutions did not detract from the enduring impact of *yetzias Mitzrayim* and the *cheirus* established then, because *Klal Yisrael* attained a permanent intrinsic stature as a liberated nation whose aspirations and character could never be altered, notwithstanding artificial obstacles that might hinder the pragmatic expression of this national persona. (It is interesting to integrate the celebrated perspective of Ibn Ezra regarding *Bnei Yisrael*'s slave and liberated mentality into this analysis.) In this sense too, it is a truism that "ואותנו הוציא משם – and He brought us out from there" (*Devarim* 6:23) – that both the collective *Klal Yisrael*, and also each generation and individual, not only benefited from but was the actual object of *Hashem*'s transformative, providential intervention in *yetzias Mitzrayim*. (See also Maharal, *Gevuros Hashem*, on this theme.) Certainly, the prominence of *hoda'a* and *shevach* in סיפור יציאת מצרים is related to its enduring and profound transformative impact, and especially its primary spiritual orientation.

Surely it is no coincidence that the ultimate symbols of the holiday of *cheirus* and *geula* were the *korban pesach*, a *korban* suffused with the theme of *emuna* and religious commitment (see "*Korban Pesach*: A Symbol of Faith and Commitment"), and *matza*, the focus of *hallel* and *hoda'a* (see also "*Matza* as an Expression of *Hoda'a*"). On *chag hamatzos* we truly celebrate the motifs of autonomy and freedom, albeit in its most religiously aspirational and halachically authentic form.

Sippur Yetzias Mitzrayim's *Mikra Bikkurim* as a Statement of Faith

Relating the events and significance of the exodus from Egypt (סיפור יציאת מצרים) on the 15th of *Nisan* constitutes a complex *mitzva* that entails multiple motifs and methods. The *seder* and the *Haggada* employ numerous overlapping devices to organize and project the different yet interconnected components that convey the totality of the experience and its importance. The four *kosos*, the various *simanim* of the *seder*, the two sections of *Hallel*, the interplay between details of the story, Torah study, and the concrete performance of specific *mitzvos* (see Rambam, *Hilchos Chametz uMatza* chapters 7 and 8, how they differ, and where they overlap, as well as Avudraham, and *Kol Bo*'s comment on "*ba'avur zeh*") contribute immeasurably to the inimitable sweep of this special evening. Rambam (*Hilchos Chametz uMatza* 7:1, 4, 8) thrice uses the expression "כל המרבה הרי זה משובח," employed by the *Haggada* only to laud additional *sippur*, to extol also a more comprehensive explication of the text of "ארמי אבד אבי," as well as to encourage the demonstrative *heseiba* expression of *cheirus*, in addition to the more maximal engagement with the *sippur* component.

"*Sippur Yetzias Mitzrayim*…" was originally published in 2017 on TorahWeb.org

Given the central role of the story itself, and particularly the apparent requirement for detail and specificity (see the *Haggada*'s extensive discussion of the *makkos*, and Rambam's repeated formulation [7:1, 3] "מה שאירע ומה שהיה – what happened and what occurred"), it is striking that the *Haggada* does not cite extensively from the Torah's own narrative of the events of the exodus. With the exception of a few proof-texts, the *parshiyos* in *Shemos* that record the pivotal events that we reenact on the night of the *seder* are largely omitted as a text. It is equally intriguing that having largely bypassed the official texts and the contemporaneous record, the *mitzva* of *sippur* instead focuses on explicating ("*doreish*") the sweeping retrospective assessment of the *parasha* of *mikra bikkurim*, beginning with "ארמי אבד אבי," in *Devarim*.

Indeed, Rambam particularly accentuates the prominence of explicating the *mikra bikkurim* text. While the *Mishna* (*Pesachim* 116a) mentions the requirement to investigate and interpret "ארמי אבד אבי" after citing the imperative of "מתחילין בגנות" and "מסיים בשבח" (which the Talmud links to עבדים היינו and/or *mitechila* etc.), Rambam (7:4, 8:3) understood and ruled that this exercise in Torah study and explication is itself a dimension of מתחילין בגנות etc. Moreover, as noted, Rambam extends the assessment of "כל המרבה משובח" also to this intriguing component of the *seder-sippur*! In *Sefer HaMitzvos* (*asei* 157, 132; in contrast to *Hilchos Chametz uMatza* 7:1) Rambam formulates סיפור יציאת מצרים and מקרא ביכורים in ways that subtly yet unmistakably overlap. His common emphasis on *shevach* and *hodaa* certainly links the two themes. (See also *Hilchos Chametz uMatza* 6:7, *Targum Yerushalmi*, *Devarim* 26:3, and Rambam's emphasis on "והגדת לבנך" in #157, in contrast to *Hilchos Chametz uMatza* 7:1.) It is noteworthy that Rambam utilizes language in his discussion of *mikra bikkurim* (#132) that evokes the role of this *parasha* on the *seder* night ("ולספר – to recount," "ומתחיל בענין יעקב אבינו ומסיים בעבודת המצרים – he begins with the matter of our father Yaakov and concludes with the Egyptian slavery," "מהפרשה כולה" – from the entire section.") (See also Ramban, *Sefer HaMitzvos*, *hashmatas esin* #15. He compares the roles of *mikra bikkurim*, *sippur yetzias Mitzrayim*, and *birchos haTorah*! See also *Sefer HaMitzvos* of R. Saadia Gaon on *mikra bikkurim*. He argues that *bikkurim* might have a status of *korban tzibbur*, like *korban pesach*, because both were brought *bekinufya*! I hope to elaborate these themes elsewhere.)

Upon further reflection, the decision to de-emphasize the text of the *parshiyos* in *Shemos* is consistent with the fundamental character of סיפור יציאת מצרים. This singular *mitzva* was not intended as a passive *kerias haTorah*, but as a dynamic, multifaceted and even individualistic-personal rendering of the exodus experience. Notwithstanding and also because of the importance of structure (*seder*), comprehensiveness and specificity in the relating of this pivotal chapter in *Klal Yisrael*'s history, it was equally important that the story be told and even re-enacted, rather than be read. The aspiration "לראות את עצמו כאלו הוא יצא ממצרים – to see himself as if he left Egypt," which Rambam also significantly expands (7:6), precludes a single voice or a fixed text. The educational imperative ("ברוך שנתן תורה לעמו ישראל ברוך הוא") and the ambition to touch and impact a wide range of ages, backgrounds and temperaments – "כנגד ארבעה בנים דברה תורה" (and *Hilchos Chametz uMatza* 7:2) – demand multi-media, as previously noted, dialogue, and a flexible voice ("כפי צחות לשונו"; *Sefer HaMitzvos*, *asei* 157), and more. It is important to be comprehensive and specific in סיפור יציאת מצרים, but equally to avoid textual regimentation or rigidity.

At the same time, the *parasha* of *mikra bikkurim* enhances the סיפור יציאת מצרים precisely because it motivates us to explicate and analyze the text (*doreish*), thereby to penetrate the spiritual challenges, accomplishments and religious trajectory of *Klal Yisrael*. Precisely because of the distance and perspective it affords, it escapes the limitations of a more passive *keria*. Moreover, *mikra bikkurim*, proclaimed in *Eretz Yisrael* at a time of agricultural triumph, provides broad national and religious perspective for what could have been conceived as a very narrow, personal and natural celebration. The capacity to evaluate *bikkurim* in light of *Klal Yisrael*'s extraordinary odyssey, especially accentuating the role of the exodus as a powerful source of *emuna* and *hoda'a*, established this text, and especially its further midrashic analysis, as the ideal centerpiece of סיפור יציאת מצרים. *Mikra bikkurim* unequivocally underscores that the praise and thanksgiving triggered by *yetzias Mitzrayim* was not a superficial and narrow response, that would have been absolutely disconnected and irrelevant to an institution like *bikkurim*, but a profound recognition of the pervasive, transformational character of this event, and especially its status as a cornerstone of faith. The explication of פרשת ארמי אבד אבי, combined with the detailed rendering of the story, and the concrete implementation of *mitzvos ma'asiyos* on this singular evening indeed facilitates the *hallel* of "הללו עבדי ה."

Rabbi Yonason Sacks

Perspective on the *Omer* and *Shtei Halechem*

The *Mishna* (*Menachos* 68b) compares the *minchas ha'omer* which is offered on *Pesach* to the *shtei halechem* which is brought on *Shavuos*. "העומר היתה מתיר במדינה ושתי הלחם במקדש" – the *omer* would permit the new grains to be used outside the *Mikdash*, whereas the *shtei halechem* allowed these grains to be offered in the *Mikdash*." Both offerings, as we are taught in *Parashas Emor* (*Vayikra* 23), permit the use of the new grain.

Although both *menachos* are mentioned in *Parashas Emor*, the Torah in *Parashas Pinchas* distinguishes between the *omer* and *shtei halechem*. *Parashas Pinchas*, which enumerates the *korbanos haregel*, the festival offerings, includes the *shtei halechem* but omits the *omer*. Indeed, in *tefillas Musaf* on *Shavuos* we mention the *shtei halechem*. On *Pesach*, however, we don't include the *minchas omer* in our *Shemoneh Esrei*.

These distinctions point to a fundamental difference between the *shtei halechem* and the *omer*. Whereas the *shtei halechem* are included in the *korbanos haregel* of *Shavuos*, the *omer*, although offered on the second day of *Pesach*, is not an inherent part of the *korbanos haregel* of *Pesach*.

This essential difference is indicated by Rambam as well. Rambam (*Hilchos Klei HaMikdash*, chap. 4) describes the division and rotation of the *kohanim* who serve in the *Beis HaMikdash*. Each *mishmar* would serve for a week and was entitled to various parts of the *korbanos*. The *korbanos haregel*, however, were divided among all the *kohanim*. When Rambam delineates the *korbanos haregel*, he includes the *shtei halechem* but omits the *omer*. Although the *shtei halechem* was shared by all the *kohanim*, the *omer* was given to the *mishmar hakavua*, the *mishmar* of that week.

The difference is also evident from the *Gemara* in *Arachin* which

---

"Perspective on the *Omer*..." was originally published in 2005 on TorahWeb.org

discusses the obligation of reciting *Hallel* on *yom tov*. Why do we recite a complete *Hallel* on *chol hamoed Sukkos*, but only a *chatzi Hallel* on *chol hamoed Pesach*? The *Gemara* assumes that on each day of *Sukkos* different *korbanos* were offered, unlike *Pesach*, שאין חלוקים בקרבנותיהם – there is no differentiation in the sacrifices. On the second day of *Pesach* in *Eretz Yisrael*, only *chatzi Hallel* is recited despite the fact that the *omer* was offered on this day! Apparently, since the *omer* is not found in *Parashas Pinchas* and is not counted among the *korbanos haregel*, only a *chatzi Hallel* is said.

Rav Betzalel Zolty explains that this distinction can be used to resolve a further difficulty in Rambam. The *Gemara* (*Menachos* 83b) explains that although ideally the *shtei halechem* and the *omer* are brought from the new grain; if no new grain can be found, grain which grew during the previous year can be used. Seemingly this statement is applicable to both the *omer* and the *shtei halechem*. Rambam, however, cites this *halacha* only regarding the *shtei halechem* (*Hilchos Temidin uMusafin*, chap. 8) and not earlier (chap. 7) when discussing the *omer*. Apparently *yashan*, last year's crop, can only be used for the *shtei halechem* and not for the *omer*! Rav Zolty suggests that the need for *chadash*, new grain, is rooted in the fact that the *omer* and *shtei halechem* serve to permit the use of the new grain ("העומר היתה מתיר במדינה ושתי הלחם במקדש"), only *chadash*, the new grain, can function as a *matir*. Accordingly the *omer*, which served as a *matir*, can only be brought from *chadash*. The *shtei halechem*, however, function as a *matir* as well as *korbanos haregel*. This second element, *korbanos haregel*, allows the *shtei halechem* to be brought from *yashan* if no *chadash* can be found.

The *Arba Kosos*

Although the Talmud *Bavli* addresses the *halachos* of the *arba*

"The *Arba Kosos*" was originally published in 2009 on TorahWeb.org

kosos, it never cites a source for the *mitzva* (see Ran, 19a in Rif, s.v. *me'arba'a*, who asserts that the *arba kosos* were instituted so that each of the four sections of the *seder* would be recited over wine). The Talmud *Yerushalmi* (*Pesachim* 10:1), however, cites numerous possible sources:

> R. Yochanan said in the name of R. Benaya: [the four cups] correspond to the four expressions of redemption… R. Yehoshua ben Levi said: they correspond to the four cups of [the butler of] Pharaoh's dream… R. Levi said: they correspond to the four kingdoms. The Rabbis say: they correspond to the four cups of affliction which *HaKadosh Baruch Hu* will eventually serve to the nations of the world…And corresponding to them, *HaKadosh Baruch Hu* will serve *Bnei Yisrael* four cups of comfort.

The *Midrash Rabba* (*Shemos* 6:4) states that the four expressions of redemption mentioned by R. Benaya in turn correspond to the four decrees which Pharaoh wrought against *Bnei Yisrael*. Moreover, Meiri (*Pesachim* 99b, s.v. *velo*) adds that each of the four expressions signifies a redemption within itself: "*Vehotzeisi*" refers to the redemption from the physical servitude of *Mitzrayim*. "*Vehitzalti*" refers to redemption from the "normal" subjugations of kingdoms, such as taxes and tributes to the king. "*Vega'alti*" teaches that *HaKadosh Baruch Hu* will bring about the complete domination of the Jewish people over their foes. And "*velakachti*" alludes to the giving of the Torah, which is the "*tachlis hakol* – the ultimate purpose of everything."

Interestingly, Rashi seems to acknowledge multiple sources for the *mitzva* of *arba kosos*. In the opening *mishna* of *perek Arvei Pesachim* (*Pesachim* 99b), Rashi cites the four expressions of redemption as the definitive source for the *arba kosos*. Later in the *perek*, however (*Pesachim* 108a), when explaining R. Yehoshua ben Levi's ruling that women are obligated to drink the *arba kosos*, Rashi cites the dream of Pharaoh's butler. These differing sources pose some uncertainty regarding Rashi's own opinion. *HaGaon* R. Betzalel Hacohen (*Haggahos Mareh Kohein, Pesachim* 108a) explains Rashi's sources contextually: because R. Yehoshua ben Levi himself issued the ruling on *Pesachim* 108a, Rashi cites R. Yehoshua ben Levi's own opinion in the Talmud *Yerushalmi* regarding the dream of Pharaoh's butler. On the *mishna*, however, Rashi cites the four expressions of redemption because only they can adequately account for the *mishna*'s subsequent ruling that "even an indigent pauper must purchase (or receive) four cups of wine on *seder* night." The four expressions of redemption highlight the fact that the *mitzva* of *arba kosos* constitutes "*pirsumei nissa*," publicizing a miracle. The critical value of *pirsumei nissa* overrides fiscal concerns, obligating even the most penurious members of *Klal Yisrael* to fulfill the *mitzva*. R. Hacohen infers from Rashi's citation of alternate sources that the opinions in the *Yerushalmi* are not necessarily in disagreement. Rather, each source adds an additional dimension to the nature and importance of the *mitzva*.

As noted, the Talmud *Bavli* conspicuously omits any source for the *arba kosos*. Perhaps this omission may relate to a deeper understanding of the conceptual nature of the *arba kosos*. R. Chaim Soloveitchik (cited in *Chiddushei HaGriz, Hilchos Chametz uMatza* 7:9) observes that, objectively, the *arba kosos* may be said to consist of two components: "recital" of the various parts of the *seder* over a cup of wine, and "drinking" of the wine itself. While all opinions agree that both "recital" and "drinking" constitute critical components of the *mitzva*, the *rishonim* seem to debate which one of these two components constitutes the essence of the *mitzva*, and which one serves a more technical, ancillary role. This analysis may account for a number of fundamental disputes between the *rishonim*, and may shed light on the *Bavli*'s omission of any source for the *arba kosos*.

One area in which this investigation may express itself pertains to the question of whether one must actually drink in order to fulfill the *mitzva* of *arba kosos*. *Tosafos* (*Pesachim* 99b, s.v. *lo*) argues that the *mitzva* of *arba kosos* may be fulfilled through the vehicle of "*shomeia ke'oneh*," which renders listening tantamount to speech. By simply listening to the recital of the *beracha*, one fulfills the obligation, even without drinking any wine. In this respect, *Tosafos* analogizes the *mitzva* of *arba kosos* to the *mitzva* of *kiddush* throughout the year, which also does not necessitate actual drinking on the part of the listener. Rambam (*Hilchos Chametz uMatza* 7:7), however, disagrees. In order to fulfill one's obligation of *arba kosos*, one must actually drink four cups of wine. Unlike *kiddush* of the rest of the year, mere listening is insufficient.

R. Yitzchak Zev Soloveitchik explains that this *machlokes* may reflect a fundamental difference of opinion regarding the nature of *arba kosos*. *Tosafos*, who accept the mechanism of "*shomeia ke'oneh*" in lieu of actual drinking, view "recital" as the main component of the *mitzva*. The presence of the cup serves to embellish and to confer significance to the verbal elements of the *seder*. Drinking itself is merely a technical requirement which follows the recital. As such, one could theoretically fulfill one's obligation without drinking any wine at all. Rambam, however, perceives the actual drinking of the wine as the definition of the *mitzva*. Hence, although "*shomeia ke'oneh*" can compensate for lack of speech, it cannot redress the lack of drinking by the listener, and is thus an insufficient means for fulfilling one's obligation.

Tosafos' opinion, that the primary component of the *arba kosos* exists in the "recital," not the actual drinking, is also evinced in their comments to *Masseches Sukka* (38a, s.v. *mi*). *Tosafos* note that although women are generally exempt from the positive time-bound *mitzva* of *Hallel*, women are nonetheless obligated to recite the *Hallel* of *seder* night. *Tosafos* prove this obligation from the fact that women are obligated in *arba kosos*: if the role of *arba kosos*, *Tosafos* reason, is to serve as an "enhancer," conferring greater significance to the recital of *Hallel* and *Haggada*, it follows that anyone obligated in the *arba kosos* must certainly be obligated in the recital of *Hallel* and *Haggada* itself. *Tosafos'* reasoning presupposes the assumption that the essential component of the *arba kosos* is to enhance the recital of the *Hallel* and *Haggada*, not the actual drinking itself.

This *machlokes* may also account for the necessary *shiur* of *arba kosos*. Rambam (*Hilchos Chametz uMatza* 7:9) rules that one must drink a "*rov kos*," the majority of a cup, in order to fulfill the *mitzva*. Ramban (quoted in *Beis Yosef Orach Chayyim* 472:9) concurs, adding that even if the volume of the cup is extremely large, one must drink the majority of that particular cup. This *shiur* exceeds the regular "*melo lugmav*," cheekful, necessary for *kiddush* throughout the year. The uniqueness of this *shiur* may also relate to the nature of *arba kosos*. If the essence of *arba kosos* lies in the "recital," enhancing the portions of the *seder* which are recited over wine, *arba kosos* should be no different than *kiddush*, and a cheekful should suffice. If, however, the emphasis of *arba kosos* lies in the actual drinking of the wine, one could well envision a new *shiur arba kosos* of "*rov kos*" (and the Talmudic principle of "*rubo kekulo*" equates drinking the majority of the cup with drinking the entire cup).

A further ramification of this analysis may emerge regarding whether or not the wine of the *arba kosos* must be diluted. In Talmudic times, wine was sold in a strong, undiluted form, which only attained optimal drinking taste after being diluted with water. According to *Tosafos*, who perceive the essence of the *mitzva* in the recital as opposed to the actual drinking, dilution of the wine is not critical (although it is certainly commendable). According to Rambam's opinion, however, the drinking itself constitutes the central aspect of the *mitzva*. As such, perhaps greater importance is placed on the details of the drinking, and diluted wine would be essential to completely fulfill the *mitzva*.

Finally, this analysis may also account for the *Bavli*'s omission of any source for the *mitzva* of *arba kosos*. If the drinking of the wine itself constituted the central component of the *mitzva*, a source should seemingly be necessary to teach the new *halacha*. If, however, the cups serve merely to enhance the recital of the *Hallel* and *Haggada* of the *seder*, perhaps the *mitzva* of *arba kosos* is subsumed under the larger *mitzva* of *Hallel* and *Haggada*. Because *arba kosos* does not constitute an independent *mitzva*, no independent source is necessary.

Yachatz

Citing the Torah's epithet for *matza*, "*lechem oni*" "poor man's bread," the *Gemara* in *Masseches Pesachim* (115b) derives that the *matza* of *seder* night must be broken: "מה דרכו של עני בפרוסה – just as a poor person eats a broken piece of a loaf, so too *matza* must be eaten as a broken piece." In addition to the *Gemara*'s textual derivation, *Chazal* perceive numerous symbolic elements in the breaking of the *matza*. The *Da'as Zekeinim al HaTorah* (*Shemos* 12:8), for example, suggests that the breaking of the *matza* may represent the splitting of the *Yam Suf* and the Jordan River. Similarly, Chida (*Haggadas Simchas HaRegel*) adds that the splitting of the *matza* into two halves may symbolize the teaching of *Pirkei DeRabbi Eliezer* (ch. 48), that *HaKadosh Baruch Hu* "halved" the time of the Egyptian servitude from 430 years to 215 years. These various understandings of *yachatz* underscore that both slavery and salvation are within the broken *matza*, thereby highlighting the central theme that salvation can instantly emerge from the most abject situations of suffering.

While all agree that the *matza* must ultimately be broken, the *rishonim* debate precisely *when* the *matza* should be broken. Rambam (*Hilchos Chametz uMatza* 8:6) implies that one breaks the *matzos*

"*Yachatz*" was originally published in 2009 on TorahWeb.org

immediately before reciting the *beracha* of "המוציא לחם מן הארץ." R. Avraham Gershon Zaks (*Haggadas HaGershuni, yachatz*) suggests that this is consistent with Rambam's general understanding of *lechem mishneh* during the *seder*. Although *lechem mishneh* generally requires two whole and intact loaves, Rambam rules that *lechem mishneh* of *seder* night consists of one whole and one half *matza*, in keeping with the *Gemara*'s teaching of "מה דרכו של עני בפרוסה". Apparently, Rambam understands the *halacha* of broken *matza* as defining the *mitzva* of *lechem mishneh*. Therefore, explains R. Zaks, it is perfectly consistent to maintain that the breaking of the *matza* should be performed adjacent to the *beracha* and consumption of the *lechem mishneh* as well. R. Zaks adds that this explanation also accounts for Rambam's omission of any broken *matza* requirement for the *afikoman*. Because the *halacha* of broken *matza* relates specifically to *lechem mishneh*, the *halacha* does not necessarily apply to *afikoman*, which is not consumed as *lechem mishneh*.

Most *rishonim* and *acharonim* disagree with Rambam, maintaining that the breaking of the *matza* must immediately precede *maggid*. Several explanations are suggested for this timing. The *Beis Yosef* (*Orach Chayyim* 473) suggests that the *matza* is broken at this point in order to recite "הא לחמא עניא," which describes the poor man's bread. Alternatively, the breaking and hiding of the *matza* serves to pique the curiosity of the children, encouraging them to ask questions. The *Shulchan Aruch HaRav* (ibid., 36) suggests a further possibility. The *Gemara* derives a connection between the consumption of *matza* and the recital of the *Haggada*, noting that *matza* is "לחם שעונין עליו דברים הרבה" – bread upon which many things are recited." Based on this relationship, one must recite the *Haggada* over *matza* which is halachically fit for fulfillment of the *mitzva* of *achilas matza*. Because *achilas matza* requires that the *matza* be broken, by extension, the recital of the *Haggada* must be performed over a broken piece as well.

Ran (*Pesachim* 25b in Rif, s.v. *mihu*) cites Rav Hai Gaon, who understands the early breaking of the *matza* as a function of the general *halachos* of *lechem mishneh*. As Netziv explains (*Responsa Meishiv Davar* I:21), *lechem mishneh* generally requires two intact loaves of bread. For purposes of *lechem mishneh*, however, "intact" is defined in a relative sense: if the *mevarech* breaks a whole loaf prior to reciting the *beracha*, the loaf is certainly *not* considered "intact." If, however, the *mevarech* receives a loaf which has *already* been broken, the loaf is halachically considered "intact," since the completeness of the loaf is defined relative to its form at the time of reception. Hence, explains Netziv, by breaking the *matza* a significant amount of time prior to the actual *beracha*, the *mevarech* can be considered to have received *matza* which was already broken. As such, the broken *matza* is halachically considered "whole" for purposes of *lechem mishneh*, and one thereby fulfills both the need for "poor man's bread" as well as the need for "wholeness" for *lechem mishneh*.

One other possibility for the early breaking of the *matza* is suggested by R. Shlomo Zalman Auerbach (*Halichos Shlomo, Pesach* 9:29). Although *halacha* dictates that *kiddush* must immediately precede the *seuda* of *yom tov*, the recitation of *maggid* on *seder* night seems to create a *hefseik*, separating the *kiddush* from the *seuda*. By breaking the *matza* before the recital of *maggid*, one links the *maggid* to the meal, demonstrating that *maggid* is considered *mitzarchei achila*, for the purposes of eating. The *maggid* is therefore not considered a *hefseik*, but rather a bridge between the *kiddush* and the meal, despite the possible passage of several hours in between.

Regarding the actual execution of *yachatz*, the *rishonim* debate which of the three *matzos* should be broken. The *Smag* (283) and the *Rokeiach* (241) rule that the top *matza* should be broken, in accordance with the Talmudic dictum of "אין מעבירין על המצוות – we do not pass over *mitzvos*." Of note, Rashi (*Yoma* 33a, s.v. *ein*), quoting the *Mechilta*, maintains that the very source for this principle comes from the *mitzva* of *matza*. As the *Mechilta* expounds, "ושמרתם את מצות – you shall guard the **matzos**" can be read "ושמרתם את המצוות – you shall guard the **mitzvos**." Thus, if a *mitzva* presents itself, one should not let it pass. While *Tosafos* (ibid.) understand this derivation to be *mideOraysa*, Radbaz (*Responsa* I:559) opines that it is a mere *asmachta* (see also *Divrei Malkiel*, *Orach Chayyim* 16).

Despite the cogent argument of the *Smag* and *Rokeiach*, the accepted *halacha* follows Rosh (*Pesachim* 10:30) and the *Mordechai* (*Pesachim* 38) who maintain that the middle *matza* is broken. In defense of Rosh and the *Mordechai*, the *Bach* (*Orach Chayyim* 473, s.v. *veyikach*) explains that breaking the middle *matza* does not violate the principle of אין מעבירין על המצוות. *Eating* the *matza*, as opposed to *breaking* the *matza*, constitutes the primary *mitzva* of *seder* night. When it comes to eating the *matza*, the *beracha* of "המוציא לחם מן הארץ" is recited on the top *matza*, while the second *beracha* of "על אכילת מצה" is recited on the broken second *matza*, in perfect adherence to the principle of אין מעבירין על המצוות. Thus, by breaking the middle *matza*, one ensures that he will *not* "pass over the mitzvos," as this breaking ensures that the first *beracha* of "*hamotzi*" will be appropriately recited on the first *matza*.

Suffering and Salvation

In his commentary on the *Haggada*, Abarbanel explains that all four questions of the *ma nishtana* revolve around a single idea: the apparent contradiction of symbols on *seder* night. On one hand, the consumption of *matza* and *maror* evokes a sense of destitution and subjugation. On the other hand, the dipping and leaning indicate royalty and freedom. By noting all four symbols, the perplexed child really asks: on *seder* night, are we slaves or are we free?

"**Suffering and Salvation**" was originally published in 2011 on TorahWeb.org

Abarbanel explains that the *seder* employs contradictory symbols because *Pesach* represents an instantaneous transition in which *Bnei Yisrael* experienced both slavery and freedom on a single night. By acknowledging the dire subjugation, a person comes to truly appreciate the magnitude of the salvation. Hence, the *matza* and the *maror* evoke bitter memories of suffering in order to augment the joy of redemption.

The *Beis HaLevi* (*Parashas Beshalach*) highlights this value of contrast in explaining an initially perplexing *midrash*:

אמר משה: ב"אז" חטאתי שאמרתי ו"מאז באתי על פרעה... הרע לעם הזה", ב"אז" אני אומר שירה – Moshe stated: With [the word] *az* I sinned, when I stated, "Since (*ume'az*) I came to Pharaoh... he has been evil to this nation" (*Shemos* 5:23); and with [the word] *az*, I sing praise ("*az yashir Moshe*"; *Shemos* 15:1).

Moshe *Rabbeinu* employed the very same term, "*az*," to describe both the unbearable slavery in *Mitzrayim* as well as the ineffable joy of the exodus. This linguistic repetition suggests that Moshe *Rabbeinu* praised *HaKadosh Baruch Hu* not only for the eventual salvation, but also for the servitude which preceded the salvation: if not for the prior servitude, no salvation could be possible. The *Beis HaLevi* adds that this notion also underlies the *pasuk*: "אודך כי עניתני ותהי לי לישועה – I thank You, for You afflicted me, and were for me a salvation" (*Tehillim* 118:21). In this *pasuk*, Dovid *haMelech* thanks *HaKadosh Baruch Hu* not only for his salvation, but also for his affliction. Only in the context of the prior affliction can one truly appreciate the salvation.

Rambam appears to perceive an additional value in recalling the suffering which precedes salvation: beyond stimulating greater appreciation for the salvation itself, our acknowledgment of the prior danger attunes us to the specific reality that *HaKadosh Baruch Hu* listens to our *tefillos* and comes to our rescue. In the beginning of his *Yad HaChazaka*, Rambam explains that the reason for reading the *Megilla*, which describes not only the salvation of *Klal Yisrael* but also the initial danger of Haman's decree, is "כדי להודיע לדורות הבאים שאמת מה שהבטיחנו בתורה כי מי גוי גדול אשר לו א-לקים קרובים אליו כה' א-לקנו בכל קראנו אליו (דברים ד:ז) – to make known to future generations that what He promised in the Torah is true, 'For what nation is there that has God so near to it, as the Lord our God is at all times that we call upon Him (*Devarim* 4:7),'" to affirm the fact that *HaKadosh Baruch Hu* listens and responds to our pleas. Similarly, in the context of *yetzias Mitzrayim*, we not only mention the salvation, but also the initial enslavement, in order to accentuate the fact that *HaKadosh Baruch Hu* listens to our prayers and comes to our rescue. Perhaps this is the intent of the *pasuk*, when it describes "ויאנחו בני ישראל... ויזעקו ותעל שועתם אל הא-לקים... וישמע א-לקים את נאקתם – the Jewish people sighed... and they cried out... and their cries went up to God... and God heard their cries" (*Shemos* 2:23-24). Immediately after *Bnei Yisrael* cried out, "Hashem heard their cries."

The value of celebrating both the suffering and the salvation of *Pesach* night is expressed in other symbols of the *seder* as well. The single symbol of *matza* represents both "*lechem oni* – poor man's bread," and "לחם שעונין עליו דברים הרבה – bread upon which the *Hallel* and expressions of thanksgiving (see *Rashi Pesachim* 36a) are recited." The *maror* of *seder* night also expresses a similar dichotomy. While it certainly evokes bitter memories of slavery and subjugation, the *Gemara* also explains that one should eat lettuce ("*chasa*") "משום דחס רחמנא עילוון – because *HaKadosh Baruch Hu* treated us with mercy." Thus, the single symbol of *maror* also represents both slavery and salvation.

This duality expresses itself in the *rishonim*'s understanding of the wording of "הא לחמא עניא": Rashbam understands the phrase "די אכלו אבהתנא בארעא דמצרים" as a reference to the *matza* eaten with the *korban* pesach as *Bnei Yisrael* emerged as a free nation on the night of *yetzias Mitzrayim*. Rashbatz, however, identifies the phrase as an allusion to the *matza* eaten *before* the redemption, over the course of the bitter servitude in *Mitzrayim*. These oppositional interpretations of "הא לחמא עניא" appear to mirror the dual symbols embedded within *matza* itself – slavery and freedom in a single symbol (see also Ramban, *Devarim* 16:2, who echoes this sentiment, suggesting that "מצה תרמוז לשני דברים, *matza* symbolizes two things.")

Rambam's version of "הא לחמא עניא" may also underscore this duality. In his text of the *Haggada*, Rambam prefaces "הא לחמא עניא" with the phrase "בבהילו יצאנו ממצרים" – with rapidity, we left Egypt," then proceeds with "הא לחמא עניא די אכלו אבהתנא בארעא דמצרים – this is the bread of affliction…." The initial part of the phrase evokes our speedy departure from *Mitzrayim* as a free nation. The second phrase recalls the horrors of our slavery. The juxtaposition of these two elements suggests that from the depths of slavery and exile can spring hope and salvation.

A similar idea is expressed in Rashi's explanation of "ברוך שומר הבטחתו לישראל ברוך הוא – blessed is He Who keeps His promise to Israel." The *Haggada* does not specify to which promise it refers. Ritva opines that the *ba'al Haggada* refers to the ברית בין הבתרים (the "covenant between the parts") in which *HaKadosh Baruch Hu* promised that Avraham *Avinu*'s descendants would be redeemed. Rashi, however, maintains that the promise refers to the servitude itself. According to Rashi's reading, it would appear that the very experience of suffering itself warrants praise and *beracha*. In this respect, Rashi's understanding of "ברוך שומר הבטחתו" may be aptly compared to the *Beis HaLevi*'s understanding of "*az yashir*."

Similarly, this lesson is implied in the passage "וירד מצרימה: אנוס על פי הדבור – 'he [Yaakov *Avinu*] went down to Egypt': compelled by Divine decree." *Chazal* underscore that Yaakov *Avinu* did not leave *Eretz Yisrael* willingly. Ra'avan writes that in theory, Yaakov *Avinu* should have been forced down to *Mitzrayim* in iron chains to fulfill the decree of *HaKadosh Baruch Hu*, if not for the mercy and compassion which *HaKadosh Baruch Hu* shows to His loved ones. The *Midrash* (*Bereishis Rabba* 86) similarly analogizes Yaakov's descent to a cow being forced to the slaughterhouse. Although the cow will initially resist with all of its might, it will ultimately submit if it sees its calf being brought to the slaughterhouse. Similarly, *HaKadosh Baruch Hu* forced Yaakov *Avinu* to descend to *Mitzrayim* by first bringing his beloved son, Yosef, down to *Mitzrayim*.

Rashbam infers the compulsory nature of Yaakov *Avinu*'s descent from *HaKadosh Baruch Hu*'s placation of his fears: "אל תירא מרדה מצרימה – have no fear of descending to Egypt" (*Bereishis* 46:3). Through this statement, *HaKadosh Baruch Hu* assuaged Yaakov's fears by guaranteeing him that everything that He does is for the best, as R. Akiva states in *Masseches Berachos* (60b): "כל דעביד רחמנא לטב עביד."

In a related vein, the Sanzer Rebbe (cited by R. Asher Weiss, *Haggadas Minchas Asher*, p. 393) cited this theme in explanation of the common practice of covering one's eyes at the beginning of *Kerias Shema* (see *Berachos* 13b). In affirming "ה' א-לקינו ה' אחד," we note the singularity and absolute unity of *HaKadosh Baruch Hu* in this world. Although *din* (strict judgment) and *rachamim* (paternal compassion) appear as distinct attributes to our imprecise perception, these entities are truly one and the same. We thus cover our eyes to represent the fallibility of our limited vision. As we acknowledge the unity of *HaKadosh Baruch Hu*, we will not allow ourselves to be "blinded" by the apparent existence of suffering and travail in this world.

Rabbi Zvi Sobolofsky

After *Kerias Yam Suf*: Where Do We Go From Here?

Immediately following *kerias Yam Suf* the Jewish people became frustrated because they lacked water in the desert. The water they did find was bitter and not drinkable until God instructed Moshe to throw wood in the water to sweeten it. *Chazal* interpret this lack of water in a spiritual sense as well as a physical sense. The Torah tells us that the Jewish people traveled three days without water after leaving *Yam Suf*. *Chazal* understand this to mean that the Jews went three days without Torah – the spiritual "water" – and this caused them to complain against God. To prevent three days from passing without Torah, *Chazal* instituted *kerias haTorah* on Monday, Thursday and *Shabbos*.

This symbolic understanding of the story seems difficult. The Jewish people are criticized for traveling three days without Torah, however at this time they had not yet received the Torah! Furthermore, it is difficult to understand the meaning of the aforementioned "bitter water" if we interpret this story in a symbolic sense.

The *Kli Yakar* offers an insight into the symbolic meaning of the events surrounding the bitter water. The Jewish people, having experienced *kerias Yam Suf*, just witnessed the climax of *yetzias Mitzrayim*, whose ultimate purpose, as they knew, was to receive the Torah at Mount Sinai. The correct response to *kerias Yam Suf* was an eager desire to get to Mount Sinai. Yet we find the exact opposite occurred. *Chazal* tell us that Moshe had to drag the Jewish people away from the riches of the Egyptians that floated to the shore of the *Yam Suf*. Even when they finally began their journey away from the *Yam Suf*, they traveled slowly, without anticipation. They were criticized for going three days without Torah because they should

---

"**After *Kerias Yam Suf*...**" was originally published in 2001 on TorahWeb.org

have begged God to give them the Torah immediately. They couldn't be punished for not learning Torah yet since they had not yet received it, but they could be rebuked for not asking to receive it sooner.

What caused this delay in the receiving of the Torah? The *Kli Yakar* explains that the fear of something new overcame the Jewish people. All beginnings are hard, and this trepidation to begin something new prevented them from running to Mount Sinai. They viewed the Torah as something difficult which would be bitter, and therefore delayed their trip to Mount Sinai.

Moshe was instructed to show them that although the Torah may appear difficult at first, perhaps even bitter, it will turn sweet as soon as one accepts it.

This lesson of the events following *kerias Yam Suf* speaks to each of us. As *Pesach* comes to an end and each of us has experienced *yetzias Mitzrayim* and *kerias Yam Suf* another year, how do we approach the *yom tov* of *Shavuos*? Do we delay in our commitment to a life of Torah and *mitzvos* because we are afraid it will be too hard, or do we get ready to approach *Shavuos* and *kabbalas HaTorah* with enthusiasm? This is the challenge for each of us as *Pesach* draws to a close.

Time Is of the Essence

Many of the *mitzvos* associated with *Pesach* revolve around proper timing. There are very specific guidelines of time that govern the proper observance of the *korban pesach*. The *korban* must be offered during the afternoon of the 14th day of *Nisan*. It is also critical that it be eaten at the proper time. The precise time for eating is a dispute whether it is until midnight of the 15th of *Nisan* or until the morning. If the *korban*

"Time Is of the Essence" was originally published in 2009 on TorahWeb.org

is not completed at the right time, the leftover meat becomes disqualified, subjecting one who eats it to the severe punishment of *kareis*.

Similar to the requirement of eating the *korban pesach* at the correct time, there exists an obligation to perform the other *mitzvos* of the *seder* at precisely the right time. *Tosafos* (*Pesachim* 99b) observe that unlike *Shabbos* and other *yamim tovim*, when it is permissible to eat the meal earlier than when it is actually nightfall, the *matza* must be eaten after dark. By whatever time the *korban pesach* must be completed, so too must the *matza* be eaten. The *poskim* extend this insistence on proper timing to the *maror*, the telling of the *Haggada*, the saying of the *Hallel* and the drinking of the four cups.

The basic difference between *chametz* and *matza* is also a function of time. Exactly the same ingredients of flour and water make up both. It is only the factor of time that differentiates between them. Even the prohibitions of eating and possessing *chametz* depend upon the clock. At one moment in time on *erev Pesach*, one can no longer eat *chametz*. An hour later, one can no longer benefit from *chametz*. Finally, at noon, the prohibition of owning and eating begin according to the Torah itself.

More than any other *yom tov*, time plays a critical role in the proper observance of *Pesach*. What is the significance of this? Why does the proper commemoration of *yetzias Mitzrayim* require observances that are so time-oriented?

During *davening* and *kiddush* of each *yom tov*, we mention that we celebrate these days as a remembrance of *yetzias Mitzrayim*. Although the *shalosh regalim* are linked to *yetzias Mitzrayim* historically, what is the connection between the observance of *Rosh HaShana* and *Yom Kippur* and *yetzias Mitzrayim*? Even though there is no historical connection, we declare that these two *yamim tovim* are also "זכר ליציאת מצרים." Apparently there is a dimension not dependent upon historical events that links the entire concept of *yom tov* with *yetzias Mitzrayim*.

The first *mitzva* given to the Jewish people as a nation as they are about to leave *Mitzrayim* is *kiddush hachodesh* – sanctifying the new moon. Is this just a necessary prerequisite, since one cannot observe *Pesach* on the 15th of *Nisan* if *Rosh Chodesh Nisan* is not declared? Apparently, there is a greater significance to why we were given *kiddush hachodesh* on the eve of attaining our freedom. There is one feature that truly demarcates between a slave and a free man. A free man is master of his own time, whereas a slave's time belongs to his owner. The *Halacha* teaches us that one cannot sanctify an object he does not own. Not only is this true of material possessions, but it is true of time as well. Before the Jewish people were freed, it was inconceivable that they should be able to sanctify *Rosh Chodesh*. The *mitzva* of *kiddush hachodesh* was the beginning of the transformation from slavery to freedom. The very observance of *yom tov* is a testimony to *yetzias Mitzrayim*. The ability to create "*kedushas hazeman*" of *Rosh HaShana* and *Yom Kippur* is a declaration of "זכר ליציאת מצרים" even if there is no historical connection between them.

The relationship between time and freedom is highlighted by the statement of *Chazal* that only one who is involved in Torah study is truly free. *Talmud Torah* is a *mitzva* that has no limitations of time. One who fulfills this *mitzva* properly by salvaging every moment is truly in control of time and is a free man. One who wastes the most precious gift of time by not sanctifying it properly cannot be called a free man.

The celebration of *Pesach* centers on time more than any other *yom tov* of the year. It is specifically at this time, when we commemorate our transformation to becoming free men, that the sanctification of time becomes a primary theme of the *yom tov*. We who now are in control of time can use time properly in the service of *Hashem*. As we observe the *mitzvos* of the *seder* in their proper time and are careful concerning the prohibitions of *chametz*, we are declaring that this is the celebration of "זכר ליציאת מצרים".

Kashering Our Utensils and Our Hearts

Kashering utensils has always been an integral part of *Pesach* preparation. As we prepare our kitchens for the upcoming celebration of *Pesach*, the deeper lessons behind these intricate laws can guide us in our service of *Hashem* throughout the year. These *halachos* are derived from *Parashas Matos* and *Parashas Tzav*. It is not coincidental that we read the *pesukim* about kashering on the *Shabbos* before *Pesach*; it is a time to delve into the halachic and hashkafic messages of this area of pre-*Pesach* preparation.

Chazal derive that there are two fundamentally different ways to *kasher*, one known as *hagala* and the other as *libbun*. *Hagala* is the kashering through boiling water, whereas *libbun* uses an actual flame. We are taught in *Masseches Avoda Zara* that the appropriate method to use depends upon how the non-kosher or *chametz* food initially entered into the utensil. The halachic principle of כבולעו כך פולטו – how it was absorbed is how it can be removed – governs the laws of kashering. For example, a utensil such as a grill, which absorbed taste through use with a direct flame, cannot be removed of this absorption by mere boiling water.

The imagery of applying different degrees of heat to remove non-kosher or *chametz* can be applied in a similar way to the process of *teshuva*. When negative actions and thoughts become a part of one's being, *teshuva* requires a similar degree of effort to remove them and thereby "kasher" one's soul. Sins that were committed with less enthusiasm, and thereby did not penetrate as deeply into one's being, can be atoned for by a *teshuva*

"Kashering Our Utensils and..." was originally published in 2015 on TorahWeb.org

process commensurate with the original actions. Those which entered with more intensity require a greater degree of "heat" to be removed; as powerful as the sin was, so must be the *teshuva* to be effective.

In *Parashas Tzav* we are taught that a *kli cheres*, an earthenware vessel, cannot be kashered. Earthenware is so porous that once a taste has absorbed into its walls, it can never be totally removed. However, this limitation only applies to kashering by *hagala*, but *libbun* is effective even on earthenware. *Tosafos* (*Pesachim* 30b) explain that although taste absorbed in earthenware can never completely be removed, the process of *libbun* is equivalent to remaking the utensil. Since these vessels are originally formed in a furnace, the *libbun* process mimics this and therefore suffices to *kasher* earthenware.

The remaking of a vessel that is permeated with non-kosher taste serves as a model for *teshuva*. *Chazal* speak of a person changing his name when doing *teshuva*, since by doing so he demonstrates that he is a new person. When *teshuva* for specific sins is not sufficient, an entire transformation is necessary. *Tosafos* describes *libbun* as "נעשה כלי חדש – a new utensil has been made." A complete *teshuva* requires an entirely new outlook on life.

When one purchases utensils from a non-Jew, in addition to kashering those which were previously used, one must immerse them in a *mikva*. Just as utensils undergo a process of purification in a physical *mikva* before being usable, a soul must be immersed in the symbolic water of Torah. The halachic details of *tevila*, which require a complete immersion and necessitate removal of *chatzitzos* (barriers that separate between the utensil and the water of the *mikva*), are similarly present in a symbolic way in the *tevila* in the waters of Torah. A total immersion in Torah study without any barriers completes the process of purification of one's soul.

As we clean and *kasher* our homes for *Pesach*, let us look inward and prepare our hearts and souls in sanctity and purity.

Yetzias Mitzrayim: **Pesach** and Beyond

In the *kerias haTorah* for the last day of *Pesach*, we are commanded to remember the events of *yetzias Mitzrayim* all the days of our lives. What is the relationship between this daily obligation and the annual *mitzva* of telling the story of *yetzias Mitzrayim* on the night of the *seder*? From a halachic vantage point, there are real differences between these two *mitzvos*. According to Rambam, one must mention the *mitzvos* of *pesach*, *matza* and *maror* in order to fulfill one's obligation of telling the story on *Pesach* night. Other *rishonim* are of the opinion that the mentioning of these three *mitzvos* is not an integral part of the story, but rather enhances these *mitzvos* themselves. Even according to Rambam, there is no need to speak about these *mitzvos* on a daily basis. Rav Chaim Soloveitchik notes that unlike the daily obligation, the story at the *seder* must be told in a question-answer format. Additionally, the *Pesach* story is related by contrasting the negative states of slavery and paganism that were replaced with freedom and worship of *Hashem*. Every day, however, we simply make a quick reference to the basic event of *yetzias Mitzrayim*, but do not elaborate upon it as we do at the *seder*.

Although these daily and annual obligations are different, there is an important connection between them. Rashi comments on the *mitzva* of remembering *yetzias Mitzrayim* daily that this is accomplished by eating *matza* at the *seder*. How does the once-a-year *matza* enable us to remember *yetzias Mitzrayim* daily?

Rambam describes the feelings one should have at the *seder*, and

---

"*Yetzias Mitzrayim: Pesach...*" was originally published in 2018 on TorahWeb.org

considers viewing oneself as if he/she is leaving *Mitzrayim* to be the essence of the *seder* night experience. Rambam cites the *pasuk* concerning *Shabbos* as the source that we should view ourselves as slaves who have been freed. How can a *pasuk* concerning *Shabbos* be the source for how to observe the *Pesach seder*?

By linking the unique night of the *seder* to the daily and weekly remembrances of *yetzias Mitzrayim*, the Torah is instructing us how to draw inspiration throughout the year. Every day and every night when we make a quick reference to *yetzias Mitzrayim*, we should think back to how inspired we were at the *seder*. Similarly, when we recite *kiddush* on a weekly basis and declare *Shabbos* is a remembrance to *yetzias Mitzrayim*, we should conjure up memories of the *kiddush* we recited at the *seder*.

The relationship between annual *mitzvos* and daily ones is not unique to remembering *yetzias Mitzrayim*. The *mitzvos* of the *Yamim Noraim* are similarly once-a-year obligations whose themes reverberate throughout the year. *Tekias shofar* for *Rosh Hashana* is a dramatic once-a-year way that we declare that *Hashem* is the King of the world. As we make a similar declaration twice daily by reciting *Shema*, we should draw on the *Rosh Hashana* experience. Similarly, although *Yom Kippur* provides the greatest opportunity for *teshuva*, *teshuva* is not limited to the dramatic day of *Yom Kippur*. Every day, when we ask *Hashem* for forgiveness in our *tefilla*, we should try to remember the state of *teshuva* that had been reached during the *tefilla* of *Yom Kippur*. The *yamim tovim* of *Sukkos* and *Shavuos* also have intense experiences of rejoicing in *Hashem*'s presence and appreciating the great gift of Torah. Yet, every day we should experience joy in the service of *Hashem* and appreciation for His Torah. Once again, we can attain these feelings by drawing on the great moments of these *yamim tovim*.

Since the *yamim tovim* set the tone for the entire year, it behooves us to take maximum advantage of these special days. How we commemorate

Pesach will impact on every *Shabbos* of the year, as well as every day and night. The experience of eating *matza* on *Pesach* can last the entire year. As we approach *Pesach*, let prepare to make the most of every moment of the *yom tov*. The memories have to inspire us for the entire year.

Rabbi Daniel Stein

Making the *Pesach* Story Personal

I. Our Dual Relationship with *Hashem*

There is an undeniable bond between the *mitzva* of offering the *korban pesach* and the *mitzva* of *bris mila*. They are the only two positive commandments whose violation elicits the punishment of *kareis*, and as perhaps alluded to by the grave consequences levied against those who neglect these two *mitzvos*, they are both arguably indispensable ingredients to the Jewish experience. The *pasuk* states in *Parashas Bo*, "And should a convert reside with you, he shall make a Passover sacrifice to *Hashem*" (*Shemos* 12:48), from which the *midrash* cited by Rashi initially infers that aside from the *bris mila* and immersion in a *mikva*, every convert must offer a *korban pesach* immediately upon his conversion, no matter what time of year the conversion occurs. The *midrash* ultimately rejects this suggestion, but the *Meshech Chochma* concludes nonetheless that a convert can substitute the *korban pesach* in place of the typical *korban* offered by every convert upon their conversion. The relationship between *korban pesach* and *bris mila* is further underscored when we consider the unique exclusion "but no uncircumcised male may partake of it" (ibid.), that no uncircumcised Jewish male may participate in the *korban pesach*. Perhaps these two *mitzvos* are so intertwined and so central because they represent two critical dimensions to our relationship with *Hashem*. (See also R. Michael Rosensweig's "*Korban Pesach*: A Symbol of Faith and Commitment" in this volume.)

The *bris mila* represents a personal commitment to serving *Hashem*, modeled after Avraham *Avinu* who was the first person to perform *bris mila*, and who independently discovered and forged a relationship with *Hashem* amidst a polytheistic culture, whereas the *korban pesach*

"Making the *Pesach* Story Personal" was originally published in 2017 on TorahWeb.org

corresponds to the birth of the Jewish nation and is a response to our shared experience of leaving *Mitzrayim* as a people. This is the platform through which we relate to *Hashem* not as individuals, but as a member of the *Bnei Yisrael*. Every Jew as well as every successful convert must subscribe to these two notions. It is not sufficient to create a personal relationship with the Almighty represented by the *bris mila*, but we must also intimately identify with the history of the Jewish people signified by the *korban pesach*. Additionally, the *Gemara* (*Yevamos* 47a) mandates that we question interested candidates for conversion, "'What reason have you for desiring to become a convert; do you not know that Israel, at the present time, is persecuted and oppressed, despised, harassed and overcome by afflictions?" Rav Soloveitchik once suggested that perhaps we inform all potential converts of our standing within the world not because we seek to discourage them, but rather to give them the opportunity to connect with our national identity and destiny, which is a critical component of the conversion process and our relationship with *Hashem*.

II. The Blood of the *Korban Pesach* and the Blood of *Bris Mila*

Indeed, it was in the merit of these these two *mitzvos*, and these two aspects to our relationship with *Hashem*, that we were redeemed from *Mitrzayim*. Rashi (*Shemos* 12:6) cites the *midrash* which interprets the *pasuk* "but you were naked and bare" (*Yechezkel* 16:7) as reflecting the Jewish people's inferior spiritual status and their unworthiness to be redeemed. In order to elevate *Bnei Yisrael* and justify their redemption, *Hashem* provided us with these two *mitzvos*, "And I passed by you and saw you downtrodden with your blood, and I said to you, 'With your blood, live,' and I said to you, 'With your blood, live'" (ibid., 6), referring to the blood of the *korban pesach* and the blood of *bris mila*. *Targum Yonasan* continues that for this reason the blood from both these *mitzvos* was mixed and placed on the doorpost during the plague of the firstborn. This is perhaps alluded to in the language of the *pasuk*, which repeats the word "blood" twice: "And the **blood** will be for you for a sign upon the houses where you will be, and I will see the **blood** and skip over you" (*Shemos* 12:13), referring to both the blood of the *korban pesach* as well as the blood of *bris mila*. Alshich *Hakadosh* adds that for this reason the blood was placed "on the two doorposts and on the lintel" (12:7). The two doorposts represent Moshe and Aharon, the leaders of the Jewish nation and our relationship with *Hashem* as part of *Bnei Yisrael*. The lintel corresponds to *Hashem*, representing our direct, individual, and personal commitment to *Hashem*.

However, the blood of these two *mitzvos* was mixed and placed on the doorpost together, perhaps indicating that these are not two separate notions and dimensions to our relationship with *Hashem* but one and the same. Each aspect of this relationship informs and compliments the other. In that sense, we must personalize our commemoration of *yetzias Mitzrayim* through our participation in the *korban pesach*, and by extension the entire *seder* experience. We must take the national story of *yetzias Mitrzayim* and make it our own individual narrative as well, by peppering it with instances of Divine intervention and Divine providence that we have personally witnessed and benefited from in our own lives. It has been widely observed that the text of *Haggada* has more commentaries than almost any other Jewish text, rivaled only by the Torah itself. Every group, every sect, and every yeshiva within the Jewish community has its own observations and interpretations of the *Pesach* story and the text of the *Haggada*. Perhaps this reflects the measure of personal input that we are required to bring to bear on the night of the *seder*. Through the lens and inspiration of retelling and reexperiencing the story of *yetzias Mitzrayim* on the night of the *seder*, every one of us is enjoined to reflect on our own personal encounters with the hand of *Hashem*, the *yad Hashem*, and how that has facilitated our own personal arc and destiny.

III. Moshe's Unique Story

After the plague of hail, Moshe threatened Pharaoh that if he did not immediately release the Jewish people, he would suffer a plague of locusts. Ramban and *Ba'alei HaTosafos* note that prior to all the other plagues, *Hashem* informed Moshe about the nature of the ensuing plague. However, with regards to the plague of locusts, we don't find any such prior notification. How was Moshe able to correctly predict that the next plague would be locusts if *Hashem* didn't inform him beforehand? Ramban claims that just like the other plagues, *Hashem* must have informed Moshe earlier even though it is not recorded in the text itself. The *Ba'alei HaTosafos* suggest that all the plagues were alluded to on Moshe's staff through the abbreviated inscription *detzach, adash, be'achav*. Rav Shimshon from Ostropol brilliantly suggests that the plague of locusts, *arbeh*, is foreshadowed in the words "come to Pharaoh," "בא אל פרעה" (*Shemos* 9:1). The word "*bo*" is spelled *beis aleph*, and the letters *beis* and *peh* as well as *aleph* and *ayin* are interchangeable since they are formed with the same part of the mouth. Therefore, he suggests that the pasuk "בא אל פרעה" was instructing Moshe to switch the letters *beis* and *aleph* of "בא" for their counterparts in the word "פרעה" spelled *peh reish ayin heh*, which if rearranged yields the letters *aleph reish beis heh*, or *arbeh*, locusts. The *Chasam Sofer* takes an even more novel approach when he submits that the plague of locusts was in fact Moshe's own idea! After the first seven plagues were successfully dictated by *Hashem* and implemented by Moshe, Moshe was given the latitude to concoct his own punishment for the Egyptians, and he chose locusts. This provided Moshe with a personal and unique perspective on *yetzias Mitrayim*, and a part of the story that was not shared with anyone else.

Perhaps for this reason the *pasuk* states, "In order that you tell into the ears of your son and your son's son how I made a mockery of the Egyptians... and **you** will know that I am *Hashem*" (*Shemos* 10:2). The *pasuk* begins in the singular, "your son," and concludes in the plural "you will know." The Belzer Rebbe explains that this is because in the generation of those who left Egypt, the only person whose children did not experience *yetzias Mitzrayim* firsthand was Moshe, whose children who were still in *Midyan* at the time. Therefore, the *pasuk* begins in the singular, because initially the only person out of all of *Bnei Yisrael* who had a *mitzva* to recount the story of *yetzias Mitzrayim* to his children was Moshe. (This might explain why Moshe's name does not appear throughout the entire text of the *Haggada*, because Moshe himself was the original narrator of the story.) Nonetheless, the *pasuk* concludes in the plural, because in subsequent generations, all Jews are bound by the duty to teach their children the story of the exodus. However, just like Moshe not only told his children the generic story of the *yetzias Mitrzayim*, but also his own personal individual account, so too each one of us must share with our children our own unique perspective and personal insight. Only if we color the story of *yetzias Mitzrayim* with our own individual experiences and encounters with the *yad Hashem*, thereby fulfilling the first part of the *pasuk*, "tell into the ears of your son," can our children be successful in attaining the conclusion of the *pasuk*, "and you will know that I am *Hashem*."

IV. *Shabbos HaGadol*

The *Tur* explains that the *Shabbos* prior to *Pesach* is known as *Shabbos HaGadol*, the "Great *Shabbos*," because it was on the *Shabbos* prior to *yetzias Mitrzayim* that *Bnei Yisrael* designated their sheep for the *korban pesach*, thereby fulfilling the *pasuk* "draw forth or buy for yourselves sheep for your families and slaughter the Passover sacrifice" (*Shemos* 12:21). This was indeed a great miracle because the sheep were worshipped as a deity in Egypt, and yet the Egyptians did not protest when *Bnei Yisrael* designated thousands of sheep for slaughter. However, the *Midrash* observes that the *pasuk* begins "draw forth," because even amongst *Bnei Yisrael*, there were still individuals who were worshipping *avoda zara*. Therefore, before designating a sheep for the *korban pesach*, Moshe instructed them to withdraw their hand, and to cease and desist their practices of *avoda zara*. However, this is somewhat difficult to understand; after all, *Bnei Yisrael* were now standing at the culmination of the process of the redemption. How could it be that Moshe waited until this late stage before instructing them to abandon their practices of *avoda zara*?

Rav Kalonymus Kalman Shapira (*Eish Kodesh*) explains that of course *Bnei Yisrael* had renounced their practices of idol worship long ago, but upon their introduction and exposure to the *mitzva* of *korban pesach*, Moshe was encouraging them not to view the *mitzva* as someone else's *mitzva*, or as someone else's religion, as *avoda zara*, a foreign service, but rather to embrace and make the *mitzva* of *korban pesach* their own. Similarly, we must embrace and transform the national story of the *seder* night, represented by the *korban pesach*, into our own personal narrative. The *Pirkei DeRabbi Eliezer* comments that the *pasuk* repeats twice, "and I said to you, 'With your blood, live,' and I said to you, 'With your blood, live,'" because just like the redemption from *Mitzrayim* was precipitated by the unification of the *mitzvos* of *bris mila* and *korban pesach*, representing the individual relationship with *Hashem* and our national relationship with *Hashem*, so too the final redemption will only materialize when we successfully integrate these two experiences and commitments. Therefore, on the *Shabbos* before *Pesach* we are reminded to personalize the *Pesach* story, to make it our own, because only in this way can we merit to transmit the story to the next generation and ultimately to be *zocheh* to a *geula* once again, במהרה בימינו אמן!

Rabbi Dr. Abraham J. Twerski

Zeman Cheiruseinu:
An Independence Day Celebration?

I learned much from working with an addicted population.

I know how you celebrate an Independence Day. Parades, picnics, hot-dogs, patriotic speeches, and fireworks – that's it. Whoever heard of an Independence Day that lasts a week, and for which you must prepare weeks in advance, cleaning the house and sterilizing the kitchen as if it were an operating room? That's a bit of an overkill for an Independence Day, isn't it?

Oh, well. Jews like to do things differently. But then, every Friday night we say in *kiddush* that *Shabbos* is in commemoration of our deliverance from Egypt. We don't invoke July 4th every week!

But we're not finished yet. *Tefillin* and *tzitzis* are in commemoration of our deliverance from Egypt. Now it's a daily thing! In fact, many other *mitzvos* are in commemoration of our deliverance from Egypt. We must concede that as an Independence Day celebration, this is a bit much.

I came to the realization of what *zeman cheiruseinu* is all about when a young man who was recovering from years of heavy drug addiction attended his father's *seder*. When his father began reciting the *Haggada*, "עבדים היינו," "we were slaves to Pharaoh," the son interrupted him. "Abba," he said, "can you truthfully say that you yourself was a slave? I can tell you what it means to be a slave. All those years that I was on drugs, I was enslaved by drugs. I had no freedom. I did things that I never thought I was capable of doing, but I had no choice. The drugs demanded it, and I had to do it. Today I am a free person."

"Zeman Cheiruseinu..." was originally published in 2010 on TorahWeb.org

When the young man related this to me, Passover suddenly took on an entirely new meaning. Yes, we can be slaves to a tyrannical ruler. But we can also be slaves to drugs, to alcohol, to cigarettes, to food, to lust or to gambling. Any time we lose control of our behavior, we are slaves. If we are not in control of our anger, we are slaves to anger. People who cannot detach themselves from the office are slaves to it. A person can be a slave to making money or to pursuing acclaim. These are enslavements that are no less ruthless than being slaves to Pharaoh. We may surrender our precious freedom and allow our drives and impulses to exercise a tyrannical rule over us.

It is now clear what *zeman cheiruseinu* is all about. It is much more than political independence, and we can see why we are reminded of this not only during the week of Passover, but every Friday night and even multiple times during each day. We are at all times at risk of surrendering our precious independence and allowing ourselves to become enslaved.

Make no mistake. A slave cannot exercise proper judgment and has no free choice. A person who wants to live and knows that cigarettes can kill him but is unable to stop smoking is a slave, and this is true of many behaviors which we may not consider addictions. Our thinking becomes distorted, as I explained in *Addictive Thinking*, and we rationalize our self-destructive behavior.

The young man's comment to his father's reading of the *Haggada* stimulated me to write a commentary, *Haggadah: From Bondage to Freedom*, in which I pointed out that far from bring a narrative of an historical event, the *Haggada* is a text of identifying our addictive behaviors and a guideline on how to break loose from these enslavements and be free people.

Animals are not free. They can not make a choice between right and wrong. They must do what their body desires. The uniqueness of man is that we are free to choose how to act. "Give me liberty or give me death" is more than a patriotic declaration. To the degree that we lose our freedom to choose, to that degree an element of our humanity dies. The teaching of Passover is to cherish freedom and not to submit to tyranny, even to the tyranny within ourselves.

Rabbi Mayer Twersky

And It Happened at Midnight

Among the songs with which the first *seder* concludes is "ויהי בחצי הלילה" ("And It Happened at Midnight"). This song catalogs various miracles and instances of Divine revelation which occurred on the night of the 15th of *Nisan* throughout the generations. However, the relevance of this song to the *seder* and the story of the exodus is unclear. What element of that story is amplified by enumerating seemingly unrelated events, which occured over a span of hundreds of years? How is our experience of this night enhanced by adumbrating its history?

At first glance, the 15th of *Nisan*, the date of the exodus, is special owing to its historical prominence; the exodus endowed this day with its everlasting significance. While this conventional understanding is not entirely incorrect, it is certainly deficient. A brief excursus on the Jewish conception and philosophy of time will provide a fuller understanding of and a deeper appreciation for the uniqueness of the *seder* night.

Judaism recognizes the duality of time. On one hand, time is quantitative, an instrument for measuring motion. A single day marks one complete rotation of the earth on its axis, a month measures a cycle of lunar movement, and similarly, all units of time are linked to motion (cf. *Pesachim* 94a: "What distance does an average person cover in a day? Ten parsangs.").

On the other hand, time is also qualitative, possessing inherent qualities. *Shabbos*, for example, possesses *kedushas hayom*; it is inherently holy, because "God blessed the seventh day and sanctified it" (*Bereishis* 2:3). So too each of the Jewish holidays is distinctively, intrinsically holy. Moreover, it is the unique *kedushas hayom* (inherent holiness) of each holiday which generates that holiday's prescriptions and proscriptions. Thus, for example, the unique

---

"And It Happened at Midnight" was originally published in 2009 on TorahWeb.org

kedushas hayom of the 15th of *Tishrei* obligates us to dwell in *sukkos*, and so on.

The *kedushas hayom* of each holiday generates that holiday's spiritual themes and creates its religious opportunities. Consider the following analogy. Within the agricultural cycle, certain periods of the year are especially conducive to planting, others to harvesting, etc. (cf. *Berachos* 18b). So it is within the religious, temporal cycle. By virtue of their inherent spiritual qualities, certain days of the year are especially conducive to certain religious experiences. Accordingly, our sages identify the עשרת ימי תשובה (the ten days from *Rosh HaShana* to *Yom HaKippurim*) as especially conducive to repentance, and in this period repentance is especially efficacious (see *Rosh HaShana* 18a).

The holiday of *Pesach* is infused with a *kedushas hayom* of *geula* (redemption), and the *seder* night is singularly suited for experiencing the *Shechina* (Divine presence). This intrinsic redemptive quality of the 15th of *Nisan* is responsible for the timing of all the miraculous events and instances of Divine revelation which have occurred on this night. Especially significant are the miracles and incidents of Divine revelation which antedate the exodus, because they clearly attest to the innate quality and intrinsic character of the day. The 15th of *Nisan* does not owe its uniqueness to the exodus; on the contrary, the timing of the exodus was determined by the intrinsic uniqueness of this day.

The Torah describes the night of the exodus as *leil shimmurim* – a night of anticipation. Our Sages explain that it is "a night that from the six days of creation has been anticipated" (*Rosh HaShanah* 11b). In other words, at the moment time was created, this night was cast as a time of *geula* and *gilui Shechina*.

The song "And It Happened at Midnight" seeks to sensitize us not only to the acquired historical significance, but also to the intrinsic spiritual character of the day. In so doing, it urges us not to be content with passively commemorating the exodus, but to strive to actively experience the wondrous, wonderful *kedushas hayom* of *gilui Shechina*.

Matza and *Maror*

"They should eat the flesh on that night – roasted over the fire – and *matzos*; with bitter herbs they shall eat it" (*Shemos* 12:8).

Hillel's understanding of this verse serves as the source for his original and our mimetic practice of eating *matza* and *maror* together (*Pesachim* 115a; *vide Haggahos* Maharav Ranshburg ad loc.). *Prima facie*, this *mitzva* appears to be anomalous because it seemingly incorporates antithetical elements within a single *mitzva*. *Matza* symbolizes and commemorates redemption; "[it is a *mitzva* to eat] *matza* because [our ancestors] were redeemed" (*Pesachim* 116b). *Maror*, on the other hand, symbolizes and commemorates bitter servitude; "[it is a *mitzva* to eat] *maror* because the Egyptians embittered the lives of our ancestors in Egypt" (ibid.). What message does this seemingly anomalous *mitzva* convey?

In truth, the dialectical merging of the symbols for redemption and servitude occurs within the *mitzva* of *matza* itself. Not only is *matza* the quintessential symbol of redemption, but simultaneously it evokes images of suffering and slavery. In fact, we accentuate this dimension of *matza* in our introduction to *maggid*, "This is the poor man's bread that our ancestors ate in Egypt" (*vide* Ramban to *Devarim* 16:2).

Upon reflection, this apparent anomaly points us to a profound, enhanced understanding of the relationship between suffering and redemption within *Hashem*'s providential scheme. Redemption does not represent the end or negation of suffering; instead it is the culmination

---

"*Matza* and *Maror*" was originally published in 2001 on TorahWeb.org

of suffering. Redemption is an outgrowth rather than a reversal of suffering. Accordingly, *matza* simultaneously symbolizes both suffering and redemption. Moreover, *matza* and *maror* merge because in *Hashem*'s master providential plan, suffering forges redemption.

Bnei Yisrael emerged from the iron furnace of Egypt poised to become a unique nation, the chosen people. Their national character – merciful, modest and kind (*Yevamos* 79a) – had been forged in the suffering of *Mitzrayim*. Accordingly, the Torah constantly reinforces our collective memory "that you were strangers in the land of *Mitzrayim*" (*Shemos* 22:20). The *matza* of the 15th of *Nisan* "because they were redeemed" (*Pesachim* 116b) was clearly the culmination of the *matza* of suffering and servitude (*vide* Ramban to *Devarim* 16:2).

This perspective on the relationship between suffering and redemption has sustained and nourished *Klal Yisrael* throughout the generations. May it continue to sustain and nourish us, individually and collectively, until the coming of *Mashiach*, במהרה בימינו אמן.

Emuna and Masora

The *yom tov* of *Pesach* has two foci: *emuna* and *masora*. The belief and knowledge of *HaKadosh Baruch Hu* is predicated upon our experience of *yetzias Mitzrayim*: "I am *Hashem*, your God, who has taken you out of the land of *Mitzrayim*, from the house of slavery" (*Shemos* 20:2). "The basic principle of all principles and the pillar of all sciences is to realize that there is a First Being who brought every existing thing into being.... To know this truth is a *mitzvas asei*, as it is said, 'I am *Hashem* your God...'" (Rambam, *Hilchos Yesodei HaTorah* 1:1, 6.) In *Mitzrayim*, we witnessed *Hashem*'s providence over the world, and were taught about reward and punishment.

"***Emuna** and **Masora***" was originally published in 2005 on TorahWeb.org

When we fulfill the daily *mitzva* of זכירת יציאת מצרים, we remind ourselves of the lessons of faith, and reaffirm our faith (*vide* Ramban, end of *Parashas Bo*). And on *Pesach*, when we re-experience *yetzias Mitzrayim*, we relive these vivid lessons of faith.

Thus we are privileged to have the *mitzva* of *achilas matza*, in the oft quoted words of the *Zohar Hakadosh*, bread of faith.

As such, the *yom tov* of *Pesach* is a time especially conducive to cultivating and deepening our *emuna* in *Hashem*.

The second focus of *Pesach* is *masora*, transmitting and teaching our *emuna*. "And you shall tell your son on that day saying, 'it is because of this that *Hashem* acted on my behalf when I left *Mitzrayim*'" (*Shemos* 13:8). "The Torah speaks with reference to four sons…"

In truth, these two foci are inextricably linked; *shtayim shehein achas*. The symbiotic relationship between *emuna* and *masora* can and should be understood on different levels. The most basic level is this: Parents (and educators) want to give their children the absolute best. They want to equip their children for the future, for life. They want to give their children what is most important, most precious. Accordingly, a genuine *ma'amin* strives to transmit his *emuna* to his children/disciples. *Emuna* is the lens through which life should be viewed, understood and experienced. *Emuna* provides an unfailing guide to how life should be lived.

But the symbiotic relationship between *emuna* and *masora*, between "אנכי" and "והגדת לבנך," reaches deeper. *Emuna* provides an all-encompassing vision of the past, present and future. The world was created for Torah, for the Jewish people who accepted and live Torah. Life does not merely muddle along. Life – existence – is purposeful, and the ultimate purpose is "לתקן עולם במלכות שקי" – to perfect the world through the sovereignty of *Hashem*."

For this reason *masora* is a pivotal, indispensable component of *emuna*. In transmitting our faith to future generations, we sow the seeds of *geula*, "*lesakein olam bemalchus Shakai*." One who experiences "אנכי ה' א-לקיך" must translate and channel that experience into "והגדת לבנך."

Ramban, in his *hassagos* to Rambam's *Sefer HaMitzvos*, emphasizes this link between *emuna* and *masora*. It is, writes Ramban, a *mitzvas lo saaseh* to never forget *maamad Har Sinai*, which is the basis of our *emuna* in Torah. This *mitzva*, according to Ramban, also entails transmitting that memory and concomitant belief to future generations. *Emuna* and *masora* are inseparable.

Avraham *Avinu* was a paragon, and hence is a paradigm, of faith. He triumphed, *Chazal* teach us, over ten *nisyonos*. His life was an odyssey of *emuna*. And yet, the Torah chooses one particular moment to describe him as a *maamin*. The Torah records Avraham *Avinu*'s reaction to *Hashem*'s promise that he, despite being barren and already at an advanced age, will yet father a child who will inherit his legacy. Avraham *Avinu*'s reaction: "והאמן בה'" – and he believed in *Hashem*" (*Bereishis* 15:6). It is only at this juncture, when *Hashem* promises him a child, that Avraham *Avinu* is given the opportunity to manifest complete *emuna* – *emuna* with a vision for the future.

A Jew is called upon to live a life of *emuna*, anchored in the past of "אשר הוצאתיך מארץ מצרים" and confident of a future of "לתקן עולם במלכות שקי."

The Gift of Speech

A blessing of the leap year is that the cycle of *kerias haTorah* focuses our attention on *lashon hara* as we prepare for *Pesach*. The

---

"The Gift of Speech was originally published in 2008 on TorahWeb.org

parshiyos of *Tazria* and *Metzora* deal extensively with *halachos* of *tzara'as*, a skin disease which, according to *Chazal*, is inflicted as a punishment for the sin of *lashon hara*. Thus, as we keep pace with *parashas hashavua*, our attention is focused on *lashon hara* and its consequences. The focus on *lashon hara* is especially welcome because it dovetails beautifully with our *Pesach* preparations.

Galus Mitzrayim was precipitated and prolonged by *cheit halashon*, sins of speech. In terms of long-term causes, the *lashon hara* which Yosef *haTzaddik* spoke about his brothers to his father incited their hatred and set in motion events which ultimately resulted in *galus Mitzrayim*.

In terms of short-term causes, *Chazal* comment on the *pasuk* in *Parashas Shemos* "אכן נודע הדבר – surely the matter is known" (*Shemos* 2:14), that Moshe *Rabbeinu*, upon his encounter with Dasan and Aviram, experiences an "ah ha!" moment. Moshe *Rabbeinu*, according to *Chazal*, now understood that the Jewish people were deserving of servitude because they engaged in hurtful, harmful speech, even informing on each other.

With this background we can approach a fascinating teaching of the *Zohar Hakadosh*. The *Zohar Hakadosh* teaches that in *Mitzrayim*, *dibbur* (speech) was in *galus*. Exile is not merely a physical and political reality and category; exile is also a spiritual reality and category. The faculty of speech, according to the *Zohar*, was in *galus*. *Klal Yisrael* abused the gift of speech, and as a result, they were plunged into *galus*, not only bodily but also spiritually. The gift of speech was also exiled.

What does *galus* of speech entail? Speech serves as an instrument of communication. As such, speech represents communication. When the *Zohar Hakadosh* teaches that in *Mitzrayim dibbur* was in *galus*, this means that the ability to communicate had been exiled. Sans communication, interpersonal connections can not be forged or maintained. The *galus* of *dibbur* generates crushing solitude.

A major feature of the slavish existence is solitude. As a result of his servitude, the slave is cut off from others. He leads a lonely, solitary existence.[18] The commensurability (מידה כנגד מידה) of slavery as a punishment for *lashon hara* is clear. *Lashon hara* creates divisiveness. The punishment for creating divisiveness through evil speech is slavish solitude with the concomitant loss of the ability to communicate. And thus, along with the Jewish people, *dibbur* was exiled.

When *galus* is precipitated by the abuse of speech, *geula* is conditional upon the refinement and purification of speech. And thus as we attempt to re-create and re-experience the *geula* of *Mitzrayim* on the night of the *seder*, we harness our ability to speak to engage in *sippur yetzias Mitzrayim*. "אתי דיבור ומבטל דיבור- speech will come and nullify speech." The redemptive speech of *sippur yetzias Mitzrayim* offsets the destructive speech of *lashon hara*.

And thus we are fortunate that the *parashas hashavua* in a leap year focuses our attention on the egregious sin of *lashon hara* as we anticipate the *yom tov* of *Pesach*. Focusing upon the causes and consequences of *lashon hara* should constitute a vital part of our *Pesach* preparations. The present forum is not suited for a discussion of the ignobility, pettiness, voyeurism ("seeking the sordid or scandalous"; *Merriam Webster Collegiate Dictionary*) or mean-spiritedness which animate *lashon hara*. Nor is the present forum suited for a depiction of the hurt, hatred, humiliation and divisiveness which result from *lashon hara*. Nevertheless, as part of our *Pesach* preparations, the following notes of caution should be sounded: It is forbidden to engage in *lashon hara* – as disseminator or receiver – in any medium: oral, written or electronic. It is well-known that the *Chafetz*

---

[18] This idea is reflected in the *halacha* that "עבד אין לו חיים," that an *eved kena'ani* is not halachically related even to his biological children.

Chayyim delineates exceptional circumstances wherein *lashon hara* is warranted and thus constitutes a *mitzva*. But we ought to be exceedingly wary of ignobility, pettiness, voyeurism or mean-spiritedness self-righteously masquerading as a *mitzva*.

Miracles and Wonders

The *Mishna* in *Pesachim* teaches that the format for סיפור יציאת מצרים is מתחיל בגנות ומסיים בשבח – one begins by recounting our disgrace and concluding with our glory (116a; translation adapted from Artscroll). Shmuel opines that *genus* refers to the fact that "עבדים היינו," we were slaves. (This stands in contradistinction to Rav's opinion that *genus* refers to our ancestors having been idolatrous. We incorporate both opinions in the *Haggada*.) The *Gemara* does not explicitly state what the contrasting, corresponding *shevach* is. *Prima facie*, it is obvious. The contrasting, corresponding *shevach* is that we are now free. And, in fact, Maharal of Prague (*Gevuros Hashem*) explicates Shmuel's view in this way.

Rambam, however, interprets very differently. He writes (*Hilchos Chametz uMatza* 7:4) that the counterpoints to עבדים היינו are the "miracles and wonders that were performed for us [in *Mitzrayim*] and in our freedom." Rambam's interpretation is puzzling. The formulation מתחיל בגנות ומסיים בשבח suggests sharp contrast, thesis and antithesis. How are miracles the antithesis of slavery?

The answer lies in understanding the spiritual deficit and handicap of slavery. "כי לי בני ישראל עבדים, ולא עבדים לעבדים" – *Bnei Yisrael* are My slaves, and not slaves to slaves [says *Hashem*]." The dependence, vulnerability and accountability which a slave feels vis-a-vis his human master obstruct his relationship with *HaKadosh Baruch Hu*. Being the

---

"Miracles and Wonders" was originally published in 2012 on TorahWeb.org

beneficiary of *nissim* and *niflaos* (miracles and wonders) not only reflects a direct relationship with *HaKadosh Baruch Hu*, but a privileged one. Thus from a spiritual perspective the נסים ונפלאות שנעשו לנו are indeed the ultimate antithesis of עבדים היינו.

If we simply read the words of Rambam carefully, we will realize that נסים ונפלאות are not merely an important aspect of the *shevach* of סיפור יציאת מצרים. In fact, they constitute the defining focal point of the *mitzva*: "It is a positive biblical commandment to recount and delve into [translation based on Rav Soloveitchik's explanation of "*lesappeir be-*"] the miracles and wonders performed for our ancestors on the 15th of *Nisan*" (Rambam, *Hilchos Chametz uMatza* 7:1)

Rambam's quintessential definition of סיפור יציאת מצרים is absolutely remarkable. סיפור יציאת מצרים, according to Rambam, is NOT about the exodus per se. In fact Rambam does not even allude to, much less mention, freedom in his definition of מצות סיפור יציאת מצרים. *Sippur yetzias Mitzrayim* is the story of an enslaved, formerly idolatrous people who become so close to *HaKadosh Baruch Hu* that He bestows נסים ונפלאות upon them. The fact of liberation per se is only significant insofar as the freedom was a byproduct of נסים ונפלאות and enabled our new, privileged relationship with *HaKadosh Baruch Hu*. סיפור יציאת מצרים is the story of spiritual transformation. An enslaved (and thus, remote), formerly idolatrous people through נסים ונפלאות become *Hashem*'s chosen people (Rambam, *Hilchos Chametz uMatza* 7:4), enjoying privileged treatment and a relationship.

Without any sermonizing or editorializing, there is a profound, compelling "take-home message." Any material, financial or political attainment, even something as essential as freedom, has no inherent significance if not translated into spiritual attainment. May we all leave *Pesach* with such a *rechush gadol*. חג כשר ושמח.

A Lesson in Humility

The *Mishna* provides the format for *sippur yetzias Mitzrayim*: מתחיל בגנות ומסיים בשבח. We begin by shamefully recounting our degradation: we were idolatrous and slaves. We conclude by thankfully celebrating our privileged status: *HaKadosh Baruch Hu* miraculously redeemed us and sanctified us as His chosen people.

What is the source for this format, and what is its underlying significance? Rambam does not explicitly address this question. His words, however, implicitly provide a beautiful answer.

> Both these festivals, I mean *Sukkos* and *Pesach*, inculcate both an opinion and a moral quality …. As for the moral quality, it consists in man's always remembering the days of stress in the days of prosperity, so that his gratitude to God should become great and so that he should achieve humility and submission. Accordingly, *matza* and *maror* must be eaten on *Pesach* in commemoration of what happened to us. Similarly, one must leave the houses and live in *sukkos*, as is done by the wretched inhabitants of deserts and wastelands, in order that the fact be commemorated that such was our state in ancient times: "כי בסכות הושבתי את בני ישראל – that I made the children of Israel dwell in *sukkos*…" (*Vayikra* 23:43). (*Guide* III:43)

Rambam had already developed this idea earlier in the *Guide* as well:

> As for the reading on the occasion of the offering of the *bikkurim*, first fruits, it also is conducive to the moral

---

"**A Lesson in Humility**" was originally published in 2014 on TorahWeb.org

quality of humility, for it is carried out by him who carries the basket on his shoulders. It contains an acknowledgement of God's beneficence and bountifulness, so that man should know that it is a part of the Divine worship that man should remember states of distress at a time when he prospers. This purpose is frequently affirmed in the Torah: "וזכרת כי־עבד היית – and you shall remember that you were a servant" (*Devarim* 5:14, 15:15, 24:22), and so on. For there was a fear of the moral qualities that are generally acquired by all those who are brought up in prosperity – I mean conceit, vanity and neglect of the correct opinions: "פן תאכל ושבעת ובתים טבים תבנה – lest when you have eaten and are satisfied, and build good houses…" (*Devarim* 8:12). It is because of this apprehension that the commandment has been given to carry out a reading every year before Him, may He be exalted, and in presence of His Indwelling, on the occasion of the offering of *bikkurim*. You also know already that the Torah insists upon the plagues, which befell the Egyptians, being always remembered: "למען תזכר את יום צאתך – that you may remember the day that you came out…" (*Devarim* 16:3). And it says: "למען תספר באזני בנך – and that you may tell into the ears of your son…" (*Shemos* 10:2). (*Guide* III:39)

The Torah protects us from becoming haughty and feeling entitled. When enjoying prosperity, we are to remember days of penury. When experiencing success, we are to recall suffering. For this reason, the pilgrim, upon bringing *bikkurim* does not simply say "thank you, *HaKadosh Baruch Hu*." Instead he is מתחיל בגנות ומסיים בשבח by reliving our degradation and only then thanking *HaKadosh Baruch Hu* for the prosperous harvest.

We also eat *matza* (= *lechem oni*) and *maror* and remember *yetzias Mitzrayim* for this reason as well. Accordingly, *Chazal* instructed that we recount סיפור יציאת מצרים in the humbling format of מתחיל בגנות. Moreover, the central text for the *sippur* is "ארמי אבד אבי," the *parasha* of *mikra bikkurim*, which serves as the source for מתחיל בגנות.

Rabbi Mordechai Willig

The *Hallel* of *Purim*, *Pesach*, and the Final Redemption

I

In the period between *Purim* and *Pesach*, it is instructive to analyze a passage in the Talmud which deals with both holidays. The *Gemara* says in *Megilla* (14a), "If *shira* was said when we were delivered from slavery to freedom at *yetzias Mitzrayim*, then when we are delivered from death to life we must certainly say *shira*." This is the source for the *mitzva* of reading the *Megilla* on *Purim*, and it would obligate us to say *Hallel* on *Purim* if not for three technical reasons that the *Gemara* lists.

Rashi adds that *Hallel* is *shira*, and the *shira* of *yetzias Mitzrayim* is *Shiras HaYam*. This means that *Shiras HaYam* teaches a *halacha* for all generations, i.e., if *Am Yisrael* is delivered from a threat to its life, there is an obligation to say *Hallel*.

An obvious question can be raised. The *Shiras HaYam* describes supernatural miracles. But on *Purim*, no laws of nature were broken. How then can the *Gemara* derive the obligations of *Purim* from *yetzias Mitzrayim*? Perhaps only miracles which break natural law obligate us to say *shira*, but not hidden miracles like those of *Purim*. In addition, the *Gemara* in *Megilla* 10b asks a second question. The angels wanted to say *shira* the night that the miracle of *kerias Yam Suf* occurred, but *Hashem* said, "My creatures are drowning in the sea, and you want to say *shira*?!" Now, if the angels were told not to say *shira* because the Egyptians were drowning, then why do we say *shira*? And why do we read the *Megilla* on *Purim*?

The *Meshech Chochma* (*Shemos* 12:16) answers as follows: "*Purim* is not celebrated on the anniversary of the victory against our enemies. *Am Yisrael* does not rejoice over the downfall and death of its foes. We

---

"The *Hallel* of *Purim*, *Pesach* and ..." was originally published in 2001 on TorahWeb.org

celebrate *Pesach* because we were saved, not because our enemies perished, and we rejoice and read the *Megilla* on the day that we rested, the day after the war, when no one died, but we were saved."

For this reason, *Hashem* included the command to observe the seventh day of *Pesach* among the *mitzvos* given to us before we left Egypt, even though the *mitzva* did not apply in *Mitzrayim*. *Hashem* did this to show that the holiday is not to commemorate the drowning of the Egyptians, as its observance was commanded prior to the historical event. It follows from the *Meshech Chochma*'s idea that the *Shiras HaYam*, which we read on the seventh day of *Pesach* is recited over our deliverance, and not because of the death of our enemies.

We can now answer the first question as well. Should the *shira* be required because of the downfall of our enemies, we would not be able to derive *Purim* from *Pesach*. After all, the Egyptians were killed by miraculous events culminating with *kerias Yam Suf*, whereas Haman and his followers were destroyed by natural means.

In reality, however, the *shira* is required only because we were saved from our enemies. In this context, what is important is not how our enemies perished, but how great the threat against us was. Therefore, if we said *shira* when we were saved from slavery, we must certainly say *shira* when saved from death.

II

We do not recite the full *Hallel* on the seventh day of *Pesach*. The *Gemara* in *Arachin* (10b) explains that *Pesach* differs from *Sukkos*, when *Hallel* is said every day, because on *Pesach* the same *musaf* offering is brought each day, whereas on *Sukkos* each day has a different *musaf*. However, the *Midrash* says that *Pesach* differs because on the seventh day we cannot say full *Hallel*, since the Egyptians drowned. It would be wrong to recite full *Hallel* on *chol hamoed* and not on the seventh day, which is *yom tov*, so it is omitted on all days after the first.

The *Midrash* seems to contradict the *Gemara*, as it gives a different reason as to why we do not say full *Hallel*. Many answer as follows: the *Gemara* explains why *Pesach*'s status as a *yom tov* does not obligate us to say *Hallel* even on the seventh day. The reason is that *Pesach* is one long *yom tov*, and therefore does not require a new recitation of the full *Hallel* each and every day, whereas *Sukkos* is eight different *yamim tovim*, each of which warrants a recitation of the full *Hallel*. The fact that the *musaf* is identical all seven days of *Pesach*, but changes each day of *Sukkos*, indicates this distinction.

The *Midrash* relates to a different issue: why we do not say *Hallel* because of the miracles of *kerias Yam Suf*. The reason is that when *Hashem*'s creatures drown in the sea, we should not say *shira*.

Two questions remain. One, why then did our ancestors say *shira*? And two, why do we say *Hallel* on the first night of *Pesach* even though our enemies died?

We can answer this question based on a comment of Netziv. The *Chasam Sofer* writes that *Hallel* on *Chanuka* is a Torah obligation, as evidenced from the *Gemara* which derives the *mitzva* to say *Hallel* from *Shiras HaYam*. Netziv quotes the *Gemara* in *Berachos* (14a) that *Hallel* is a rabbinic commandment. How can we reconcile this statement in *Berachos* with the *Gemara*'s proof from *Shiras HaYam* that *Hallel* is a Torah obligation?

Netziv writes that the Torah obligation exists only when the miracle occurs. On the subsequent anniversaries, the obligation is rabbinic.

The Rabbis did not introduce *Hallel* on days when our enemies died. Therefore, there is no full *Hallel* on the seventh day of *Pesach*.

Only *Purim*, which is celebrated on the day following the battle, could have qualified as a day of *Hallel*.

Our ancestors recited *Hallel* when the sea split because at that point *Hallel* was a Torah obligation which had to be discharged even though our enemies died on that day. On the first night of *Pesach* we must consider ourselves to have just left Egypt at that moment (as ruled by Rambam). Therefore, there is a Torah obligation to say *Hallel*, an obligation that overrides the problem that arises because our enemies died that night. And so the *shira*, which is like full *Hallel*, was said when the sea was split, and full *Hallel* is said every year on the first night of *Pesach*, but not on the seventh day.

Unfortunately, death threats made by the enemies of *Am Yisrael*, especially in *Eretz Yisrael*, are not a thing of the past. As we celebrated *Purim* this year, we were affected by the recent murder of innocent Jews by vicious enemies, and the continued threat to our security. We pray to *Hashem* to deliver us from the threat of death to a life of peace, not because we want our enemies to be destroyed, but because we want to be saved.

The *Midrash* teaches us that the *Shiras HaYam* is similar to the *Hallel* we will all sing when the final redemption comes. May we be privileged to join in that great song, במהרה בימינו אמן.

Vehiggadeta Levincha

The paradigmatic *mitzva* of Jewish parenting, combining rich experiential and deeply inspirational tradition with fundamental and yet profound education, is the *Haggada*. The word "*haggada*" is based on the *Torah*'s command, "והגדת לבנך ביום ההוא לאמר – You shall tell your son on that day, saying…" (*Shemos* 13:8).

"Vehiggadeta Levincha" was originally published in 2003 on TorahWeb.org

The *Or HaChayyim* asks a fundamental question. The first and last words of this five-word phrase seem contradictory. On the verse, "כה תאמר לבית יעקב ותגיד לבני ישראל – *thus shall you say to the house of Jacob and tell the children of Israel*" (*Shemos* 19:3), Rashi quotes the *Talmud*, "תאמר - בלשון רכה, ותגיד - דברים הקשין כגידין" – '*Tomar*' – *in gentle language*, '*vesaggeid*' – *things that are as harsh as wormwood*" (*Shabbos* 87a).

The verb *amar* means gentle language. The verb *higgid* means harsh language. If so, "והגדת...לאמר" is an internal contradiction. Do we speak to our children harshly, "והגדת," or gently, "לאמר"? The *Or HaChayyim* suggests several answers. I would like to share with you a suggestion of my own.

In general society, the practices of which are often adopted by *Torah* Jewry living in that time and place, two radically different methods of child-raising exist. The first is disciplinarian. Children must be taught the rules and punished if they fail to keep them. In this way, the theory goes, they can achieve great things, as their potential is directed by wiser adults and not wasted on the foolishness of youth. This 19th-century attitude, captured in works by authors as varied as Charles Dickens and Mark Twain, views discipline as an end in itself, and as the very essence of the upbringing of a proper, virtuous and accomplished child.

Recently, an opposing theory has emerged. Discipline is terrible for a child's development and self-esteem. It stunts his ability to grow and achieve his potential; hence the term "positive parenting," in which the word "no" is almost removed from the vocabulary. Children are to be persuaded that something is wrong, and not prevented forcibly from engaging in it. Misbehavior is handled by soft talk explaining that an action is wrong. There are no punishments, physical or otherwise.

In five immortal words, the *Torah* rejects both extremes. Parenting must begin with והגדת, with the discipline of harsh words. Red lines must be drawn and a child who crosses them must be punished. A child who is never disciplined grows into an undisciplined adult, incapable of conforming even to the mores of general society, and certainly not to the more exacting norms *of Torah and mitzvos*. American neo-conservative thinkers have attributed many teenage social ills to unrestricted permissive parenting. These ills include drug abuse, sexual promiscuity, diminished attention span, and general underachievement. Apparently, children are not wise enough to set limits and develop their potential on their own. In *Torah* society, in Israel and the United States, this type of education has led to the abandonment of *Torah* observance in great numbers of youth growing up in *Torah* homes. Unrestricted exposure to modern general culture, given the twin developments of the decadence of society and the greater availability of modern media in the home and beyond, has overpowered the natural tendency of copying the lifestyle of the parents. Does this mean that the *Torah* endorses the disciplinarian approach? After all, we know that many youngsters were brought up that way and became high achievers and upstanding Jews.

The answer is a resounding no, and for two reasons. First, such an upbringing stunts growth. In the short-term, it produces results: higher grades in school, better behavior at home and in *shul*. But in the long-term, such an education does not allow a child to do his own thing, to develop his unique talents and personality.

Second, such a *chinuch* carries a significant risk of rebellion. Perhaps, in earlier times, when we lived in a world of conformity, this risk was minimal. But now, a child who behaves and achieves because he is forced to do so may rebel as soon as the ability to force him is lost. Is discipline an end in itself, enabling a parent to control a child's development, and brag of a high-achieving, well-behaved child? *Chas veshalom!* Discipline is only a prerequisite for the primary challenge of parenting –

expressing love and warmth, sharing your innermost soul, talking gently and passionately about love of God, love of *Torah*, love of Israel, love of all creatures. Yes, והגדת is no more than a necessary prerequisite for the lifelong responsibility and opportunity of לאמר, of teaching with love and by example, as the wondrous passage of one's children into adults takes place. In these five words, the *Torah* has taught the secret of successful Jewish parenting. Discipline your child only in order to teach him, gently and lovingly, for a lifetime. That is all. The rest is commentary. Rabbi Shlomo Wolbe, *zt"l* wrote a book entitled *Planting and Building in Education: Raising a Jewish Child*,[19] which expresses similar ideas. When one builds, a precise architectural plan must be followed. There is no room for imprecision or improvisation. This represents the indispensable infrastructure of *Torah* education. A child must be clearly taught: you may not do this, you must do that. All children must conform to the basics.

The essence of education, however, is planting, enabling a child to develop in his own way, to utilize his own strengths and character traits, to grow on his own. This is "חנך לנער על פי דרכו – educate a child according to his own way" (*Mishlei* 22:6). As the Vilna *Gaon* comments, forcing a child against his nature, even if successful at first, is a recipe for unmitigated disaster.

Like planting, *chinuch* requires patience. When bringing up my own wonderful, sometimes-rambunctious children, of whom my wife and I are exceedingly, and I hope rightfully, proud, I would repeat over and over again – patience. Rav Wolbe's words, which we heard then on tape, confirmed this idea. "חינוך הוא לטווח הארוך – *chinuch* is a long-range project." Punishment is a quick fix, but love is the only long-term option.

A word on spanking. The Talmud (*Moed Katan* 17a) prohibits spanking an older child, "בנו הגדול", based on "ולפני עור לא תתן מכשל"

---

[19] Feldheim, 2000, Nanuet, NY and Jerusalem.

(*Vayikra* 19:14). *Rashi* in *Moed Katan* explains that the child may rebel and sin, and the parent is responsible for that sin. The *Shulchan Aruch* (*Yoreh De'ah* 240:20) quotes this *halacha*. *Rema*, based on a different passage in the *Talmud* (*Kiddushin* 30a), defines an older child as older than 22 or 24 years of age. This certainly strikes us as counterintuitive.

In fact, the *Ritva* interprets *gadol* to mean 13, *bar mitzva*, after which it is common that a youth will respond to a spanking by cursing or striking his parents, both capital offenses.

Rav Wolbe claims that today, striking a three-year-old causes a *michshol*, a stumbling block, and is prohibited. In previous generations, children were more tolerant and had a more positive self-image, and were not damaged by spanking. Today, many children are damaged for life by spanking, especially since rebellion fills the air.

While this is a far-reaching and novel approach adopted in, and for, our times, a precedent exists in the words of the *Ritva*: "לא גדול גדול ממש, אלא הכל לפי טבעו, שיש לחוש שיתריס כנגדו בדיבור או במעשיו כי אפילו לא יהא בר מצוה אין ראוי להביאו לידי מכה או מקלל אביו, אלא ישתדלנו בדברים – Even if a child is not *bar mitzva*, if, because of his nature, there is a reasonable chance that he will rebel with words or deeds, and ultimately curse or strike his parent, it is prohibited to hit him. Rather, one must persuade him with words." Thirteen is simply an average age beyond which spanking may lead to rebellion and is, therefore, forbidden. If today the age is three, then that is the cutoff, as Rav Wolbe says.

Let me conclude with an insight from Rav Simon Schwab, *zt"l*, in *Ma'ayan Beis Hashoeiva*. The prohibitions against hitting and cursing parents, "ומכה אביו ואמו מות יומת... ומקלל אביו ואמו מות יומת" (*Shemos* 21:15, 17) are separated by the prohibition against kidnapping, "וגנב איש ומכרו ונמצא בידו מות יומת" (*Shemos* 21:16). Why?

Perhaps the *Torah* was anticipating the question: how can a child reach such a low level that he hits or curses his father? The answer is that the father continues to control his son by spanking or otherwise beyond the age of 22 or 24. In such a case, the father is effectively enslaving his son with intimidation. If so, he is considered one who stole a person, his own son, by denying his freedom of choice and action. This is the root cause of the son's tragic descent and rebellion to the point that he may hit or curse his father. The son is put to death, but the blame lies with the father.

On *Shabbos HaGadol*, when we read the *Haggada*, and on *Pesach*, when we focus on the *mitzva* of והגדת לבנך, we must remember that the primary mode of *chinuch* is *amira*, talking softly and warmly to our children. May our best efforts to raise our children properly be blessed with success.

Pesach: The Holiday of Faith

I

Pesach, from its very inception, represented the antithesis of idolatry: "Draw your hands away from idols and take for yourselves a sheep of *mitzva*" (Rashi, *Shemos* 12:6). "And the people believed" (*Shemos* 4:31); belief in *Hashem* and His messengers, Moshe and Aharon, began the redemption process.

"This is the law of the *korban pesach*: any stranger may not eat from it" (*Shemos* 12:43). "Any stranger" includes one who knowingly rejects all, or even part, of the Torah (Rashi, *Gur Aryeh*). The opening law stated regarding the *korban pesach* emphasizes the indispensability of faith in *Hashem* and His Torah on *Pesach*. The wicked son is excluded from the *korban pesach*, even though he too left Egypt, because his lack of faith disqualifies him from the final *geula*.

The *Beis HaLevi* (*Parashas Bo*) comments that *Pesach* is linked to

---

"Pesach: **The Holiday of Faith***"* was originally published in 2007 on TorahWeb.org

the ultimate redemption. Since denial of the validity of the Oral Torah led to the destruction of the second *Beis HaMikdash*, acceptance of this belief is a prerequisite for its rebuilding.

II

What should our response be to those who deny the Oral Torah? The *Beis HaLevi*, in addressing the Reform movement which claimed that some *mitzvos* no longer applied, demanded that we strengthen our own faith! "If your children will say to you, 'What is this service to you?' You shall say, 'It is a *pesach* offering to *Hashem*, Who skipped over our houses, etc.'" (*Shemos* 12:26-27). You shall say so to yourselves, the believers, to counteract the negative influence of deniers.

Jews living in the diaspora are called "worshipers of *avoda zara betahara*" (*Avoda Zara* 8a). We are involved in idolatry unintentionally and without paying attention (Rashi). Exposure to the various deviations from basic Torah fundamentals and practice demands reinforcement of these basics by the faithful. This is the essence of a parent's obligation on *Pesach*.

III

We can try to apply these concepts to contemporary times. For example, today, most of those who condone, or even promote, intermarriage or homosexuality do not knowingly reject the Torah. They were never taught properly, and might theoretically be eligible for the *korban pesach* (see Rambam, *Hilchos Mamrim* 3:1-3). We should attempt to influence such individuals with words of peace until they return to the strength of Torah (ibid.). Rambam's strategy of causing the elimination of *resha'im*, and the *Haggada*'s advice to ignore a *rasha* and thereby set his teeth on edge (Gra), no longer apply.

According to the *Chazon Ish* (*Yoreh De'ah* 2:16), strong-arm tactics have no place in our world. Employing such tactics against one who knowingly rejects Torah is counterproductive, and, therefore, prohibited when most Jews are not observant. Rather, we should attempt to bring them back to Torah with love. This *kiruv* imperative, however, makes the danger of our being influenced by anti-Torah beliefs and practices more potent and insidious. The need to strengthen our faith and commitment, as well as our children's, is greater than ever.

IV

Even greater vigilance is necessary for individuals and groups that delve into the reasons for *mitzvos*. For them, the danger of falling into denial is not merely due to exposure to outside influences. Rather, it is a risk of sophisticated inquiry. The *Beis HaLevi* (*Parashas Ki Sisa*) warns that one who thinks he knows the reason for *mitzvos* is more prone to stumble. Such a person requires alacrity and additional safeguards; otherwise, his logic may lead him even to idolatry.

"*Hashem* will save those who are cunning in their knowledge as humans, but who make themselves like animals" (*Chullin* 5b). This refers to Jews who are rational and intellectual, yet also accept Torah based on simple faith. This acceptance characterized our "נעשה ונשמע" response at *Har Sinai*. It stands in sharp contrast to the erroneous rationalization that led to the sin of the Golden Calf.

While a religious philosophy espousing openness to new and modern ideas and interpretations may be acceptable, it certainly increases one's chances of crossing the line into the unacceptable. Untraditional teachings may not always deny basic traditional principles; nonetheless, they increase the risk of denial of such principles.

V

Perhaps this is symbolized by the special offerings which bracket the *sefira* period. The *omer* offering is barley, a simple animal food representing simple faith. This *halacha* was passed down orally from Moshe *Rabbeinu*. The lack of a scriptural source for this law highlights the need for *emuna peshuta*.

Rambam (*Hilchos Temidin uMusafin* 7:11) records the oral tradition that the *omer* is brought on the second day of *Pesach*, following the first day of *Pesach* which is referred to by the Torah as "*Shabbos*" (*Vayikra* 23:15). During the second *Beis HaMikdash*, the deniers of *Torah shebe'al peh* understood the aforementioned "*Shabbos*" literally. *Chazal* went to great lengths to defend the oral tradition against its deniers.

By contrast, the *shtei halechem* brought on *Shavuos* is wheat, human food. It is *chametz* (*Vayikra* 23:17), representing the complexity associated with the vastness of Torah given on *Shavuos*.

The simple faith of *Pesach* is a prerequisite for the sophistication of *Shavuos*. In this light, not only are the seven weeks from *Pesach* to *Shavuos* themselves "*temimos*," complete (*Vayikra* 23:15), but they also symbolize *temimus*, wholeheartedness, which should define our relationship with *Hashem* (see *Devarim* 18:13). Only after unquestioningly accepting *Hashem* and His Torah may we turn our formidable God-given intellect to analyze the nuances and profundities of that Torah in all its grandeur.

The opening line of *Hallel*, recited each day of *Pesach*, refers to *Am Yisrael* as servants of *Hashem*. When we left Egypt, we ceased to be servants of Pharaoh and became His servants (*Megilla* 14a, *Yerushalmi Pesachim* 5:4). As we celebrate *Pesach*, we must eliminate any vestige of slavish loyalty to modern ideologies which compromise our service of *Hashem*. May we be blessed to become true *avdei Hashem*.

Seeing Clearly

I

The story of *Pesach* is inextricably linked to the heroic life of Moshe *Rabbeinu*. Ultimately, the Torah teaches, "Never again has there arisen in Israel a prophet like Moshe, whom *Hashem* had known face to face" (*Devarim* 34:10). As such, we cannot strive to be as great as Moshe. Nonetheless, every Jew can be as righteous as Moshe (Rambam, *Hilchos Teshuva* 7:2). What does this mean?

"Moshe received the Torah at Sinai and gave it to Yehoshua" (*Avos* 1:1). Only Moshe received all of Torah; all others were given it, but something was lost in transmission. Only Moshe saw clearly; all others saw reflections or dreams (*Bamidbar* 12:6, 8). Moshe was the humblest person (*Bamidbar* 12:3). Since he had absolutely no personal agenda, he saw clearly.

Moshe's humility was greater than Avraham's (*Chullin* 89a). *Hashem* called "Moshe Moshe" (*Shemos* 3:4), without the line that usually exists between the two repetitions of a name, such as exists in (*Bereishis* 22:11) "Avraham, Avraham" (*Shemos Rabba* 2:6). The separating line represents the gap between the person's potential, represented by the first name, and the actual person, represented by the second name. Only Moshe, who was exceedingly humble, reached his full potential (Rav Chaim of Volozhin, *Avos* 1:1). No prophet will ever be like Moshe, but for everyone else there is the possibility of being righteous like Moshe, reaching his/her full potential through great humility.

Moshe's name is omitted from the *Haggada*. *Klal Yisrael* feels bad, and poignantly searches for their hero to thank and credit him (see *Shir*

"Seeing Clearly" was originally published in 2008 on TorahWeb.org

HaShirim Rabba 3:2). But Moshe, in his humility, prefers anonymity.

II

"*Hashem* saw that [Moshe] went to see, and He called out to him from the bush and said 'Moshe Moshe'" (*Shemos* 3:4). Moshe left his palatial setting and went out to his brothers to see their burdens (*Shemos* 2:11). "He focused his eyes and heart to be distressed over their suffering" (Rashi). "*Hashem* said, 'You left your affairs and went to see the pain of *Yisrael* and help them. I will, in kind, leave the angels and speak with you'" (*Shemos Rabba* 1:27). Moshe saw *Hashem* because he went to see the pains of his brothers. His love and active concern for them resulted from his humility, which led him to ignore his comfort and focus on the problems of *Klal Yisrael*. Rashi explains "*Hashem* saw *Bnei Yisrael*" (*Shemos* 2:25) to mean He focused on them and did not hide His eyes. Moshe's focus on the burdens of *Am Yisrael* was a reflection of *Hashem*'s focus.

"At the image of (ותמנת) *Hashem* does he [Moshe] gaze" (*Bamidbar* 12:8). Netziv understands this phrase to equate Moshe's manner of looking with that of *Hashem*, i.e., Moshe's look of empathy and clarity resembled *Hashem*'s. Moshe saw Torah clearly because of his humility and lack of any personal agenda, and similarly saw all of the world, and its people, clearly for the same reason.

III

"One with a good eye will be blessed, for he has given of his best to the poor" (*Mishlei* 22:9). This refers to Moshe. *Hashem* gave the *pilpul* (in-depth analysis) of Torah to Moshe, but he had a good eye and shared it with all of *Klal Yisrael* (*Nedarim* 38a).

The same good eye that sees the Torah clearly and sees the best in people gladly shares the most precious commodity, Torah, with others. Moshe, the great prophet, was happy to share the great gift of prophecy as well: "Would that the entire people of Israel be prophets" (*Bamidbar* 11:29). By sharing *pilpul* with, and wishing prophecy upon, *Klal Yisrael*, Moshe's uniqueness may be diminished, but his humility, and the love of *Am Yisrael* that it engendered, motivated his ultimate spiritual altruism.

As an advocate for *Am Yisrael*, Moshe demanded that *Hashem* exercise the same "good eye" when dealing with His wayward people: "Even if a slave doesn't obey his master, a magnanimous master gazes upon him with a pleasant face. So too, You should not look at their stubbornness, as it says (*Devarim* 9:27), 'Do not turn to the stubbornness of these people'" (*Bamidbar Rabba* 16:28).

Only one who posses a good eye should be given a כוס של ברכה (read [*Mishlei* 22:9] "*yevorach*" as "*yevarech*"; *Sota* 38b). One who sees the good side of others can bless for them and can bless them, as Moshe did. On the *seder* night, the *ba'al habayis*, who has demonstrated his good eye by inviting the poor, leads the *zimmun* (*Orach Chayyim* 479:1).

IV

Moshe took the bones of Yosef with him (*Shemos* 13:19). Chasidic masters interpret that Moshe took the essence (*atzmiyyus*) of Yosef with him (*Itturei Torah*). Yosef had an *ayin tov* (good eye) to the extent that the *ayin hara* (evil eye) had no power over his descendants (Rashi, *Bereishis* 49:22). He fed the entire world (*Bereishis* 42:6) and had mercy on the very brothers who mistreated him (Rashi, *Bereishis* 42:8). When Yosef brought evil reports to his father about his brothers, his sole intention was *lesheim Shamayim*, for *Hashem*'s sake, so that Yaakov could help his brothers improve.

Yosef's brothers viewed him as a threat to *Am Yisrael*, akin to their uncles Esav and Yishmael, and sold him *lesheim Shamayim*. And yet, despite their ostensibly pure motivation, this sale is the paradigmatic interpersonal sin (*Meshech Chochma, Vayikra* 16:30). How did their *lesheim Shamayim* intentions lead to a grave sin? The brothers were jealous of Yosef (*Bereishis* 37:11), and their jealousy did not allow them to see clearly. Without jealousy they would have seen that Yosef was a *tzaddik* (Rashi, *Shemos* 1:5), and would have either forgiven his evil reports to their father, or brought their complaints to their father for his resolution. Yosef did not anticipate his brothers' jealousy because he lacked it completely. He forgave and assisted those who harmed him. It is this *ayin tov* essence that Moshe took with him.

On *Pesach*, we must learn from the generosity of spirit of the great leaders who saved us, both in Egypt and when leaving Egypt. This includes avoiding jealousy that clouds our wisdom and leads to serious interpersonal failings, fostering a sense of humility which allows us to reach our potential, and seeing and feeling the pain of our brothers, especially in *Eretz Yisrael*, and endeavoring to assist them.

We should try to emulate Moshe and see *Am Yisrael*, even its wayward members, as *Hashem* does, in a positive light, even as we entreat Him to focus on our tribulations and not our sins (*Selichos*, day 2). Hopefully, if *Klal Yisrael* learns and internalizes these lessons, *Hashem* will quickly fulfill, "in *Nisan* they will be redeemed" (*Rosh HaShana* 11b).

Above Time and Beyond Time

"'You shall guard the *matzos*' (*Shemos* 12:17). Do not read 'the *matzos*' but rather 'the *mitzvos*.' Just as we do not allow the *matzos* to become *chametz* [by tarrying so that the dough rises], so too we do not tarry in performing *mitzvos*. Rather, if [the *mitzva*] comes to your hand, do it immediately" (Rashi).

This analogy is problematic. If one tarries and the dough becomes *chametz*, it is not *matza* at all, while if one tarries in performing a *mitzva*,

---

"Above Time and Beyond Time" was originally published in 2016 on TorahWeb.org

it is still a *mitzva*, albeit one that is missing the extra dimension of alacrity.

Rav Hutner (*Pachad Yitzchak, Pesach, ma'amar* 1) answers this question based on Maharal's explanation of Rashi. By delaying the time of the *mitzva*, one views the *mitzva* as being under the influence of time. Time is a part of the creation, but the refined soul of a Jew, which is heavenly, cannot be satiated by all the delicacies of this world (*Koheles Rabba* 6:7). Therefore, the soul is above time, which was created as part of this world.

Alacrity represents the attempt to minimize the time gap between the opportunity to perform a *mitzva* and its completion. We left Egypt in a hurry, since this was the creation of *Am Yisrael* (*Maharal, Gevuros Hashem*, chap. 51) as an entity above time. We are above time not only as an eternal nation, but also as a nation that attempts to break the barrier of time via alacrity in the performance of *mitzvos*. Failure to do so is not merely foregoing an extra enhancement of the *mitzva*; rather it reduces the *mitzva* to something under the influence of time instead of being, as it should be, above time. As such, it can be compared to tarrying when preparing the dough and allowing it to become *chametz*, which is an entirely different entity than *matza*.

Remarkably, the very hurriedness which was necessitated by our creation as a nation above time led to the fact that the dough we took out of *Mitzrayim* was *matza* and not *chametz* (*Shemos* 12:34). Moreover, the conclusion of the *pasuk* which demands alacrity (12:17), alludes to the eternity of our nation as being above time: "You shall guard this day for your generations as an eternal law."

Eternity, in practice, demands that the transcendent importance of *mitzvos* be taught to the next generation. *Pesach* is the time of, "You shall tell your son" (*Shemos* 13:8). Words do not suffice for this. A child must absorb his parents' attitude that *mitzvos* are the most important actions of a Jew. Alacrity is required to demonstrate this idea. Failure to be quick and focused in performing *mitzvos* risks a child's indifference to, and even abandonment of, *Hashem*'s commands, thus endangering the eternity of *mitzvos* in one's family.

At a *siyyum* we say "We run to the words of Torah, and they run to meaningless things." The *Pachad Yitzchak* contrasts the alacrity of the non-Torah world with the Jew's requirement to attempt to break the barrier of time by hastening to perform *mitzvos*.

Our children keenly observe our pace in approaching Torah and *mitzvos*, as well as our pace in dealing with worldly matters. In the world around us, people run to work, a necessary enterprise, but even more so to enjoyable sports and entertainment events. If we do so, and do not run to Torah and *mitzvos*, it conveys an attitude which can have negative impact on ourselves, and certainly on our children.

The difference between *chametz* and *matza* is exceedingly small, כחוט השערה (*Chasam Sofer, derush* 35, for *Shabbos HaGadol*). On *Shabbos Parashas Hachodesh*, as we prepare for *Pesach*, our alacrity and our attitude to the *mitzvos* we perform can make all the difference, both for ourselves, as we run to the life of the next world, and for the eternity of our generations.

Eating to Live

I

The very first *mitzva* given to every individual of *Am Yisrael* was the *korban pesach*. As opposed to all other offerings, eating the meat is a separate *mitzva* unto itself (*Shemos* 12:8, Rambam, *Sefer HaMitzvos, asei* 56). In contrast to other offerings, if it becomes impure and cannot be eaten, it may not be offered (*Pesachim* 78b). Conversely, when the

---

"Eating to Live" was originally published in 2018 on TorahWeb.org

majority of *Am Yisrael* is impure and the *korban pesach* is brought in an impure state, it is eaten that way since the whole reason to offer it is to eat it (*Pesachim* 76b).

The Torah teaches us that eating, the most basic human need for survival, can be done before *Hashem* (*Devarim* 14:23), as a *mitzva*. Although this activity is one which man shares with the animal kingdom (*Chagiga* 16a), man must elevate his eating to a dignified level.

This is a uniquely Jewish perspective. A non-Jew can offer a sacrifice, but only an *olah*, which is totally burned on the *mizbeach* (*Menachos* 73b). "Eating before *Hashem*" does not exist in a bifurcated lifestyle in which worldly actions are not included in religious life.

Esav told Yaakov, "Pour into me ("*haliteini*") now some of the red, red soup" (*Bereishis* 25:30). Rashi writes, "I will open my mouth, and pour a lot into it, as we have learned (*Shabbos* 155b), 'we may pour (*malitin*) food into a camel's mouth.'" Rav Yerucham Levovitz (*Da'as Torah*) explains that many laws apply to eating in order to raise it from an animalistic act to a human one. The portion size and the pace distinguish humans from animals. A Jew must eat for the sake of doing *Hashem*'s will, just as we must do when eating *kodshim* from the *mizbeach*. Woe unto a person whose eating is not superior to that of an animal.

When Yaakov received the *berachos* instead of Esav, he was told by Rivka to bring meat from the *korban pesach* to Yitzchak (Rashi, *Bereishis* 27:9). Yitzchak planned to give Esav worldly *berachos* and Yaakov spiritual ones (*Bereishis* 27:28, 29; 28:4). Rivka arranged for Yaakov to receive the physical *berachos* as well. Her plan was for Yaakov to sublimate earthly matters by including them in *avodas Hashem*, and this is symbolized by the *korban pesach* which she gave to Yaakov in order to receive, and thereby elevate, worldly *berachos* (Rav Chaim

Yaakov Goldvicht). Divine Providence ruled in accordance with Rivka's view (Rav Yosef Dov Soloveitchik).

II

"A *tzaddik* eats to satiate his soul" (*Mishlei* 13:25). As a rule, the Torah discourages asceticism, and yet running after food is deemed sinful and requires *teshuva* (Rambam, *Hilchos Teshuva* 7:3).

Recently, medical science has taught that overeating is injurious not only to the soul but to the body as well. In the U.S., overweight and obesity are primary causes of mortality and morbidity, perhaps even exceeding smoking (see "The Health Risks of Obesity: Worse Than Smoking, Drinking or Poverty," RAND Health, 2002). The typical eating habits of Orthodox Jews on *Shabbos* and *yom tov*, especially *Pesach*, can have negative medical consequences. The Torah prohibits dangerous activities, and this includes smoking (Rav Ovadia Yosef, *Yechaveh Da'as* 5:39). Unhealthy eating is difficult to define precisely, but egregious gluttony, which clearly reduces longevity, is prohibited.

Ramban (*Vayikra* 19:1) describes a lustful individual who avoids technical prohibitions as a "נבל ברשות התורה - a degenerate operating within the technical requirements of Torah." "קדשים תהיו - be holy" (19:2) requires moderation in food and alcohol. If excessive eating or drinking endangers one's health, it no longer is ברשות התורה. Rambam (*Hilchos De'os* 4:1) rules: "It is the way of *Hashem* to be healthy, as illness prevents understanding and knowledge of the Creator. Therefore, one must distance himself from things that harm the body, and conduct himself with things that heal and strengthen. One should not eat unless he is hungry".

Our bodies do not belong to us, but rather to *Hashem* (Radvaz, *Hilchos Sanhedrin* 18:6), as we say in *Selichos*, "...and the body is Yours"

(See *Le'or HaHalacha* by Rav Shlomo Yosef Zevin, pp. 318-328). We are commanded to follow medical advice and avoid dangerous practices. We must **eat to live** longer and healthier lives, and avoid **living to eat**, especially if it shortens or harms our lives.

III

"You may not break a bone in it [the *korban pesach*]" (*Shemos* 12:46). The *Sefer HaChinuch* (*mitzva* 16) explains that it is not honorable for princes to eat like dogs that break bones. To remember the exalted level we reached on *Pesach*, we must eat like princes would, and not like animals.

The *Chinuch* famously continues that a person's heart is influenced by his deeds. One should not indulge in the pleasures of those who engage in gluttony and scoffing, as these actions, even if not technically prohibited, affect one's heart and soul negatively.

Rambam (*Hilchos Yom Tov* 6:18) states that when one eats and drinks on *yom tov*, he is also obligated to feed the poor and the stranger (*geir*). If one does not feed the poor and the embittered souls, his is not a *simcha* of *mitzva* but of his stomach, which is a disgrace.

This can explain the juxtaposition of the subsequent *pesukim* (*Shemos* 12:47, 48). "All of *Adas Yisrael* shall do it [the *korban pesach*]," including a *geir*. One who doesn't break bones recognizes that eating should not be gluttonous but refined. Sharing with those who do not have the means assures that all of *Am Yisrael*, including the poor and the *geir*, will fulfill the *mitzva* of *korban pesach*. This elevates the *korban pesach* of the donor, as he eats it like a prince, who bears and feels responsibility to provide for the unfortunate.

The original *korban pesach* was eaten only in one's home (*Shemos* 12:46) in a princely fashion (see *Sefer HaChinuch* 15). Ideally, the *seder* should be at home, with extended family and appropriate guests.

For those who, for whatever reason, spend *Pesach* in hotels, the words of the *Chinuch* are doubly important. Unfortunately, a culture of overindulgence, reported by participants and reflected in advertisements, can negatively influence a person's heart and soul on *Pesach*.

True שמחת יום טוב requires moderation in eating and drinking, the avoidance of idle chatter and scoffing, and significant time learning Torah (Rambam, *Hilchos Yom Tov* 6:19). In some cases, as the *Chinuch* writes, this requires resisting temptations and social pressures. For those expending great sums for hotels and/or travel, the amount of money given before *Pesach* to feed the poor should increase commensurately.

On *Pesach* 5778, let us all be mindful of the elevated status we achieved on *Pesach* years ago and thereby merit the rebuilt *Beis HaMikdash* and the renewal of the *korban pesach*.

Rabbi Benjamin Yudin

Not Just Lip Service

This week we begin *Sefer Vayikra*, which concentrates on *korbanos*. Since we have not had a *Beis HaMikdash* for almost two thousand years, the topic of *korbanos* seems remote, removed and foreign to us. I'd like to begin by listing the many ways that the *korban pesach* impacts upon us.

1. While the *yom tov* of *Pesach* does not begin until the night of the 15th of *Nisan*, one is forbidden to eat *chametz* on *erev Pesach* from midday (*Devarim* 16:3), as that is the time when the *korban pesach* was slaughtered.

2. One is not to own *chametz* on *erev Pesach*, as the Torah says, "you shall not slaughter my blood offering (i.e., the *korban pesach*) while in possession of *chametz*" (*Shemos* 23:18).

3. The *Mishna* (*Pesachim* 4:1) teaches that from midday on *erev Pesach* it is forbidden to work, as one is restricted from working whenever their *korban* was brought. Thus, *erev Pesach* starting from midday, i.e., the time for bringing the *korban pesach*, is to be treated like *chol hamoed*, even outside of *Eretz Yisrael*.

4. Unlike *Shabbos*, which one may begin from *plag hamincha* (a halachic hour and a quarter prior to sunset) and eat the *Shabbos* meal while it is still day (Friday), one is not to begin the *Pesach seder* until night. The reason for this is that the Torah ordains that the *korban pesach* is to be eaten at night (*Shemos* 12:8), and all the other *mitzvos* of the night go into effect with the time of the *korban pesach*.

5. The custom of wearing a *kittel* at the *seder* is explained by Netziv

---

"Not Just Lip Service" was originally published in 2007 on TorahWeb.org

in his *Haggada* as a remembrance of the white robe one donned when eating *kodshim* (sacrifices).

6. The custom of having the *zeroa* on the *seder* plate is to recall the *korban pesach*. The placing of the hard-boiled egg is to remember the *korban chagiga*.

7. We wash our hands prior to eating *karpas*. The vegetable is dipped in salt water (דבר שטיבולו במשקה), and such dipped items require hand-washing when one eats the wet food. The *Taz* points to this practice and sharply criticizes those who are not careful to wash their hands before eating a wet fruit or vegetable all year long. One could defend the practice of "*urchatz*" not only to arouse the curiosity of the young, but to conduct ourselves on this night in keeping with the way that all practiced when we had a *Beis HaMikdash*.

8. Rav Chaim Brisker *zt"l* explained that the purpose of the custom of hiding the *matza* designated as *afikoman* after *yachatz* is not only to maintain the interest and excitement of the children, but also is connected to the *korban pesach*. The *afikoman* is eaten at the end of the meal as a remembrance of the *korban pesach*, and the *korban pesach* needed *shemira* (guarding); *hesech hadaas* (lapse in awareness) could disqualify the *pesach* lest it became *tamei*. To avoid such disqualification, the *korban pesach* was kept in a safe place until the time it was eaten; hence our *minhag* to hide the *afikoman*. It would therefore make sense for the one conducting the *seder* to hide the *afikoman*, not the children.

9. While we point to the *matza* and *maror* when we explain their significance as part of "*Rabban Gamliel haya omer*," we do not point to the shank bone, lest we assign it the actual status of a

korban pesach.

10. The *mitzva* of eating *maror* today is only a *mitzva mideRabbanan*. It is *deOraysa* only when it accompanies the *korban pesach*.

11. The custom of *Ashkenazim* is to abstain from eating roasted meat at the *seder*, lest one assume they are eating the *korban pesach*, which would be a violation of *kodshim bachutz*.

12. In keeping with the opinion of Rosh, the *afikoman* is eaten at the end of the meal, just as the *korban pesach* was eaten "*al hasova* – when they were full," and serves as a remembrance of the *korban pesach*. According to Rashbam, the *afikoman*, the fulfillment of the *mitzva* of *matza*, is eaten at the end of the meal as a remembrance of the *matza* that was eaten with the *korban pesach* at the end of the meal. Both Rosh and Rashbam agree that it is preferable that the *afikoman* be eaten prior to *chatzos*, as was the *korban pesach*.

13. Rav Yosef Salant *zt"l* (in *Be'eir Yosef*) explains that the practice of opening the door after *birkas hamazon* is not only to welcome Eliyahu *haNavi* ushering in the future redemption. One had to eat the *korban pesach* on the ground level, as the roofs and upper floors in *Yerushalayim* did not share the *kedusha* of the rest of the city that enables the consumption of the *korban pesach*. The door was kept closed during the meal lest one take the *korban pesach* outside or upstairs, and after the meal the Jews went onto the rooftops to sing *Hallel*. We open our doors today in remembrance of this sequence.

There is one additional way that the *korban pesach* impacts upon our *seder*. The word *seder* means a prescribed order of events. Out of the 15 components of this *seder*, the first 14 are all some type of action (including the 14th – *Hallel* – the recitation of the second half of *Hallel*). The last component is somewhat challenging. *Nirtza* means acceptance, and we *daven* that our *seder* will be accepted On High. For this reason Chida in his *Haggada* (*Simchas HaRegel*) lists only fourteen components, counting *Hallel* and *nirtza* as one.

However, in light of the impact of the *korban pesach* on our *seder*, the final component takes on great meaning. *Nirtza* comes from the *pasuk* "ונרצה לו לכפר עליו – it shall become acceptable to him, to atone for him" (*Vayikra* 1:4). The term *ritzui* is only found after and in conjunction with *korbanos*. We don't ask for *ritzui* after affixing a *mezuza*, wearing *tefillin*, etc. We do, however, conclude every *Shemoneh Esrei* with the prayer of "*retzei*." Since our daily *tefillos* substitute for the daily *korbanos* in the *Beis HaMikdash*, we conclude our *tefillos* appropriately with a supplication of *ritzui*.

If our rabbis looked upon the *seder* only as the performance of a set of *mitzvos* (*matza*, *haggada*, *daled kosos*, *maror*, etc.) there would be no place for *nirtza*. However, the text of *nirtza* exclaims, "as we have carried out the *pesach* observance of this *seder*, so may we merit to fulfill the actual *korban pesach* in the future." We are asking *Hashem* to accept our *seder* as a partial fulfillment of the *korban pesach*, and thus the inclusion of *ritzui* is appropriate.

This special request, that our *seder* partially replace a *korban pesach*, can only take place in an environment of *kedusha*. While it is true all year that "when we were privileged to have a *Beis HaMikdash* the *mizbeach* was *mechapeir*; now "שולחנו של אדם מכפר, every person's table atones" (*Berachos* 55a), this is especially true at the *Pesach seder*. I have witnessed how not-yet-observant families who participated at a *Pesach seder* found the experience to be transforming, to the point that they embraced a Torah-observant lifestyle. Make your *seder* count. Not only during *maggid* should there be an exciting give-and-take among all the participants, but even the discussions during the meal should be channeled to reflect "אשרינו מה טוב חלקנו ומה נעים גורלנו".

Guess Who's Coming to Dinner?

The *Mishna* (*Pesachim* 116b) mandates that in every generation a person is obligated to look at himself as though he personally departed from Egypt. Rambam (*Hilchos Chametz uMatza* 7:6, 7) cites this command as the reason for our reclining and drinking four cups of wine at the *seder*. The Alter of Slabodka is purported to have said that this is the most challenging *mitzva* of the night of *Pesach*.

At first glance, the *mishna* is teaching that the level of *hakaras hatov* we must all have at the *seder* is not simply for what *Hashem* did for our ancestors and that we would not be where we are today were it not for His kindnesses afforded them; rather, we must look at the exodus and express a personal *hakaras hatov* for what He did for us.

The *birkas hagomel*, thanksgiving blessing, is mandated by the Talmud (*Berachos* 54b) for the following four survivors: (a) one who completed a sea journey; (b) one who completed a hazardous land journey such as crossing a desert; (c) one who recovered from a serious illness; (d) one released from captivity. Interestingly, our meal at the *seder* is upgraded to a *seudas hoda'a*, meal of thanksgiving, as upon leaving Egypt we successfully experienced all four. Alshich asks, if the motivation and cause for the thanksgiving is appreciation for what *Hashem* has done, than in reality we should be reciting this blessing constantly, as His kindnesses are with us always. Therefore, he teaches that it is not only the salvation from these threatening circumstances, but, as the verse in *Tehillim* (107:24) which is the scriptural source for this blessing states, "They have seen the deeds

---

"Guess Who's Coming to Dinner?" was originally published in 2012 on TorahWeb.org

of *Hashem*." When one hears of the salvation that another experienced, it bolsters their faith in God and His personal involvement in the affairs of man. When however, an individual experiences a personal life-saving situation, they are giving thanks for the privilege of **seeing** God firsthand. A miraculous outcome for someone else solidifies my belief intellectually, but when I am the direct recipient of His kindness, my *emuna* is elevated to a tangible experiential level.

Tehillim (33:1) states: "'רננו צדיקים לה – sing joyfully, O righteous, because of *Hashem*." The *Midrash Shochar Tov* points out that it does not say "*el Hashem*" which would mean sing **to** *Hashem*, rather *baHashem*; as soon as they are privileged to **see** the Divine, they sing. Thus, we find immediately prior to the miraculous rescue at *Yam Suf* (*Shemos* 14:31), "Israel **saw** the great hand that *Hashem* inflicted upon Egypt," and immediately thereafter, (15:1), "then Moshe and the children of Israel sang this song." We also find at the opening day ceremony to the inauguration of the *Mishkan* that the Torah teaches (*Vayikra* 9:24), "A fire went forth from before *Hashem*, the people **saw**, and sang glad song." Similarly, the prophet Micha promises "as in the days when you left the land of Egypt, I will **show** him [the Jewish people] wonders" (7:15). And lastly, we also pray daily in every *Shemoneh Esrei*, "may our **eyes** witness Your return to Zion."

The Talmud (*Berachos* 12a) explains why the *Shema* in the morning is followed by the blessing of "אמת ויציב," while that of the night is followed by "אמת ואמונה", by citing the *pasuk* (*Tehillim* 92:3) "to relate your kindness in the morning and your faith at night." Why do we focus on "kindness" in the morning but on "faith" at night? Daytime represents clarity, when one can see and comprehend with certainty; things are "clear as day," as the saying goes. This refers to the kindnesses and miracles that He performed for us. Nighttime, however, indicates the doubt and uncertainty we may have as to when and how we will be extricated from our communal and personal challenges. As such, nighttime is a time to draw upon one's faith that redemption, *geula*, will come.

The majority of *mitzvos* – *shofar, lulav, tefillin, Hallel* – are day-*mitzvos*, reflecting the positive and open relationship between *Hashem* and Israel. Why, asks the Vilna Gaon in his *Oros HaGra*, are the *mitzvos* of *Pesach* – eating the *korban pesach, matza,* and *maror* – all night *mitzvos*? His answer is that the night of *Pesach* is philosophically and halachically a day. Similarly, the Gaon explains that although the Torah says (*Shemos* 13:8), "you shall tell your son on that **day**" when describing the *mitzva* of סיפור יציאת מצרים, we fulfill this *mitzva* at night, since this night is axiologically a day. We experienced on this night His presence with such clarity that the character of this night was forever transformed from a night of faith to a virtual daytime of seeing.

Thus, the charge to "**look** at oneself as if they personally left Egypt" means not only to attempt to put oneself back in time over three thousand years ago, but rather to know with absolute surety that *Hashem*, the Honored Guest at our *seder*, will solve our communal and personal pressing problems.

Listen to Your *Matza*

The Torah (*Devarim* 15:3) refers to *matza* as "*lechem oni.*" The second word, which we pronounce as "*oni* – answering," is written in the Torah "*ani* – poor." When interpreted using the written form of the word (i.e., the *kesiv* – "*ani*") the phrase means "poor man's bread." Shmuel (*Pesachim* 36a) understands the pronounced version of the word (i.e., the *kri* – "*oni*") to be the source that we are to recite many recitations over, and in conjunction with, the *matza*. The Talmud further understands "*lechem ani* – poor man's bread" to prescribe the meager ingredient list of flour

---

"**Listen to Your *Matza***" was originally published in 2013 on TorahWeb.org

and water and to exclude *matza* made with wine or oil as well as what we call today "egg *matza*." In addition, we are taught that just as when an impoverished individual receives a loaf of bread, he saves a half for the future, so too the *matza* is characterized by it being a *perusa*, a broken half.

We integrate both themes, *oni* and *ani*, at the *Pesach seder*. We begin the recitation of *maggid* with "הא לחמא עניא," thus highlighting *matza*'s role as the bread of affliction over which we are going to recite (*oni*) the *Haggada* (specifically, *maggid* and the first two paragraphs of *Hallel*). Immediately prior to *maggid* we break the middle *matza* at *yachatz*, just as a poor man would save part of his loaf of bread, in order to present the *matza* in its true form following the *kesiv – ani*. We further integrate the *kri* and *kesiv* by proclaiming that the *matza* is the bread of the poor, and we invite the poor to join us in our celebration.

The *Mishna* (*Pesachim* 116b) teaches that in every generation we are to view ourselves as if we personally left Egypt. Rav Yosef Salant *zt"l* suggests (in *Be'eir Yosef*) that by proclaiming that this is the bread of the poor, we relive the evening of the exodus, reminding ourselves that our ancestors were slaves and poor and ate *matza* for centuries prior to the exodus, helping us focus on that frame of mind, and allowing us to feel as if we personally left Egypt. It is thus understandable that the declaration "הא לחמא עניא די אכלו אבהתנא בארעא דמצרים – this *matza* that our ancestors ate in the land of Egypt" has two connotations. The first connotation is that we ate *matza* as slaves, and the second is that we ate *matza* on the way out of Egypt. It speaks of our servitude and our freedom. Perhaps, then, another reason for splitting the *matza* at *yachatz* is to call attention to the dual theme of *matza* and note that the larger half is for the *afikoman*, the sign of our freedom and deliverance.

The *Be'eir Yosef* additionally notes that while there is the *mitzva* to invite the poor and needy and those who are alone to all *yom tov* meals (as

Rambam emphasizes in *Hilchos Yom Tov* 6:18), the special *mitzva* on the night of *Pesach* to have the needy at your table is a further fulfillment of demonstrating that you personally left Egypt in that very state. It is the actual reliving of the moment. Hence, the inclusion of "כל דכפין ייתי ויכול – let all who are hungry and needy join us."

There is one more fascinating connection between the *kesiv* of *ani* and *kri* of *oni*. The Torah informs us that the Jewish people demonstrated incredible faith by leaving Egypt without provisions. True, we are taught that the Egyptians gave the former slaves silver and gold vessels and garments; however, they did not have food except for the *matza* they took with them. Rashi (*Shemos* 16:1) teaches that miraculously the *matza* lasted and sustained them for 31 days and 61 meals! By proclaiming and pointing to the *matza*, the poor's man bread, we are encouraging the poor that just as He provided for all of us who were needy at that time, may He similarly provide for those still impoverished.

הא לחמא עניא thus bespeaks our historical past, our faith and our optimism.

The Sacred Ingredient

While the taste of *matza* is still in our mouths from the *afikoman* (and according to the Gaon of Vilna [*Ma'aseh Rav*, 185] there is still a *mitzva kiyyumis lechatchila* to eat *matza* each day of *Pesach* and thereby reify the biblical description of eating *matza* for seven days [*Shemos* 23:15]), I would like to share an insight into the *Haggada* that is relevant to all of *Pesach* and indeed the entire year.

Right before we begin Rav's *Haggada* of "מתחלה עובדי עבודה זרה היו אבותינו – originally our ancestors were idol worshipers" (*Pesachim*

"The Sacred Ingredient" was originally published in 2014 on TorahWeb.org

116a), we declare, "יכול מראש חודש – one might think that the obligation to discuss the exodus commences on the first day of the month of *Nisan*." What would prompt one to celebrate on *rosh chodesh*? At first glance, as the Torah teaches (*Shemos* 12:2), it was on *Rosh Chodesh Nisan* that the Jewish nation experienced a revelation of *Hashem* to Moshe and Aharon to be communicated to them. This Divine occurrence and relationship is certainly worth celebrating. However, I believe there is much more.

The first *mitzva* given to the fledgling nation in Egypt was not only their unique calendar, but the ability and mandate to sanctify. The *Midrash* (*Shemos Rabba* 15:2) teaches that prior to this first *mitzva*, any and all *kedusha* in this world came from *Hashem*. With the exodus, that changed, and the Jewish people "shall be holy for Me, for I *Hashem* am holy, and I have separated you [the Jewish people] from the peoples to be Mine" (*Vayikra* 20:26.) On *Pesach* we not only celebrate our emergence from slavery to freedom and royalty (*Sefer HaChinuch* no. 16), but also from slavery to sanctity. The *midrash* continues, "The nation of Israel is holy and they sanctify the month; in addition they sanctify Me".

Sefer Shemos begins with the very formation of the Jewish people; hence it is called the "Second Book" (see Netizv's introduction to *Shemos*). The first book deals with the creation of the world, and the second deals with the creation of the Jewish nation. We were created with the capacity and the charge to sanctify ourselves and the world about us. *Hashem* liberated the Jewish people with a mission: we were to accept His Torah 50 days after the exodus, and through our living and fulfilling His Torah with which He, the Holy One, is one, we become filled with sanctity.

Moreover, says Rav Chaim Volozhiner, (*Nefesh HaChayyim* 1:3) the effect of our actions is beyond our comprehension. Our positive acts, words and even holy thoughts generate *kedusha* in this world and beyond. The Talmud (*Berachos* 64a) explains the verse "and all your sons will be disciples of *Hashem*, and abundant will be the peace of your sons" (*Yeshayahu* 54:13) to mean, "Do not read 'your sons' but 'your builders.'" The *Nefesh HaChayyim* takes this most literally. Hence, the observance of *Shabbos* by Jews in one location might well prevent assimilation and intermarriage in another. This injection of *kedusha*, sanctity, according to the *Or HaChayyim Hakadosh*, is renewed annually, as the verse states, "It is God who **takes** them out of Egypt" (*Bamidbar* 23:22) using the word "takes – *motzei'am*," which includes the present.

Two cases in point: if one were to train a monkey to bake *matza*, and we would all watch the monkey move with alacrity in a completely *chametz*-free environment, and complete the baking within eighteen minutes, that *matza* could be eaten on *Pesach* (it is *chametz*-free) but could not be used at the *seder* to fulfill one's *mitzva* of *matza*. What is missing is the *lishma*, the thought and speech of man that endows this unleavened bread with the characteristic of "bread of faith" (*Zohar*).

The holiest object of the Jewish people is the *sefer Torah*. Once again it is not the calligrapher that creates a holy object. It is the *sofer*, who, before he writes a single letter, articulates that it is being written for the purpose of the sanctity of the Torah scroll. His character, persona, and his personally living the Torah endow the *sefer Torah* with sanctity.

"יכול מראש חודש"; yes, I would have thought we should celebrate on *Rosh Chodesh Nisan*, as that is the anniversary of our being endowed with sanctity. On this שבת חול המועד פסח, which has a double sanctity of both *Hashem* and man, as He established the sanctity of *Shabbos* and the Jewish nation the sanctity of the holidays, may we live up to the potential and faith that *Hashem* has invested in us.

---

*"****Hashem's** Used Vehicle"* was originally published in 2016 on TorahWeb.org

Hashem's Used Vehicle

The *kerias haTorah* for אחרון של פסח is the *parasha* of the *moadim* found in *Parashas Re'eh*. In the last verse speaking about *Pesach* (*Devarim* 16:8) the Torah teaches "...and on the seventh day shall be an assembly (*atzeres*) to *Hashem*, Your God, you shall not perform labor." Interestingly, the Torah does not provide us with a reason for this day being designated as a *yom tov*. Rav Hirsch understands the *atzeres* gathering as a gathering together of ideas and a type of recapitulation of the lessons and concepts that the *yom tov* provided for us. Seforno understands this day as a commemoration of the *shira* that the Jewish nation sang upon its deliverance; hence the day was consecrated as a *yom tov*. Thus the very character of this day may be defined by the *shira*.

The *yom tov* of *Pesach* is permeated with *hakaras hatov* – thanksgiving and recognition of the kindnesses that *Hashem* performed on our behalf. The *seder* is replete with *hakaras hatov*; we fulfill the *mitzva* of סיפור יציאת מצרים by citing and explaining the four verses from the declaration of thanksgiving that the Jewish farmer recited upon bringing his first fruits to the *Beis HaMikdash*. Furthermore, our meal is eaten between the first two paragraphs of *Hallel* and its conclusion, to demonstrate that the meal itself is a *seudas hoda'a*, a meal of thanksgiving.

Indeed, there are many lessons of *hakaras hatov* that emerge from the narrative in *Shemos*. Moshe is forbidden to strike the water to bring about the plagues of blood and frogs, and the earth to commence *kinnim*, and thus the important lesson of gratitude, even to the inanimate, was emphasized. Even prior to the *makkos*, when Moshe finally acquiesces and agrees to assume the mantle of leadership to be the emissary of *Hashem* to Pharaoh and the Jewish people, prior to going to Egypt Moshe asks permission from Yisro to leave, even though Moshe is almost 80 years old and even though it will delay his mission, because Yisro afforded him hospitality and he had to show *hakaras hatov*. Moreover, *hakaras hatov* is extended to the dogs (see *Shemos* 22:30) in appreciation of their having remained silent from barking on the night of *makkas bechoros*, thereby creating a greater distinction between the crying and wailing in the Egyptian communities and the total silence in the Jewish sector.

Hakaras hatov is such a crucial element of human decency that the Torah prohibits us from marrying an Ammonite or Moabite for all time, even if they convert to Judaism, because they did not extend any help, even bread and water, to the fledgling Jewish nation upon its leaving Egypt. They should have felt a debt of gratitude to us since our grandfather Avraham saved their grandfather Lot, and yet they did not return the kindness (*Devarim* 23:5), and thus are forever banned from marrying into the Jewish people. Rav Chaim Friedlander *zt"l* notes (*Sifsei Chayyim* vol. 2, p. 278) that the Jewish people were being nourished miraculously by the *mon* and the *be'eir* of Miriam, and therefore we did not actually need any help from Ammon and Moab; rather it was they who needed to extend basic goodness and kindness in order to show appreciation, but failed to do so. *Hashem*, who is not only our Liberator but our loving Father and Teacher, says regarding *yetzias Mitzrayim*, "Today you are leaving in the month of spring" (*Shemos* 13:4). Rashi explains that *Hashem* was not telling them the time; rather He was noting that they should see the kindness that He bestowed upon them by taking them out during the most comfortable season of the year.

I believe that שביעי של פסח, complete with the singing of *shira*, brings us to a newer, higher, pinnacle of *hakaras hatov*. At first glance the essence of the *shira* is thanking *Hashem* for saving us from the danger of the Egyptians who were seeking to either kill us or return us to Egypt for further bondage. However, the *Beis HaLevi* teaches that core idea of the *shira* is found in its very last *pasuk*, "When Pharaoh's horse came with his chariots and horsemen into the sea and *Hashem* turned back the waters of the sea upon them, the children of Israel walked in the dry land amid the sea" (*Shemos* 15:19). The prior eighteen verses are all extolling *Hashem* as the incredible warrior who, with such precision, is able to simultaneously punish each Egyptian in accordance with the level of punishment that he deserved (see Rashi, *Shemos* 15:5). The *hakaras hatov* of the *shira* is understood by the *Beis HaLevi* as one of thanksgiving to *Hashem* for using *Bnei Yisrael* as the vehicle through whom a magnificent *kiddush Hashem* occurred. *Hashem* changed the natural order, transforming water into dry land on behalf of *Bnei Yisrael*, and the entire world, without the benefit of modern communications, knew of the miraculous splitting of the Red Sea. Rachav tells the spies Yehoshua sent that "we have heard how *Hashem* dried up the water of the Sea of Reeds" (*Yehoshua* 2:10). This is even a higher and more profound form of *hakaras hatov*; it is not only thanksgiving for a physical deliverance but for spiritually elevating former slaves by allowing them to participate in bringing about honor and splendor to the King. *Yetzias Mitzrayim* connotes not only our transformation from slaves to free men, but from slaves to aristocracy. I believe this very special designation came about at *kerias Yam Suf*.

Seforno explains the *pasuk*, "That is this night of watching unto *Hashem*, for all the children of Israel for their generations" (*Shemos* 12:42), to indicate that just as *Hashem* anticipated anxiously the night of redemption in Egypt, so too, He anxiously yearns for our redemption in the future. Moreover, the *Navi* (*Micha* 7:15) prophesies that just as *Hashem* showed wonders to the Jewish nation upon our deliverance from Egypt, so will He in the future. Our prayer as we enter the last days of this holiday is for *Hashem* to once again redeem us and use us, His children, as the vehicle of educating the entire world about His existence and His magnificence.

Sefiras HaOmer

Rabbi Hershel Schachter

Aveilus, Sefira and *Hallel*

The *Gemara* (*Moed Katan* 14b) understands from the *pesukim* in *Parashas Shemini* that the *kohein gadol* does not observe *aveilus* over the death of a relative (see *Sefer Ginas Egoz*, p. 95). "The *kohein gadol* all year long is compared to everyone else on *yom tov*." Just as on *yom tov* no one observes *aveilus*, so too the *kohein gadol* does not observe *aveilus* all year long. Rav Soloveitchik explained this comparison as follows: the *Gemara* (*Chagiga* 5b), based on a *pasuk* in *Divrei Hayamim*, comments that in the presence of *HaKadosh Baruch Hu* there cannot be any sadness; *simcha* always follows when one is in the presence of *Hashem* (see *Ish HaHalacha*, pp. 210-211; *Nefesh HaRav* p. 314). Just as on the *shalosh regalim* we all have an obligation to be *oleh regel* (i.e., visit the *Beis HaMikdash* and enter into the presence of *Hashem*), so too it is the role of the *kohein gadol* to be in the *Beis HaMikdash* all day long (Rambam, *Hilchos Klei HaMikdash* 5:7) and supervise the offering of all of the *korbanos* (see *Nefesh HaRav*, p. 306). Because the *kohein gadol*, and everyone else on *shalosh regalim*, are obligated to be *lifnei Hashem*, this engenders a *mitzvas simcha*, which in turn is a contradiction to observance of *aveilus*.

The Talmud (*Yevamos* 62b) tells us that many thousands of students of Rabbi Akiva died during the period of *sefira*, and in the days of the Geonim the *minhag* developed to observe *aveilus* over the great loss in Torah caused by the death of so many Torah scholars. The *Zohar*, however, considers *sefira* to be a biblical period of mourning unrelated to the death of these Torah scholars, and explains that it is because of this biblical element of *aveilus* that we don't we recite *Hallel shaleim* on שביעי של פסח in commemoration of the *neis* of *kerias Yam Suf*, even though we do recite *Hallel shaleim* to commemorate other miracles (e.g., the miracles of *Chanuka*). Based on this *Zohar*, Sephardic *mekubbalim* introduced the

---

"Aveilus, Sefira and *Hallel"* was originally published in 2013 on TorahWeb.org

minhag, followed by many *chasidim* today, to delay beginning the counting of *sefira* on the second night of *Pesach* until after the completion of the *seder*, so that the recitation of *Hallel shaleim* at the *seder* comes before we start counting *sefira*. The *Hallel* which will be recited on the morning of the second day of *Pesach* after *Shacharis*, however, is not connected to any *neis* but is rather an expression of our שמחת יום טוב (see *Sha'ar HaKollel*, chap. 49 sec. 2). As such, the Sephardic *mekubbalim* were not concerned with this recitation of *Hallel shaleim* during *sefira*. It is not proper, however, to recite *Hallel shaleim* in connection with a *neis* during *sefira*.

When an individual is *tamei*, the *Halacha* sometimes requires him/her to wait seven clean days before going to the *mikva* to become purified. When the entire Jewish nation was spiritually impure after living among the Egyptians for so many years, it was necessary for us to have seven clean **weeks**. One reason for our counting of the *omer* today is for the purpose of purifying ourselves, as we mention in the prayer we recite after the *sefira*. One who is *tamei* is precluded from entering the *Beis HaMikdash*, and therefore, by definition, is in a mild state of mourning. *Simcha* follows when one is in the presence of *Hashem*, and *aveilus* comes when one is unable to enter into His presence.

One modern implication of the restriction of *Hallel shaleim* during the *sefira* is the question of whether to recite *Hallel* on *Yom HaAtzma'ut*. The establishment of *Medinas Yisrael* took place in the middle of the *sefira*. *HaGaon* Rabbi Meshulem Roth wrote a *teshuva* encouraging the reciting of *Hallel shaleim* on *Yom HaAtzma'ut* in commemoration of the *yeshua* and the *nissim*. Rabbi Moshe Zvi Neriah, in a letter to Rabbi Roth, raised an objection to this recitation based on the aforementioned *Zohar* and *minhag*, which dictates that *Hallel shaleim* should not be recited during the *sefira* period, even for the great *neis* of *kerias Yam Suf* (see Rabbi Neriah's *sefer*, *Tznif Melucha*).

Rabbi Yaakov Neuburger

Respect and Appreciation for One Another

In some communities, it is marked by festive trips to Meron, and in some by cheerful *"upsheirin"* parties celebrating the education of our little ones. In much of Israel, bonfires, culminating weeks of wood collecting, fill its evening with their smoky smell. Yet for many, it may just be a much-anticipated pause in the national mourning accorded the students of Rabbi Akiva. Bonfires, bows and baseballs may be its trademark, yet is it not intriguing that *Lag Ba'omer*, the *yahrzeit* of Rabbi Shimon bar Yochai, has caught our imagination altogether, and certainly in such varied ways? (Interestingly, Rabbi Shimon Bar Yochai is probably the first one to have the anniversary of his death celebrated rather than mourned – a practice expanded and maintained by *chasidim* to this day.)

What is it about this *tanna* that sets him apart from the other *tannaim*, all of whose words and thoughts we plumb daily? True, Rashbi was chosen by Heaven to be the conduit of the mystical parts of our Torah, but does that mean that he outshines Rabbi Meir, on whom we depend for most of the *Mishna*, or Rabbi Yehuda *haNasi*, who saved the Oral Law for us and future generations?

His story in *Masseches Shabbos* (33b) begins with Rashbi's biting cynicism accusing the Roman Empire of developing roads and bathhouses for self-serving and decadent purposes. His comments were soon reported, and he and his son found themselves holed up in a cave, living in fear of their lives, leaving no trace behind and having no sustenance from within. Miraculously, *Hashem* provided a carob tree and a fountain of water, enough to sustain the two scholars, as they *davened* and learned daily for twelve uninterrupted years. It was then that Eliyahu called upon them to join the world once again, as the death of the Roman Emperor made the world safe for them.

"Respect and Appreciation for..." was originally published in 2004 on TorahWeb.org

Yet, it was not long at all before father and son found themselves once again secluded in the cave. This time however, *Hashem* Himself banished them from society. What a painful censure after twelve years of eating and learning directly from *Hashem*'s hand! Apparently it was necessary because they had become a dangerous menace, questioning the validity of working in this world, "leaving a life of sanctity in order to pursue the mundane and the worldly." Coming from where they did, this was a powerful question, and the *Gemara* records that Rashbi's gaze alone would singe the innocent farmer tending to his crops.

Thus, *Hashem* sentenced father and son to seclusion once again in the cave, with the words, "I did not free you in order to destroy My world." Twelve months later, Rashbi begged to return to the world and *Hashem* acquiesced. The story could have easily ended there. After all, how things had changed! This time, Rabbi Shimon bar Yochai did not wait for Eliyahu to come. Now he and his son yearned to be part of *Hashem*'s world. Perhaps they had made peace philosophically with a world that has room for Kabbalists and farmers, for the temporal and eternal to somehow live side by side.

However, the story continues. It was Friday afternoon and a simple older gentleman, rushing home, as so many of us do weekly, bounded past Rashbi, who was probably already engrossed in the loftiest *Shabbos* thoughts that unify all worlds. This gentleman was returning home clasping in his hands two myrtle branches, proudly explaining to Rashbi that each branch represented for him an essential part of *Shabbos*. One branch reminded him of the positive commandments that we observe, and one represented the work from which we refrain. Upon hearing this insight of this seemingly ordinary person, Rashbi exclaimed, "How dear are the *mitzvos* to *Klal Yisrael*!"

In this little vignette, Rabbi Shimon Bar Yochai is far from the biting cynic that drove him away from all people, and he is certainly not the saint who has no patience for simplicity and innocence. Rather, he is obviously the saint who has developed the "*ayin tov*" that appreciates the goodness of the well-meaning gesture of every Jew, and sees within them purity and substance. Indeed, it was probably this gentleman, whose name we will never know, who introduced into our homes, out of his interest to give to his home and his God, the two candles, the primary *minhag* with which we welcome every *Shabbos*.

This attitude, which respects the inherent goodness and contribution of all those who earnestly strive to do *Hashem*'s bidding, and which was extended from the greatest Kabbalist to the farmer, is clearly the antidote to the lack of respect that the students of Rabbi Akiva had for each other which brought about their death. Certainly it deserves to bring about a pause in our mourning to give **us** pause, so that the life of Rashbi will impact upon us and enhance the respect and appreciation we have for one another.

Maintaining Torah through Healthy Respect

As our hair grows longer and less comfortable, and we constantly evaluate which events we are allowed to attend, surely we all ponder why the death of Rabbi Akiva's 24,000 students demands this period of national mourning. After all, it seems that their demise has had little impact on later generations, and yet it is marked so strikingly. True, the *sefira* period has since brought great tragedies to our people, often through hatred that was intensified by Easter sermons and acted upon during the ensuing pogroms. Nevertheless, at the outset, it was the loss of these scholars to the sin of uncivil behavior to each other that prompted our predecessors to give it a longer mourning period than even the destruction of *Yerushalyim*.

"Maintaining Torah through..." was originally published in 2005 on TorahWeb.org

There is no question that to Rabbi Akiva and his generation, and undoubtedly for several generations later, the tragic death of all the nation's scholars was devastating. It can certainly be compared to our own loss, from which we are still reeling, of generations of European scholars half a century ago. Rabbi Akiva himself testifies (*Yevamos* 66b) that if not for the group of five *talmidim*, whom he taught at the end of his life and who "established" Torah, he may have had little impact on the Torah we learn today. Our *Mishna*, and thus what we have of the Oral Law, is primarily taught and filtered through these five *talmidim*. The 24,000 students who populated the entire land perished, leaving comparatively little behind.

However the *Gemara* (*Yevamos* 66b) describes the effect of the loss of these scholars in even more profound terms. Until new students were educated and established, "the world became desolate." When else since creation has the entire natural world been described in such a desperate manner? I am reminded of the tenuous nature of the world in the early morning just prior to the giving of the Torah. There too, the *Midrash* describes that all of creation was silenced in mortal fright, knowing that its very existence would depend on our acceptance of *Hashem*'s Torah. Were we to decline, we are told, the purpose and destiny of the world would be thrown into question. Apparently, a world without an entire generation of scholars to continue our *mesora* is of questionable meaning and purpose as well, and perhaps once again our physical survival came into question.

In fact, the *Gemara* indicates that the scholars shared in the responsibility of this frightening threat to Torah. In relating indications that the death of the rabbis was not due to unrelated matters, the *Gemara* points to the fact that they all succumbed to the same plague, "*askara*," and in the same period of the year, between *Pesach* and *Shavuos*. *Askara* is a disease that, according to our tradition, attacks, among others, those who aggressively disrupt the study of Torah (*Shabbos* 33b). Apparently these scholars, who through their mutual disrespect and contentiousness threatened the viability of their very mission in life, were a target for this dreadful disease at a time when they should have been preparing to celebrate and rededicate themselves to that very mission.[20]

Now, we still have to connect the dots. How does the lack of respect among a generation of scholars translate into a threat to the *mesora*? Further, how could scholars disagree so strongly and act so disrespectfully as to incur such anger that would challenge the viability of the *mesora*?

Perhaps we have all come across individuals so absolutely dedicated and invested in their ideas that the inner pressure to defend them is enormous. To be sure, it matters little whether the pressure is borne of the risk of lost time and energy, or of a tarnished reputation. Nevertheless this pressure can blur the lines between the healthy defense of one's work and the unacceptable lapse of respect for a worthy opponent.

In a not dissimilar fashion, the absolute love and dedication that our scholars have for distilling *Hashem*'s thoughts with precision, and the responsibility that comes with it, forge a passionate commitment to their ideas. Nevertheless, as praiseworthy as this passion is, we can learn from Rabbi Akiva's *talmidim* that if it is not tempered, it can be detrimental to the completeness of Torah. This idea is expressed by Rashi in his interpretation of Shlomo *haMelech*'s insight, "Two are better than one for they get a greater return for their labor. For should one fall one can lift the other, but woe to him who is alone when he falls and there is no one to lift him" (*Koheles* 4:9-10). Rashi explains that this can refer to the study of Torah and the interdependence that *talmidei chachamim* share. It follows that the Torah, which *Hashem* made dependent on people for its retention, transmission,

---

[20] See "Respect and Appreciation for One Another," above. There we explained how the life of Rabbi Shimon Bar Yochai, whose *yahrzeit* is a break in the mourning, came to represent the respect that one must have for every individual and their ability to develop some aspect of Torah. Thus we can understand why Rashbi's *yahrzeit* was a day when the *askara* epidemic came to a halt.

and even interpretation, can be impacted upon through human error and must be corrected by other scholars as well.

Therefore, maintaining a healthy respect for fellow worthy scholars and being open to them becomes crucial to maintaining the completeness and precision of Torah. The lack of respect for one's peers can threaten the responsibility of a generation to maintain the wholeness of Torah. Evidently, these are precious ideas that must be refreshed as we get closer to celebrating *Shavuos*.

Rabbi Michael Rosensweig

Reflections on *Sefiras HaOmer*

The *mitzva* of *sefiras ha'omer* as it is formulated in the Torah appears to be somewhat ambiguous in terms of its essential character, purpose and function. One verse seems to imbue the *mitzva* with an agricultural motif, stating that the obligation to count begins "from when the sickle is first put to the standing crop" (*Devarim* 16:9). Other verses stress this *mitzva*'s sacrificial theme, obligating us to begin the *mitzva* of counting "from the day [we] bring the *omer* as a wave offering" and to complete it by bringing the *shtei halechem* as an "offering to God" on the fiftieth day (*Vayikra* 23:15-17). In fact, the sacrificial theme is echoed in the *midrash*,[21] and manifests itself most dramatically in the view subscribed to by many *rishonim* that *sefiras ha'omer* in our time is only a rabbinic obligation inasmuch as we no longer offer the *korban ha'omer*.[22] Similarly, the *Semag*'s classification of *sefiras ha'omer* under the heading of "עדות שבמקדש" calls attention to its sacrificial theme (*Semag, asei* 200).

In addition to the agricultural and sacrificial themes inherent in *sefiras ha'omer*, the Torah also presents this *mitzva* as a countdown to the holiday of *Shavuos* (*Devarim* 16:9-10). This is strikingly reflected by the fact that in contrast to other holidays, the Torah never associates *Shavuos* with a specific calendar date;[23] instead it focuses exclusively on the fact that *Shavuos* occurs at the culmination of *sefiras ha'omer*. Furthermore, the Torah only mentions *sefiras ha'omer* in the context of sections devoted to the the *shalosh regalim*; again implying that despite its connection to the sacrifice of the *omer*, *sefiras ha'omer*'s central theme is its linking of *Shavuos*

---

[21] *Midrash Rabba* on *Emor* (*parasha* 28) and Ramban on *Vayikra* 23:15.

[22] This appears to be the view of Ameimar (*Menachos* 66a). Rashi and *Tosafos* indicate clearly that this is the *pesak*.

[23] See *Rabbeinu* Bachya (*Vayikra* 23:16), Ibn Ezra (*Vayikra* 23:11).

"**Reflections on *Sefiras HaOmer***" was originally published in 1999 on TorahWeb.org

with *Pesach*. Rambam's view (*Hilchos Temidin uMusafin* 7:24) that *sefiras ha'omer* is a *din deOraysa* in our own era despite our inability to bring the *korban ha'omer* also suggests that *sefiras ha'omer* is fundamentally some form of countdown to *Shavuos*.

In fact, this viewpoint is adopted explicitly and forcefully by the author of the *Sefer HaChinuch*. He asserts that the exodus should be perceived as a mere prelude to the more important goal of receiving the Torah. Thus, by counting the days between *Pesach* (which celebrates the exodus) and *Shavuos* (which celebrates the giving of the Torah), we symbolize the eager anticipation of the newly freed Jews to receive the Torah, and affirm the overwhelming importance of Torah in Jewish life. The *Sefer HaChinuch* minimizes the importance of the *korban ha'omer* as a theme in *mitzva* of *sefira*, claiming that the Torah merely used the *korban ha'omer* as a convenient way of identifying the second day of *Pesach* (on which the *sefira* must begin); the *korban* itself, however, is essentially irrelevant to the character of the *mitzva* of *sefira*.[24]

While the *Sefer HaChinuch*'s stance has definite appeal, it still seems deficient in that it does not appear to adequately capture some of the intriguing facets of the *mitzva* of *sefiras ha'omer*. If the sole function of *sefiras ha'omer* is to mark the time between *Pesach* and *Shavuos*, then its significance lies in those holidays themselves, and *sefiras ha'omer* should not have constituted its own *mitzva*, nor should it require a *beracha*. In addition, the fact that there are definite halachic rules and regulations which govern and define the counting process itself seems to imply that the act of counting is somehow infused with meaning and inherent value. Ramban

---

[24] *Sefer HaChinuch* (273). He is initially troubled by the progressive nature of this counting process which might, on the surface, imply that the focus is commemorating the past (*Pesach*), rather than anticipating the future (*Shavuos*). However, he resolves this by suggesting that the alternative scheme would have been discouraging in that it would have accented the distance from *Shavuos* instead of its proximity, thus dampening the enthusiasm it should generate.

(*Vayikra* 23:15) accentuates this point when he contrasts *sefiras ha'omer* with another act of counting – that of a *zava* (a menstruating woman who must count seven consecutive days without bleeding before she can purify herself). A *zava* need only keep track of her count and be aware of it, but *sefiras ha'omer* demands a verbalized nightly counting, during an ideal time (at the onset of each evening), utilizing a precise formula; all of these facts seem to imply that *sefiras ha'omer* possesses its own inherent significance. Finally, Ramban (*Vayikra* 23:36) draws a parallel between the days of *sefiras ha'omer* and the days of *chol hamoed* that intervene between *Sukkos* and *Shemini Atzeres* (see also *Rabbeinu* Bachya *Vayikra* 23:16). If the days of *sefira* represent a form of *chol hamoed* between *Pesach* and *Shavuos*, then clearly this interim period serves an inherently important function.

To resolve some of these difficulties, it may be helpful view *sefiras ha'omer* from the perspective of *kedushas hazeman*. Rav Yosef Dov Soloveitchik *zt"l* developed this theme at length in an essay entitled "Sacred and Profane." He argues that time consciousness is a prerequisite to freedom. The slave who lives for the moment and does not control his own destiny, whose time is literally not his own, is exempt from all מצוות עשה שהזמן גרמן (time-restricted obligations) because he has no sensitivity to, or appreciation of, the nuances of time. Rav Soloveitchik explains the function of *sefiras ha'omer*:

> When the Jews were delivered from the Egyptian oppression and Moses rose to undertake the almost impossible task of metamorphosing a tribe of slaves into a nation of priests, he was told by God that the path leading from the holiday of *Pesach* to *Shavuos*, from initial liberation to consummate freedom, leads through the medium of time. The commandment of *sefira* was entrusted to the Jew; the wondrous test of counting 49 successive days was put to him. These 49 days must be whole. If one day is missed, the act of numeration is invalidated.

A slave who is capable of appreciating each day, of grasping its meaning and worth, of weaving every thread of time into a glorious fabric, quantitatively stretching over the period of seven weeks but qualitatively forming the warp and woof of centuries of change, is eligible for Torah. He has achieved freedom.[25]

On this basis, many of the peculiar and seemingly incongruous facets of *sefiras ha'omer* can be justified. The very act of counting acquires significance and requires a *beracha* inasmuch as it represents a process whose aim is to sensitize man to this indispensable religious dimension of time-consciousness. If we identify *sefiras ha'omer* with time-awareness, then our act of counting is more than a simple marking of time between *Pesach* and *Shavuos*, or a passive noting of time's passage (like the counting of a *zava*); rather, *sefiras ha'omer* becomes a means of effecting an important psychological and religious transformation, which is most effectively achieved by verbal articulation and daily expression. Ramban's allusion to an analogy to the concept of *chol hamoed* is particularly apt, in as much as *sefiras ha'omer* constitutes an essential period of transition between the slave mentality of the immediate post-*Pesach* era and the time-conscious mindset of true freedom that is prerequisite for receiving the Torah on *Shavuos*.[26]

In associating *sefiras ha'omer* with the themes of freedom and sensitivity to time, it is illuminating to examine, if only briefly, other *halachos* that distinguish *sefiras ha'omer*.

The Talmud (*Menachos* 65b), commenting on the words

---

[25] "Sacred and Profane," in *Gesher* III:1 (1966), p.16.

[26] The idea that autonomy and freedom are central themes of *talmud Torah* and *matan Torah* requires no elaboration. The principles of "the Jews are My slaves; My slaves, and not the slaves of other slaves," and "only someone who engages in Torah study is free" are just two of many prooftexts that illustrate this point. The connection between *yovel* and *sefira* – a prominent theme in the *Midrash* and commentaries – also takes on new meaning if the ultimate aim of *sefira* is the time-consciousness which enhances authentic freedom.

"*usefartem lachem*" ("you shall count for yourselves"), declares: שתהיה ספירה לכל אחד ואחד, that the *mitzva* of *sefiras ha'omer* devolves upon each individual, not on the Jewish nation as whole. Some *poskim* take this a step further and disqualify the use of *shomeia ke'oneh* as a mechanism with which to accomplish this *mitzva*. This view dramatizes the personal motif of *sefira* (see, for example, *Magen Avraham* 489:2). The cultivation of sensitivity and the inculcation of a mentality can be achieved effectively only on a personal level. Individual self-development must be the focus of any such enterprise, even when the ultimate goal is the transformation of a national destiny.

The *Ba'al haMa'or* (end of *Pesachim*) asks a famous question: Why should we not consider *sefeika deyoma* when counting *sefira* in the Diaspora, just as we do in requiring the observance of a second day of *yom tov*? Some *acharonim* respond that the very concept of counting would be undermined by indecisiveness. If we view *sefira* from the perspective of time-consciousness and human autonomy, this response takes on a new dimension of meaning.[27]

Finally, it is interesting to assess the method of counting and its implications against this background. The Talmud (*Menachos* 66a) informs us: "Abaye says there is an obligation to count the days of *sefira* and there is also an obligation to count the weeks." This statement reflects the two types of time-awareness: the long-term perspective and the immediate perspective. Clearly, one of the most salient features of free and progressive man is his ability to plan ahead, to work toward a long-term objective with foresight. By living for the future and preparing for it, he asserts and demonstrates a measure of autonomy over his life. By being goal- and project-oriented, he is able to infuse his life with meaning and purpose.

---

[27] In addition, *yemei sefira* as an independent and intrinsically valuable interim period would no longer be as closely linked with the precise date of the *yom tov* that precedes it and the *yom tov* that follows it.

This theme is reflected in the concept of "counting weeks."

There is, however, a definite hazard in focusing on the future to the exclusion of the present. If long-term objectives and goals totally dominate one's actions and attitudes, the urgency of the present and its unique opportunities may be lost. In compromising the integrity of the present for the sake of the future, one generally undermines the ultimate purpose as well. Thus we are instructed to treat each day as a discrete unit – to "count days." Rambam, in his *Sefer HaMitzvos* (*asei* 161) goes to great lengths to prove that despite the existence of these two distinct motifs – of days and of weeks – they in fact comprise one integrated *mitzva*.[28]

The challenge we face, then, is clear. We must endeavor to harmonize and reconcile our long-term growth (the "counting of weeks") with our immediate needs (the "counting of days"), and to cultivate a sensitivity to time in all of its various dimensions. Then we will effectively be able to partake in the transforming process of *sefiras ha'omer*, the bridge which will bring us to Sinai.

The *Sefiras HaOmer* Period: A Dimension of *Kedushas HaZeman*

Parashas Emor enumerates the full range of *moadim* (*Vayikra* 23:1-44), beginning from *Shabbos* and *Pesach* and concluding with *Sukkos*. However, the presence of a large section (13 *pesukim*; *Vayikra* 23:9-22) dedicated to the *korbanos* of the *omer* and *shtei haechem*, and the counting

---

[28] In this context, it is interesting to note that some *rishonim* adopt the position that weeks are only acknowledged at their completion, not daily (*Ba'al haMa'or*, etc.). This view accents the tension between two motifs even if they are counted as one *mitzva*. It is also tempting to interpret the argument between the *Behag* and *Ba'alei haTosafos* along similar lines. They argue whether the entire interim period of *sefira* constitutes one *mitzva*, or whether each day is a distinct unit. This issue, obviously, requires some elaboration.

"The *Sefiras HaOmer* Period...." was originally published in 2012 on TorahWeb.org

of the *omer* that connects the second day of *Pesach* with the subsequent holiday of *Shavuos*, is somewhat puzzling.

The fact that this segment comprises roughly 30 percent of the entire *parashas hamoadim* and that it dwarfs the treatments of any of the actual festivals (*Yom Kippur* commands six *pesukim*; *Sukkos* contains two different five-*pesukim* accounts) simply belies the conjecture that these themes – the *korbanos* and the *sefira* count –merely establish the timing and framework for the *Pesach* and *Shavuos* holidays. This is particularly significant according to the perspective reflected in the views of the Vilna Gaon (*Yoreh De'ah, Hilchos Aveilus, siman* 399, no. 9) and Netziv (*Ha'amek Davar, Vayikra* 23:5) that the very inclusion of a single *pasuk* (23:5) dedicated to the *korban pesach* in *Parashas Emor* establishes the 14th of Nisan as a quasi-independent *moed*.

It is noteworthy that the Torah actually interrupts the *chag hamatzos* narrative (*Vayikra* 23:6-8) by independently introducing the *omer-shtei-halechem-Shavuos* interval with the phrases (23:9-10) "וידבר ה' אל משה לאמר, דבר אל בני ישראל..." This parallels the distinctive presentations of *Rosh HaShana* (23:23, 24) after *Shavuos*, of *Yom Kippur* after *Rosh HaShana* (23:26; though significantly absent the otherwise ubiquitous addition of "דבר אל בני ישראל"!), and of *Sukkos* after *Yom Kippur* (23:33). The effect of these apparently gratuitous introductory refrains is to underscore the independent character and significance of each holiday. By extension and implication, *omer-sefira-shtei-halechem-Shavuos* emerges as a distinctive *moed* motif.

While Rambam associates the *korban ha'omer* with the *musaf korbanos* of *chag hamatzos* (*Hilchos Temidin uMusafin* 7:3) and integrates the laws not only of *ketziras* and *korban ha'omer* (7:4-21) but also of *sefiras ha'omer* (7:22-25) within the framework of the *Pesach* holiday, the Torah itself delineates these themes independently and briefly identifies them with *Shavuos* (*Vayikra* 23:21). (It is noteworthy that Rambam presents the *shtei halechem* offering in the context of the *musaf* of *Shavuos* in a new chapter [chap. 8] of *Hilchos Temidin,* although he surely also connects it with the conclusion of the *sefira*.)

Moreover, the triple usage of the ambiguous and challenging phrase "*mimacharas haShabbos*" (*Vayikra* 23:11, 15, 16), to signify the timing of these *korbanos* and the duration of the count, further reinforces the impression that these subject matters are not simply signposts for other obligations, but constitute inherently consequential and yet interconnected institutions that also unquestionably facilitate and enhance *Shavuos* (and, according to Rambam and Ramban 23:36, perhaps also *Pesach*). The routine omission of the festival *musafin* from the *Emor* account (see Ramban's discussion of this point in the beginning of chapter 23 and at the conclusion of his remarks on 23:15) further accentuates the significance of the integration of the *omer* and *shtei halechem korbanos* in unsparing detail in this *parasha*. Indeed, Ramban explicates the singular role of these *menachos* as expressions of *kedushas hazeman* – "ולכך הזכיר הקרבנות האלה בפרשה, כי הם בגלל המנחות שהם העיקר בחג הזה. ולא הזכיר המוספין בהן כאשר לא הזכירם בשאר המועדים – therefore the Torah mentioned these *korbanos* in this section, because they are the offerings that are essential to the holiday. The Torah did not mention the days' *musaf* offerings, just as it did not for the rest of the holidays in this section."

A close reading of the *parasha* reveals that in some respects *Shavuos* does not trigger, but is itself a product of, this combination of *omer-sefira* and *shtei halechem*. Chizkuni (*Vayikra* 23:21) posits that the Torah omits a date for *Shavuos* because the process of counting the 50 days of the *omer* is indispensable to generating the *kedushas hayom* of *Shavuos*. He adds that there would have been a requirement to recite *birkas hazeman* in the bringing of these *korbanos*, typical of the *zeman* requirement of any *moed*, but the link to *Shavuos* satisfies this demand (see also Avudraham, *Tefillas HaMoadim* and responsa of Radvaz). Because of the prominent role of these *korbanos* in the genesis of *Shavuos*, Seforno suggests that the Torah deems it necessary to establish unequivocally that the absence of the *korbanos* of *omer* and *shtei halechem* will not preclude the very *kedushas hayom* of *Shavuos*!

The Torah's presentation in *Emor* establishes that the *korbanos* of *omer* and *shtei halechem* and the *sefiras ha'omer* that bridges them do not simply mark the time between *moadim*, but constitute a vital contribution to the concept of *kedushas hazeman* in their own right. Partly this is due to the very bridging of the *Pesach* and *Shavuos* themes. Indeed, Ramban (*Vayikra* 23:36) depicts the *sefira* period as a *chol hamoed* between the two holidays that parallels the days between *Sukkos* and *Shemini Atzeres*.

We have also emphasized that the *parasha* in *Emor* particularly underscores that these *korbanos* and the *omer* count define the character of *chag haShavuos*. Elsewhere, we have developed the idea that *Shavuos* celebrates not only *Hashem*'s initiative of *matan Torah*, but especially *Klal Yisrael*'s preparation and worthiness for *kabbalas haTorah*. The themes of these *korbanos* (which I hope to elaborate on another occasion), and the transition from one to the other reflected by the count between two "ממחרת השבת's," highlights that process of preparation and transition. The fact that *shtei halechem* is the rare *chametz mincha* (alongside the *toda*) dramatically captures the transition from *Pesach*'s theme of physical *cheirus*, in which *chametz* as a symbol of unrestricted and undirected growth is excluded from all use and benefit, to the *Shavuos* motif of a comprehensive halachic commitment that provides the framework for authentic freedom (אין לך בן חורין אלא מי שעוסק בתורה) in which *chametz*, even in the context of *korbanos*, where it typically disqualifies, is a constructive catalyst. The fact that there is no need for a *kemitza* in the *korban shtei ha lechem* is consistent with this *kedushas hazeman* perspective as well.

If this lengthy section in *parashas hamoadim* reflects that the *sefira* period and the *menachos* of *omer* and *shtei halechem* constitute a dimension of *kedushas hazeman*, we may also clarify another difficulty in the Torah's presentation. The concluding *pasuk* in this section inexplicably repeats the general obligation to provide *peah* and *leket* to the poor. The *mefarshim* contend with the apparently gratuitous character, as well as the puzzling location, of this law. They propose different explanations for the intriguing insertion of this law in this context (see, for example, Rashi's citation of the *Sifrei*, and the comments of Ibn Ezra and Ramban ad loc.). However, we note that Rambam (*Hilchos Yom Tov* 6:18) rules that providing for the poor and vulnerable is an indispensable component in *simchas* and *kedushas yom tov*. The perspective that this entire transition period from *Pesach* to *Shavuos* is itself part of the *moed* cycle establishes this agricultural expression of *tzedaka* as a perfect coda to this challenging *moadim* section.

Sefiras HaOmer: A Process of Individual and National Growth

The Torah (*Vayikra* 23:9-22) presents the *mitzva* of *sefiras ha'omer* by linking it to the *korban ha'omer* and the *korban shtei halechem*, each of which brackets the counting imperative. This presentation spurred most halachic authorities to conclude that *sefiras ha'omer* is only a rabbinic obligation in the aftermath of the destruction of the Temple. Ameimar (*Menachos* 66a) explicitly argued that only days (not weeks) should be counted in the post-destruction era as a *zeicher lechurban*. Rashi (s.v. Ameimar) explains that the absence of the *korban ha'omer* renders the *mitzva* a *deRabbanan* (see also *Ba'al haMaor* and Ran, end of *Pesachim*). Indeed, the Tosafists (*Menachos* 66a, s.v. *zeicher*) rule that one could count *sefira* during twilight (*bein hashemashos*), since we are lenient regarding rabbinic obligations.

"*Sefiras HaOmer*: A Process..." was originally published in 2013 on TorahWeb.org

Yet Rambam disputes this contention. He emphasizes that *sefiras ha'omer* is a biblical obligation in all eras (*Hilchos Temidin uMusafin* 7:22). Evidently, he considers Ameimar's contrary view to be exceptional, as the *Kesef Mishneh* notes. Indeed, the *Midrash* (*Parashas Emor*) and many *rishonim* (*Chinuch* and others) perceive the counting of the *omer* as marking a transition from *yetzias Mitzrayim* to *matan Torah*, something seemingly independent of the requirement of *korbanos*. Moreover, the fact that the period of *sefiras ha'omer* is detailed in the *parashas hamoadim* of *Emor* establishes it as an important bridge between the festivals of *Pesach* and *Shavuos*, as Ramban (*Vayikra* 23:36) remarks. However, this challenges us to better comprehend the Torah's explicit connection between the *mitzva* of counting the *omer* and these *korbanos*, particularly as the *mitzva* applies, according to the Rambam, even in the absence of the *korbanos*.

The very presence of these two *korbanos* in the context of the festival chapter in *Emor* may provide a clue to our enigma. Typically, the details of the festival offerings are discussed in *Parashas Pinchas*, not in *Emor*, as Ramban (*Vayikra* 23:2) also notes. Ramban (23:15) and other commentators were troubled by this exception. Perhaps these *korbanos* are integrated into *Emor* because their special features effectively embody the character of the transitions involved and, by extension, they convey the goal of the counting process and period.

The *Aruch HaShulchan* (*Orach Chayyim* 489:3) certainly adopts this approach in his explanation of Rambam's controversial view. He notes that the *korban ha'omer* is unusual (like the *korban minchas sota*) in being a barley-based *korban*, while the wheat-based *shtei halechem* serves as a sharp contrast. He posits that the transition from the crude barley staple of an animal's diet to the refined human consumption of wheat symbolizes the process of spiritual refinement and the attainment of human potential that is the telos of *matan Torah*, and that is achieved only by a commitment to Torah and *mitzvos*.

There is perhaps another dimension to this transition reflected by the timing and substance of the two *korbanos*. It is surely significant that the *Shavuos* offering of *shtei halechem* alone consists of *chametz* (even the *korban toda* only contains one part *chametz*; other *korbanos* are disqualified by the presence of any *chametz*), while the *omer* is sacrificed in the context of *Pesach*, the holiday that demands an absolute eradication of even the presence of *chametz*. The Torah appears to be conveying that while the political freedom of *yetzias Mitzrayim* requires strict discipline (*shemira* of *matza*) and rejects the theme of unfettered growth symbolized by *chametz*, authentic growth and creativity can only really flourish in the context of the commitment to Torah.

The interaction between personal growth and the forging of a national identity based on common spiritual aspirations may also be relevant to the process of spiritual growth between *Pesach* and *Shavuos*, and highlighted by *omer* and *shtei halechem*. The *Gemara* (*Menachos* 65b) establishes that each individual must count the *sefira*. Some *poskim* even conclude that the principle of *shomeia ke'oneh* does not apply to this personal requirement. Yet, the obligation to count is defined by the *korban ha'omer* and *korban shtei halachem*, two *korbanos tzibbur* (public sacrifices). Moreover, these two sacrifices share an unusual common denominator: the requirement that they stem from the produce of *Eretz Yisrael*. This requirement is actually cited in the *Mishnah* (*Keilim* 1:6) as exemplifying the special sanctity of *Eretz Yisrael*! The commentators (see *Mishna Acharona*, *Eliyahu Rabba* and the emendation of the Gra) note that *omer* and *shtei halechem* (alongside *bikkurim* – see the Gra and *Eliyahu Rabba*) were selected, rather than the classical מצוות התלויות בארץ (*Kiddushin* 36a) such as *terumos* and *ma'asros* that technically depend on the soil of *Eretz Yisrael*, precisely because they underscore a broader principle. There is ample evidence in other contexts to suggest that the broader halachic requirement of *Eretz Yisrael* signifies a national dimension. It is highly appropriate, then, that *Eretz Yisrael* be featured prominently in the *korbanos* that mark the transition from the *yetzias Mitzrayim* experience of a collection of individual refugees to the moment of *kabbalas haTorah*, the event that established Jewish national identity – "היום הזה נהיית לעם, on that day you became a nation" (*Devarim* 27:9.)

Perhaps the link to the two *korbanos* further stresses that while the act of *sefira* requires the personal involvement of each individual, the ultimate purpose is to forge a nation of committed individuals that identify with the both the common and contrasting themes of these *korbanos* and the holidays that they represent. This message, according Rambam, remains biblically viable and compelling in all eras, even when the actual implementation of the *korbanos* is, alas, unattainable.

Rabbi Yonason Sacks

Between *Pesach* and *Atzeres*: Perspectives on *Sefiras HaOmer*

The exodus from Egypt serves as the basis for numerous *mitzvos* and for one of the fundamental principles of our faith. The first of the Ten Commandments links the belief in God with His having freed us from Egypt. Twice daily we are obligated to acknowledge our indebtedness to God by recalling the exodus at the conclusion of the *Shema*. In fact, R. Chaim Soloveitchik *zt"l* explains that according to Rambam, the *mitzva* of זכירת יציאת מצרים is not an independent obligation, but is rather an inherent part of the *Shema*, and as such is a component of our קבלת עול מלכות שמים.

Even our observance of *Shabbos* is tied to the exodus. Unlike Ibn Ezra, who explains the verse, "You shall remember that you were slaves in Egypt" (*Devarim* 5:14), as commanding that even slaves refrain from work on *Shabbos*, Rambam and Ramban explain this reference as a basis of *shemiras Shabbos* generally. In this sense, the Talmud (*Pesachim* 117b) insists that we incorporate the theme of *yetzias Mitzrayim* into the text of *kiddush*. Accordingly, the *Minchas Chinuch* (*mitzva* 31) asserts that although many *rishonim* maintain that any need for wine during *kiddush* is only *mideRabbanan*, one would certainly not fulfill the Torah obligation of *kiddush* with *tefilla* alone, for nowhere in the *Shabbos* evening *Amidah* do we mention the theme of *yetzias Mitzrayim*.

Even the 39 *melachos* themselves are linked to the exodus from Egypt. *Tosafos* (*Pesachim* 117b, s.v. *lema'an*) cite the *midrash* which states that on *Shabbos* we demonstrate our freedom by abstaining from the various forms of labor that we performed while slaves in Egypt.

Although *yetzias Mitzrayim* plays such a central role in our belief, it would be incorrect to view this event as an end in itself. When Moshe

---

"Between *Pesach* and *Atzeres*...." was originally published in 1999 on TorahWeb.org

Rabbeinu expresses his doubt as to his worthiness of taking the Jews out of Egypt, God assures him that the fact that the Jews would later receive the Torah makes the exodus worthwhile (see *Shemos* 3:12). The very purpose and challenge of *yetzias Mitzrayim* is to channel this newfound freedom toward the service of God. Ramban explains that the essence and purpose of *sefiras ha'omer* is to link the experience of *yetzias Mitzrayim* with that of *kabbalas haTorah*. Ramban comments that the days of *Pesach* are to be viewed as the first days of *yom tov* and the days of *Shavuos* as the last days of *yom tov*, with the intermediate days of *sefiras ha'omer* serving as a form of *chol hamoed*. For this reason the rabbinic literature often refers to *Shavuos* as "*Atzeres*," the true and fitting conclusion of *Pesach*. Accordingly, R. Ovadia Yosef (*Yechaveh Da'as* 1:24) argues that although the days of *sefira* mark the tragic passing of the students of R. Akiva (see *Yevamos* 62b), it would be incorrect to consider this period as one of *aveilus*. Essentially these are days of great joy in anticipating *kabbalas haTorah*. Perhaps it is for this very reason that the Torah makes no mention of the *mitzva* of *simcha* on *Pesach*. Only on *Shavuos*, when the true purpose of *yetzias Mitzrayim* is realized, does the Torah obligate us to rejoice.

It is in this sense that the *Aruch HaShulchan* (*Orach Chayyim* 489) explains the view of Rambam, who maintains that the *mitzva* of *sefiras ha'omer* is a Torah obligation even today. Even without the *Beis HaMikdash* and the *minchas ha'omer* (the special sacrifice that was made in connection with *sefiras ha'omer*), the need to link *Pesach* to *Shavuos*, and thereby to see freedom as a means to further and enhance one's service of God, is as significant today as it was when the *Beis HaMikdash* stood.

Although the special sacrifices of *Pesach* and *Shavuos* (the *minchas ha'omer* and the *shtei halechem*, respectively) have much in common, they are nonetheless brought from different grains. Whereas the *minchas ha'omer* is brought from barley, which the Talmud describes as *ma'achal beheima* (food for animals), the *shtei halechem* is from wheat, described as *ma'achal adam* (food for people). Perhaps this distinction as well can be understood given the link between *Pesach* and *Shavuos*. The experience of freedom, in the sense of relief from physical service and oppression, is not one which is unique to humanity. Even an animal can sense the removal of a physical burden. Hence, the *minchas ha'omer* marking this form of freedom comes from *ma'achal beheima*. *Shavuos*, however, which challenges us to use this freedom wisely, to ascend in the distinctly human endeavor of acquiring holiness and enhancing our commitment to God, has its sacrifice brought from wheat, *ma'achal adam*.

Mitzvos which are performed relatively infrequently are generally accompanied by the blessing of *shehecheyanu*, in which we thank God for allowing us to perform them. Why then is no *shehecheyanu* recited on the *mitzva* of *sefiras ha'omer*? The *Ba'al haMa'or* (end of *Pesachim*) explains that this blessing is only recited on *mitzvos* that possess qualities of joy When the *Beis HaMikdash* stood, this was true of *sefiras ha'omer*, and certainly the blessing of *shehecheyanu* was recited. In our time, however, *sefiras ha'omer* is only a *zeicher leMikdash*, devoid of joy, and therefore no *shehecheyanu* is recited.

According to Rambam and *Rabbeinu* Yeruchum, however, who maintain that the *mitzva* of *sefiras ha'omer* is a Torah obligation even today, other reasons must be given to explain the omission of *shehecheyanu*. Rabbeinu Yeruchum explains that the *shehecheyanu* recited on *Shavuos* itself covers the *mitzva* of *sefiras ha'omer* as well. The very purpose of *sefira* is to underscore the significance of *Shavuos*. In fact, whereas all other holidays are linked to specific calendar dates, *Shavuos* commences at the conclusion of the *sefiras ha'omer*. Therefore, only after counting these days and successfully bridging the gap between *Pesach* and *Shavuos* do we recite the blessing of *shehecheyanu*.

The days of *sefira* are indeed days of intense preparation and anticipation. May we be worthy recipients of *Toras Hashem*.

Rabbi Zvi Sobolofsky

Omer and *Shtei Halechem*: Two Sides of Man

Our thoughts focus on the *mitzva* of *sefiras ha'omer* as we read, in *Parashas Emor*, about the *mitzva* that we are in the process of fulfilling. *Sefiras ha'omer* begins and concludes with a *korban*. The *korban ha'omer* (barley offering), brought on the second day of *Pesach*, initiates the countdown to *Shavuos*, which culminates with the *korban* of the *shtei halechem* offered on *Shavuos*.

There are certain similarities between these two *korbanos*. Both are grain offerings which are incumbent upon the community to bring, and in contrast to other *korbanos*, they can only be brought from grain that grew in *Eretz Yisrael*. Aside from these similarities, there are certain stark differences between them. The *korban ha'omer* is brought from barley in deviation from the usual practice of offering wheat in instances of a grain offering. Although the *shtei halechem* are made of wheat, they are required to be baked as *chametz*. A *korban mincha* which is *chametz* is an anomaly because all other *menachos* have to be *matza*. The *korban ha'omer*, on the other hand, was the absolute antithesis of *chametz*. Not only was it bound by the regular prohibition of offering *chametz* in the *Beis HaMikdash*, but it was also brought on *Pesach* when it would be unthinkable to bring a *korban* which was *chamtez*. What is the Torah trying to teach us by requiring us to bring these *korbanos* which are different from other *menachos*, and so radically different from one another?

Chazal (*Pesachim* 49b) comment on the *pasuk* (*Vayikra* 11:46), "This is the Torah concerning the animal and the bird," that only one who is involved in the study of Torah (*talmud Torah*) is permitted to eat animals and birds. Why should the study of Torah be a prerequisite to being per-

---

"Omer and Shtei Halechem:..." was originally published in 2003 on TorahWeb.org

mitted to eat meat? The significance of the *omer* and *shtei halechem*, and the relationship between learning Torah and partaking of meat, are both rooted in the unique nature of man. Man is created as part of the animal kingdom with needs and desires similar to those of other animals. Yet only man is endowed with the gifts of creative thought and speech. As a member of the animal world, man has no right of dominion over other animals. It is only his unique status as an *oveid Hashem* that gives him the right to elevate other living beings by using them for *avodas Hashem*. The man who uses the gifts of thought and speech for studying Torah has the right to partake of meat. The nutrition he receives enables him to achieve the lofty goal of elevating his thoughts and speech by using them for the purpose for which they were granted to him. Eating meat without living up to the unique status of man is merely one animal attacking another.

The *korbanos* of the *omer* and *shtei halechem* reflect the dual aspects of man. The *omer* was brought from barley, which is a very basic food, primarily eaten by animals. The barley was not improved in any way; it was not made into *chametz*. In contrast, the *shtei halechem* were brought from the finest wheat flour and baked as *chametz*. These elegant loves of bread were the antithesis of the plain barley. By offering the *omer* on *Pesach*, followed by *sefiras ha'omer* culminating with the *shtei halechem* on *Shavuos*, we are demonstrating vividly the two parts of our existence. On *Pesach* we have not yet received the Torah. We have not begun the process of elevating our thoughts and speech by using them for the purpose for which they were given. We are still part of the animal kingdom, and our *korban* reflects this. It is only our preparation for *kabbalas haTorah*, and our commitment to and celebration of this *kabbalas haTorah* on *Shavuos*, that grant us the privilege of offering a *korban* that reflects our unique status as humans.

May we be *zocheh* to offer the *shtei halechem* this *Shavuos*, celebrating our unique privilege of serving *Hashem* with our minds and our words through the *mitzva* of *talmud Torah*.

Rabbi Mayer Twersky

Kabbalas HaTorah

Sefiras ha'omer, according to the *Sefer HaChinuch,* reflects our anticipation and yearning for *kabbalas haTorah.* This beautiful perspective is oft quoted, but what does it actually mean? In what sense are we going to accept the Torah this year? We can not opt out of Torah; Torah is eternally binding on all Jews. So what do we mean when we speak of a new *kabbalas haTorah* every year?

Let us consider two perspectives. In the first *perek* of *Hilchos Talmud Torah,* Rambam describes and defines the חיוב. Then in the third *perek* he writes, "מי שנשאו לבו לקיים מצוה זו כראוי – one who is inspired to fulfill this *mitzva* optimally...." In other words, one's fulfillment of *talmud Torah* can be minimalist or maximalist. The minimalist discharges his obligation of *talmud Torah*; the maximalist takes full advantage of the priceless *beracha* and privilege of *talmud Torah.* He does not simply fulfill the *mitzva*; he does so optimally.

These two approaches are not limited to *mitzvas talmud Torah*; they are applicable to all *mitzvos.* One can be "*yotzei*" his *avodas Hashem*; or, alternatively, one can strive to excel in his *avodas Hashem.*

The minimal obligation in Torah and *mitzvos* does not require a new *kabbala.* The new *kabbalas haTorah* every year provides an opportunity to commit ourselves to optimal fulfillment and observance of Torah and *mitzvos.* Perhaps our *tefilla* has hitherto been adequate; on *Shavuos* when we accept Torah, we commit to improving our *tefilla* (coming earlier, *davening* slower, etc.) Perhaps our *kevius itim* has been acceptable; *Shavuos* is a time to commit to making extra time to learn. Similarly in the realm of בין אדם לחברו.

"Kabbalas HaTorah" was originally published in 2011 on TorahWeb.org

A second perspective on our *kabbalas haTorah*: the *Gemara* teaches that, "כל מצוה שקבלו בשמחה, עדיין עושין בשמחה" – every *mitzva* that *Klal Yisrael* accepted joyously, they still fulfill joyously." Case in point: *mitzvas mila*.

This *Gemara* teaches us that *kabbala* is significant not only in creating obligation, but also in forging connection. By reaccepting the Torah, we strive to forge a deeper connection to *HaKadosh Baruch Hu* and His Torah.

In anticipation of *kabbalas haTorah*, we need to reflect upon the gift of life which *HaKadosh Baruch Hu* bestows upon us. Life in its simplest sense, but also in the sense of חיי עולם נטע בתוכנו. Such reflection can inspire us to a *kabbalas haTorah besimcha* which, בסייעתא דשמיא, will forge an even deeper connection to *HaKadosh Baruch Hu* and His Torah.

Reassuring Rabbi Shimon bar Yochai

Upon first emerging from the cave, Rabbi Shimon bar Yochai (Rashbi) and his son could not tolerate people who were plowing and planting (i.e., working to earn a livelihood). They could not make peace with the fact that these people were, "מניחין חיי עולם ועוסקים בחיי שעה" – neglecting eternity and preoccupying themselves with transience." A heavenly voice instructed them to return to their cave. Upon reemerging a year later, they encountered a man who was running with two bundles of *hadassim* (myrtle branches) right before *Shabbos*. Upon questioning, the man explained that the two bundles corresponded to *zachor* and *shamor*. Hearing this, Rashbi and his son were reassured and became at peace with the world.

How did this encounter with the old man reassure them? Rav Chaim of Volozhin in his *Nefesh HaChayyim* (I:8) indicates that Rashbi

---

"Reassuring Rabbi Shimon…" was originally published in 2016 on TorahWeb.org agrees with Rabbi Yishmael that the overwhelming majority of people should combine earning a livelihood with the study of Torah. Clearly neither Rashbi nor Rabbi Yishmael are conceding that it is a necessary evil to divert time and energy away from *avodas Hashem* to earn a livelihood. Rather, they teach that it is *HaKadosh Baruch Hu*'s will that people adequately address their mundane needs. Having been addressed, the mundane fades into the background and people can devote themselves to the spiritual (see Rashi to *Berachos* 35b, that one who neglects earning a livelihood and has to seek help will end up neglecting his *talmud Torah*.)

One who is involved with the physical and mundane because these concerns define his life is guilty of being "מניח חיי עולם ועוסק בחיי שעה - neglecting eternity." But one whose involvement is measured, framed and contextualized by his ultimate overarching spiritual goal is involved with eternity at all times.

Shabbos is *me'ein olam haba*, a miniature of the spiritual, eternal world to come. The old man running *lekavod Shabbos* - no simple task at his advanced age - reassured Rashbi and his son that their fellow Jews' real and ultimate preoccupation was the Eternal, and thereby eternity.

Rabbi Mordechai Willig

VeAhavta LeReiacha Kamocha

The *Gemara* in *Yevamos* (62b) relates the story of the death of Rabbi Akiva's *talmidim*. Twelve thousand pairs of his students died during one period because they did not respect one another. Meiri comments that these *talmidim* died between *Pesach* and *Lag Ba'omer*, and for this reason it is customary not to marry during this period.

A number of questions can be raised concerning this matter. First, why does the Talmud refer to 12,000 pairs of *talmidim* rather than 24,000 *talmidim*? Second, how is it possible that Rabbi Akiva's *talmidim* did not have basic respect for one another? Third, why is this tragedy singled out for perpetual commemoration during the period of *sefira*? Finally, how does the custom of refraining from marriage (in contrast to other forms of *aveilus*, which were not originally practiced) reflect the tragedy of the *sefira* period?

Perhaps the answer to these questions is as follows. Although Rabbi Akiva's students were generally respectful to one another, they were deficient in one area. Each *talmid* had a *chavrusa*, a friend and study partner, with whom he would learn all day, under Rabbi Akiva's guidance. The unique relationship, which blossoms when two individuals join in the difficult and incessant challenge of attempting to master the Divine law to the best of their abilities, should also produce a paramount mutual respect, far beyond the standard requirement to honor a friend. Rabbi Akiva's students lacked this lofty but essential part of the *chavrusa*.

For this reason, the *Gemara* tells of 12,000 pairs of talmidim, highlighting the lack of sufficient respect accorded to one member of the pair by the other. This lesson is so important that it bears constant reinforcement during *sefira*, which is not only the anniversary of the tragedy, but also the

---

"VeAhavta LeReiacha Kamocha" was originally published in 1999 on TorahWeb.org

period of preparation for the reacceptance of the Torah on *Shavuos*.

Each year during *sefira* we read of the *mitzva* to love one's friend as oneself (*Vayikra* 19:18). The obvious question is raised; how can one be expected to love every Jew as oneself? Rabbi Akiva's famous comment, cited by Rashi, that this *mitzva* is a great rule in the Torah ("*baTorah*"), also requires explanation.

The *Chasam Sofer* raises an additional question. The above statement of Rabbi Akiva seems to contradict his famous ruling (*Bava Metzia* 62a): "Your life takes priority over your friend's." How can this be reconciled with the command to love your friend as yourself?

To answer this question, the *Chasam Sofer* reinterprets the word "*baTorah*" in Rabbi Akiva's first statement. It does not mean that loving a friend is a great rule which is written in the Torah. Rather, it means that it is a great rule concerning the study of the Torah. While in the area of physical survival and attainment one's own life and possessions have priority, in the spiritual realm one must share his Torah knowledge equally with others.

Perhaps this idea can be modified in light of the above. Rabbi Akiva refers to the special *chavrusa* relationship which is critical to the study of Torah. While a person cannot be expected to love every Jew as he loves himself, he must love and honor his *chavrusa* as himself in all ways and at all times, and not only while sharing Torah knowledge. Otherwise, the relationship is not a truly spiritual one, and its members are worthy of punishment for not internalizing the spirituality of Torah. In this respect, Rabbi Akiva's statement reflects the terrible tragedy of his students' deaths, which illustrates the importance of loving one's *chavrusa* as oneself and the catastrophic results of neglecting this command.

The Talmudic passage containing the story of Rabbi Akiva's *talmidim* continues and promises peace to one who loves his wife as himself and honors her more than himself. At first glance, this statement is puzzling. After all, a person is commanded to love everyone as himself. Why, then, is his wife singled out?

In light of the above interpretation of Rabbi Akiva's statement and the deficiency of his students, the answer is clear. Indeed, the command to love one's friend as oneself is limited to a deep spiritual relationship between two people. A man's relationship with his wife must be a spiritual one that reflects the ideals of Torah, and, as such, requires that he love her as himself, and honor her even more than himself (see Rashi). If a husband loves and honors his wife in a way which reflects his recognition of the deep spiritual nature of their relationship, he is promised peace and happiness in marriage. Otherwise, he is doomed to suffer misery and tragedy, just like Rabbi Akiva's students. They did not recognize the full measure of the spiritual nature of their relationship with one another, and as a result, did not love and honor each other sufficiently.

It is perhaps for this reason that the custom evolved to avoid marriages during the *sefira* period. Since other aspects of *aveilus* were not practiced, the establishment of the custom to abstain from marriage was not a form of mourning for the death of Rabbi Akiva's students. Rather, it was felt that this period was not a propitious time for marriage. At a time when the true meaning of a deep one-to-one Torah relationship was ignored, it is not appropriate to begin such a relationship between husband and wife.

While the command to love and honor another as oneself may be limited to one-to-one relationships, it is clear that all relationships based on Torah require mutual love and respect, commensurate with the intensity and spirit of the relationship. Let us attempt to develop appropriate levels of love and honor toward all Jews in general, and toward spouses, parents, *rebbeim* and fellow *talmidim* in particular. In this *zechus*, may we merit a true commemoration of *kabbalas haTorah* and the hastening of our ultimate redemption.

Rabbi Benjamin Yudin

A Reaction Speaks Louder Than Words

The *Shulchan Aruch* (*Orach Chayyim* 493:1) teaches that the custom is not to marry until the 33rd day of the *omer*, for during this time the students of Rabbi Akiva died. The source of this teaching is the Talmud *Yevamos* (62b) that states that Rabbi Akiva had 12 thousand pairs of disciples and they all died during one period, because they did not treat each other with respect. The Talmud further informs us that they died between *Pesach* and *Shavuos*.

I was always troubled by the charge of "they did not treat each other with respect." Does it mean they did not say "good morning" to one another? Intuitively we sense there is more going on. Commenting on the verse "Avraham proceeded and took a wife whose name was Ketura" (*Bereishis* 25:1), the *Midrash Rabba* (61:3) quotes the teaching of *Koheles* (11:6): "in the morning sow your seed and in the evening do not be idle, for you cannot know which will succeed; this or that, or whether both are equally good." Rabbi Yishmael understood the above verse to mean that if one was privileged to study Torah in his youth, he should continue to learn Torah is his old age as well, for one can never be sure of the accuracy of his understanding of Torah. Moreover, Rabbi Akiva, inspired by the verse in *Koheles*, taught that if one was privileged to have many students in his youth, he should continue and have disciples in his old age. Rabbi Akiva, upon losing his 12,000 pairs of students, proceeded to teach Torah to seven students, who later perpetuated the study of Torah for all time. Rabbi Akiva addressed his later students and said, "My sons, my earlier students died as עיניהם צרה אלו באלו, they begrudged and resented one another. Be especially careful not to emulate their misdeeds."

"*Tzarus ayin*" is usually understood in the physical, materialistic

---

" **A Reaction Speaks Louder**" was originally published in 2003 on TorahWeb.org

realm. Too often, one is not happy with the success and accomplishments of the next one. They are bothered that the next person has what they do not. The *Midrash* is shedding light on the students' lack of respect for one another, namely their resentment of each other's spiritual growth and accomplishments. Ideally, "קנאת סופרים תרבה חכמה - jealousy between scholars increases wisdom" (*Bava Basra* 21a). One should say to himself: if that individual can *daven* with *kavana*, abstain from talking during *davening*, have regular *sedarim* with a *chavrusa*, learn *daf yomi*, visit the sick, participate in the *chevra kaddisha* and abstain from *lashon hara*, then so can I!

There is a classic case in the Talmud *Sanhedrin* (102a) where we are taught that despite the many atrocities of Yaravam, *Hashem* seized him by his garment and said to him, "Repent, and I, you and the son of Yishai will stroll together in the Garden of Eden." Thereupon Yaravam said to *Hashem*, "*Mi ba'rosh*? - who will lead the procession?" *Hashem* answered that David would be at the head. Yaravam replied that he was not going. Among other things, Yaravam had *tzarus ayin* toward David. That *Hashem* should recognize David's spiritual accomplishments over Yaravam's was something he could not tolerate. Not only was he not happy and proud of David's success, but his wishing it were not so was a form of diminution of *Hashem*'s honor and glory that David's *avoda* (spiritual growth) had accomplished. Strong condemnation of such *tzarus ayin* is expressed by *Rabbeinu* Yonah in *Sha'arei Teshuva* (3:160). He says that though an individual may be a *talmid chacham* and *shomeir mitzvos*, if he begrudges the success of his colleagues he is termed a *sonei Hashem*, one who shows some hatred toward *Hashem*.

The Talmud (*Sanhedrin* 93b) delves into the psyche of King Saul and concludes that when Doeg informs Saul that "*Hashem* is with him [David]" (*Shmuel* I 16:18), this means that David was the recipient of special Divine assistance, as witnessed by the fact that his views and opinions were established as the accepted *halacha*. Immediately Saul became disheartened and jealous of David. Saul suffered from *tzarus ayin*!

The very antithesis of *tzarus ayin* was Aharon *haKohein*. Moshe was afraid to accept the leadership position in *Bnei Yisrael* lest he offend his older brother Aharon. *Hashem* assures Moshe, "וראך ושמח בלבו – when [Aharon] sees you, he will rejoice in his heart" (*Shemos* 4:14). Aharon possessed "*tuv ayin*," a good eye; he was genuinely happy with the mission and accomplishments of Moshe. *Mishlei* 22:9 teaches, "One with a good eye will be blessed," and Aharon was the beneficiary of his generosity of spirit by receiving the breastplate of the *kohein gadol* upon his generous heart.

This very critical lesson is one that we all need to learn and master. It is not only for the great among our people, as the malady has precipitated the downfall of prestigious institutions of learning. All too often this negativism is found in homes and synagogues. Case in point: A young man or woman attends a yeshiva in Israel post-high school. They attain success in their learning and often return with a more serious attitude and demeanor toward their personal spirituality. They now actually recite blessings before eating, recite *birkas hamazon* slowly from a text, and come to *shul* on time. They find time in their schedule for daily learning of Torah and *chesed* activities. How is this received by their families? Is it encouraged and viewed through the lens of *tov ayin*? Is it *nachas* for parents to see their child advance beyond their own personal station? Or is it met with mocking and sarcastic gestures and language, often a reaction based on feelings of guilt and inadequacy?

Yaakov, in his departing words to Shimon and Levi says, "כי באפם הרגו איש" (*Bereishis* 49:6), translated literally as, "For in their rage they murdered people." Our wise among us were quick to note that *af* also means "nose." Sometimes with only a facial gesture, a turning up of the nose, we can do immeasurable damage to the effect of a speaker's words, and to the positive advances of a spiritual journey. No one said the time of *sefira* was easy!

When Is Every Day a *Mon*-day?

What's in a name? The Torah (*Shemos* 16:36) tells is that an *omer* is a tenth of an *eipha* (a dry measure). Rashi on this verse makes a calculation and informs us that a tenth of an *eipha* is the minimum amount of dough needed for the requirements of taking *challa* and for the *menachos*. What is of special noteworthiness is that the Torah and the Rabbis take note of this weight measurement of *omer* and refer to the *korban* of barley that is brought on the second day of *Pesach* (the 16th of *Nisan*) not as the offering of barley, but as the *korban omer* (*Vayikra* 23:10-12). Moreover, the *mitzva* of counting and connecting the *yom tov* of *Pesach* with that of *Shavuos* is called counting the *omer* (*Sefer HaChinuch, mitzva* 306). Why stress the *omer* in each case, when even regarding the *korban tamid*, brought twice daily, the Torah ordains (*Bamidbar* 28:5) that it be accompanied by a tenth *eipha* of fine flour as a meal offering, with no mention of the *omer*?

Rav Yosef Salant *zt"l*, in his *Be'eir Yosef*, suggests a fascinating answer. He notes that the first time the term *omer* is used in the Torah is in conjunction with the *mon* that miraculously sustained the Jewish nation in the desert for 40 years. Moshe directs them to "gather from it an *omer* per person" (*Shemos* 16:16). Moreover, when Moshe is told to hide and preserve some *mon* so that future generations will be able to actually witness the miracle food, he places an *omer*'s worth of *mon* for safekeeping in the *aron* (*Yoma* 52b). The *Gemara* (*Kiddushin* 38a) teaches that the *mon* stopped falling on the seventh of *Adar*, the day of Moshe's death, since the *mon* fell in his honor. However, unlike the other times that, as the Torah teaches, *mon* which was left overnight became worm-infested and putrid (*Shemos* 16:20), after Moshe's death the remaining *mon* lasted until *Bnei Yisrael* crossed the Jordan, until the 16th of *Nisan*. From then on they ate of the produce of the land.

"When Is Every Day a *Mon*-day?" was originally published in 2005 on TorahWeb.org

It is thus no coincidence that the Torah ordained that the *korban omer*, whose purpose is to thank *Hashem* for His kindness in renewing the harvest (and thus we present Him with this produce prior to our benefiting from it; *Sefer HaChinuch, mitzva* 306) was to be brought on the day the *mon* stopped nourishing us. Thus, the 16th of *Nisan*, the second day of *Pesach*, is the day the *korban omer* was brought.

Our bringing the *korban omer* results in our remembering the *omer* of the *mon*. As the *mon* was המוציא לחם מן השמים, the produce of *Eretz Yisrael* is המוציא לחם מן הארץ. The "*motzi*" is the same. The produce of the Land of Israel represented by the *omer* of barley is no less a Divine blessing than the *omer* of *mon*.

Rav Menachem Mendel of Rimanov suggests a novel interpretation to the name *mon*. When the *mon* descended, the Jewish nation did not know what it was. Referring to the newfound object, they said to one another "*mon hu*" (*Shemos* 16:15). Rav Menachem Mendel learns that "*mon hu*" refers not only to the object of the *mon*, but additionally to the persons who ate the *mon*, as they were constantly being elevated and spiritually uplifted by this Divine nourishment. "*Mon hu*" – *Bnei Yisrael* didn't recognize each other and the positive transformation *mon* had on the people.

Our counting the *omer* from *Pesach* to *Shavuos* is likewise to remind us of the special nourishing food for thought that the *mon* provided. There is no room for jealousy or envy if one believes his sustenance is being provided by *Hashem*. Ben Azzai taught (*Yoma* 38a) "by your name shall they call you, and in your place shall they seat you, and from your own position shall they provide you." Rashi explains that each person's livelihood (*parnasa*) is not a gift of others' goodwill; rather it is the personalized *parnasa* that *Hashem* has allotted to him.

We count the *omer* until *Shavuos*, our time of reaccepting the

Torah and our commitment toward renewed Torah study, as the *omer* itself served in that capacity. The *omer* of *mon* that Moshe hid was removed from its case many hundreds of years later by Yirmeyahu *haNavi*. In response to the excuse of the Jewish people for not studying Torah (that they needed to earn a livelihood) Yirmeyahu said: learn from the *omer* of *mon*; as He sustained them with a minimum effort and exertion, so will He provide for you.

The *omer* teaches: you make time for Him; He'll make time for you.

The *Omer*: Grateful Beyond Measure

We find ourselves in the period of the *omer*. In *Parashas Emor* (*Vayikra* 23:15) we are taught: "You shall count for yourselves, from the morrow of the rest day, when you bring the *omer* of the waving, seven weeks they shall be complete." A few basic questions are in order.

We know that an *omer* is a dry measure. We first encounter the term in conjunction with the *mon* (*Shemos* 16:16): "This is the thing that *Hashem* has commanded, gather from it for every man according to what he eats, an *omer* per person." Why, then, is the *korban* brought on the second day of *Pesach* known as the *korban omer*? Yes, an *omer*'s worth of barley was brought as a *korban*, but it seems strange that it should be called "the dry measure *korban*." Moreover, in the *beracha* instituted prior to the counting why not say "*vetzivanu al sefiras shavuos*, and He commanded us to count weeks," for indeed we are counting the weeks to the holiday of *Shavuos*; why do we instead say "*al sefiras ha'omer*, to count the *omer*"?

Rav Yaakov Tzvi Mecklenburg *zt"l* in his *HaKesav VeHaKabbala* offers a novel, fresh interpretation. He says that we should not focus on the *omer* as a dry measure, but rather as it is used in *Devarim* 24:7: "If a man is

---

"The *Omer*: Grateful Beyond..." was originally published in 2010 on TorahWeb.org

found kidnapping a person of his brethren, among the Children of Israel, *vehisamer bo* [and he enslaves him or subjugates him] and sells him, that kidnapper shall die and you shall remove the evil from your midst."

The word *omer* means to subjugate, and that is the application and understanding in relation to this time, the *korban*, and the *mitzva* of counting. The Torah refers to the *korban omer* in *Vayikra* 2:14 as a "*minchas bikkurim* – a meal offering of the first grain to *Hashem*." When people are blessed with prosperity, represented by the first grain, there is always the possibility of erroneously attributing the success of their labor to themselves, as the Torah cautions in *Devarim* 8:17, "And you may say in your heart, my strength and the might of my hand brought me all this wealth." Therefore, the Torah mandates that the *kohein* take the *omer* of barley and wave it in all directions, to indicate that this produce and bounty came from *Hashem*.

In addition, the designation of this time as "*omer*," as, for example, the title of chapter 493 of *Shulchan Aruch Orach Chayyim* is "the laws applicable in the days of the *omer*," may be interpreted in light of the above as days of subjugation, or our willingness to yield to a Higher Authority. Thus, for each individual, starting with the second day of *Pesach*, a psychological and intellectual commitment is being reinforced by their personal counting of the *omer*. In a sense, one is declaring, "count me in." This also sheds light on the *minhag Yisrael* to study *Pirkei Avos* during this time of *omer*, providing concrete formulae of true *omer* – subjugation to *Hashem*.

The *Gemara* (*Shabbos* 31a) explains the verse from *Yeshayahu* 33:6, "והיה אמונת עתיך..." as referring to the six sections of the *Mishna*. "*Emunas*" refers to the section of *Zeraim*, which deals almost exclusively with the agricultural laws of *Eretz Yisrael*. It is called "*emunas* – faith," explains the *Yerushalmi*, because the farmer who sows his seeds places his faith in *Hashem*. The subsequent teaching by Rava is that when each individual is brought before the heavenly tribunal for judgment, they will be asked: (a) Did you conduct your business honestly, or, more precisely, with faith? (b) Did you set aside fixed times for Torah study? For if one believes that his business success or livelihood is from *Hashem*, then it follows that he was afforded this blessing to enable him to set fixed times for Torah study. This is one form of the subjugation of the *omer* period.

In *Parashas Emor*, each holiday is presented and its specific laws taught in a paragraph dedicated exclusively to that holiday. The paragraph of *Shavuos*, however, concludes (*Vayikra* 23:22) with a description of seemingly irrelevant agricultural gifts to the poor such as leaving the corner of the field (*peah*) for the poor to harvest themselves and leaving the fallen gleanings of the harvest (*leket*) for the poor. The paragraph of *Shavuos* concludes this way because these laws embody the message of the *omer*. If the produce is mine, the result of my knowledge, expertise and farming acumen, then why should I necessarily share my produce with the less fortunate? However, if I recognize and acknowledge that it all comes from On High, I subjugate myself to His higher authority, and His requiring the dispensing of my assets to the poor and needy is very much in place. A greater commitment to needs of others and of the community is an implementation of the true character and essence of the *omer*.

Love Is Blind, but Respect Can't Be

In *Parashas Emor* we not only read about *sefiras ha'omer*, but we are in the middle of its observance. Ramban (*Vayikra* 23:36), teaches that from the Torah the days between *Pesach* and *Shavuos* are understandably happy days; these are days of anticipation, yearning and excitement. We are counting from our liberation to relive the moment of His revelation to

---

"Love Is Blind, but Respect Can't Be" was originally published in 2017 on TorahWeb.org

an entire nation, something which was and is unprecedented in the annals of world history. Our Rabbis remind us (Rashi, *Bereishis* 1:1) that the very purpose of creation was the giving of the Torah.

The Talmud (*Yevamos* 62b) teaches that the 24,000 students of Rabbi Akiva died during this period of *sefiras ha'omer*, and for this reason the *Shulchan Aruch* (*Orach Chayyim* 493:1-2) legislates some mournful observances, including no weddings and no haircuts during 33 days of the *omer*. The cause of their dying is given as "לא נהגו כבוד זה לזה – they did not show adequate respect for one another." The *Mesillas Yesharim* (chapter 22) takes this most literally, accusing them of a lack of *derech eretz*, *mentchlechkeit*, which is a prerequisite for Torah as taught by our Rabbis; "דרך ארץ קדמה לתורה." This is found as well in *Avos* (3:17) where Rabbi Elazar ben Azarya taught, "If there is no respect, there is no Torah," and *Rabbeinu* Yona teaches that one has to refine one's character as a prerequisite for Torah.

Maharsha understands this deficiency to be specifically in the realm of *talmud Torah*. Instead of praising one another for their unique understanding, contribution and *cheilek* in Torah, Rabbi Akiva's students viewed each other as threats and competition to their individual self-worth.

I'd like to suggest an explanation of their lack of *kavod* one to another, based upon the teaching of the *Sheim MiShmuel*. He is bothered, as are we, by the following: how is it possible for a lack of respect to exist among Rabbi Akiva's students, who not only heard the teaching of their great *rebbe* that ואהבת לרעך כמוך is a fundamental principle of the Torah, but observed Rabbi Akiva, who lived and personified this teaching as well. The Talmud (*Shabbos* 127b) describes the extraordinary character of a worker, and the *Sheiltos* (*Parashas Shemos*) ascribes this story to Rabbi Akiva. How is it possible that Rabbi Akiva's students would be deficient in this area?

The *Sheim MiShmuel* answers that there is a significant difference between love and respect. Love is an emotion that most often emerges from and pervades a natural organism. There is love within the family unit as they are just that, a unit. Love stems from the commonality that individuals share together. Thus, the students of Rabbi Akiva followed the sacred teaching of their *rebbe* and loved all Jews. The Jewish people share a common pedigree, history and destiny, all of which contribute to unite them and, in addition, the Torah commands them to love one another.

Respect, on the other hand emerges not from commonality, but the reverse. One notices the unique features that mark someone's individuality and admires these positive traits, and consciously or subconsciously desires to emulate these qualities. In order for respect to emerge and prevail, one must note how a person is different and shines above others in this particular realm. The students of Rabbi Akiva followed their teacher and his teaching to a fault. Their intense love for every Jew led them to relax any and all formality, and they viewed each *talmid* as being on par with all the other *talmidim*. This caused them to overlook the unique strengths of each, thus missing the opportunity to develop a desire to emulate that uniqueness and thereby be driven to grow, and for individual recognition and respect to emerge.

Note that the Torah, in the fifth of the *Aseres HaDibros*, does not legislate loving a parent, because it is natural to love a parent. The Torah does, however, command a child to respect a parent, for often the child will not necessarily adopt the same ideologies and lifestyle, but nevertheless, the child is to respect his parents' unique traits.

The students of Rabbi Akiva failed to recognize and learn from each other. Sad to say, we repeat the tragic mistakes of our past. Ideally, we too love all Jews, and this is the easy part. However, even within the Orthodox community, there are the divisions of modern, *yeshivish* and *chasidish*, and too often we might love them all and yet fail to sufficiently note and implement the many noble and distinguishing character traits of the other groups. Our instinctive, immediate dismissal of their identifying outer trappings too often precludes us from considering and incorporating their many positive virtues. This might well be characterized as "לא נהגו כבוד זה לזה," as not showing respect one for another.

The same page of Talmud that condemns the students of Rabbi Akiva continues and presents the ideals of marriage. A husband is to "love his wife as himself, and respect her more than himself." This is precisely what the *Sheim MiShmuel* has been teaching. The couple shares love as a single unit, but must respect the distinguishing traits of their spouse.

Reb Elimelech of Lizhensk, one of the outstanding Chasidic leaders of the 18th century, was wont to pray that we should see, appreciate and emulate the worth of others, thereby not only loving them as part of *Klal Yisrael*, but also respecting them for their individuality. May we follow in his footsteps in both prayer and deed.

Shavuos

Rabbi Hershel Schachter

Why Was the Torah Forced upon Us?

Before God was prepared to give His Torah to the Jewish people, He first wanted to know whether we were prepared to accept it. With great enthusiasm, the Jews expressed their desire to both accept and observe all of the laws of the Torah. Then, according to Talmudic tradition (*Shabbos* 88a), God pressured the Jewish people to accept the Torah, and forced it upon them against their wishes.

The commentaries on the Talmud all wonder, why it was necessary to force the Torah upon the Jews if they had already enthusiastically expressed their willingness to accept it? The *Midrash Tanchuma* (to *Parashas Noach*) elaborates upon this *aggada* and distinguishes between the different parts of the Torah. The people were prepared to accept both God's written Torah and all the הלכות למשה מסיני – laws transmitted directly from God. Their response to Moshe was that "כל אשר דבר ה' נעשה -that all that **God** has said we are prepared to accept." But the bulk of the Oral Torah is really what the Talmud and Rambam refer to as "*divrei soferim,*" *halachos* which were developed over the centuries with much rabbinic input. The rabbis were licensed to employ the various מידות שהתורה נדרשת בהן, to read "in between the lines," so to speak, of the Torah in order to present a fuller picture of each of the *mitzvos*. This the Jews at *Har Sinai* were **not** prepared to accept. They felt that this was not Divine! This is a **human** Torah, and all humans can err. Why should they agree to be subservient to the ideas of other human beings? Who says that another is so much more intelligent than I? Each Jew should be entitled to interpret the law according to his own understanding!

And it was this part of the Torah that God had to force upon us. Whether we like it or not, God expects us to follow the positions set

---

"Why Was the Torah Forced upon Us?" was originally published in 2004 on TorahWeb.org

forth by the rabbis in interpreting the Torah. Not until years later, after the story of *Purim* occurred, did the Jewish people as a whole fully accept this aspect of rabbinic authority. It was at that time that Ezra and the *Anshei Keneses HaGedola* set up the entire system of the Torah *shebe'al peh* as we know it today. They formulated the text for all blessings and prayers, *kiddush* and *havdala*, the system of 39 categories of *melacha*, etc., along with many rabbinic enactments. *Klal Yisrael* at the period of the beginning of the Second Temple wholeheartedly accepted all of these formulations and innovations of their *rabbanim*.[29]

This is the significance of the expression we use (from Rambam's formulation), that we believe (*ani ma'amin*) that the Torah **as it is observed today**, is an accurate transmission of that Divine Torah which was given to Moshe *Rabbeinu*. This added phrase, "as it is observed today," implies exactly this idea – to include all of those *halachos* in which there was rabbinic input. We have "*emunas chachamim*." We believe that throughout all of the generations there was an invisible Divine assistance given to the rabbis to develop the *halacha* in a correct fashion.

The Talmud (*Menachos* 29b) records an *aggada* that when God showed Moshe *Rabbeinu* a vision of the rabbis of future generations, Moshe became troubled by seeing Rabbi Akiva. By the time of Rabbi Akiva, the *halacha* had already so developed that it seemed to Moshe as if this were not really the Torah he was given. Moshe was very upset over the distortion, until he heard a student ask Rabbi Akiva for the source of a certain *halacha*, and Rabbi Akiva responded that that was a "הלכה למשה מסיני." In other words, all of the Torah, even in the days of Rabbi Akiva and even today, is a legitimate development of *Toras Moshe*, based on the use of the *middos*, and therefore everything is implicitly "included" in what was given to Moshe. He was given the text with the *middos*, and when applying these

---

[29] See essays by Rav Moshe Zvi Neriah in *Meoros Neriah, Purim*, pp. 164-171.

middos to the text, all the details of the *halacha* as we know it today follow automatically. The *middos* simply guide the Rabbis in their task of reading "in between the lines," in order to obtain a fuller picture of each *mitzva*.

In the *beracha* one recites after an *aliya*, we praise God for having given us His *Toras emes*, which is a reference to the text of the Torah *shebichsav*, as well as for having implanted in our midst (*"nata besocheinu"*) the ability to further develop the "living" Torah (*"chayyei olam"*) with the aid of the *middos* and through rabbinic input (see *Orach Chayyim* 149:10, and Gra, nos. 27, 28). This *beracha* was composed after the period of the *Anshei Keneses HaGedola*, at which time *Klal Yisrael* came to realize – without any coercion – the immense value of the "*divrei soferim*"; that the ability to have rabbinic input is what keeps the Torah in constant touch with an ever-changing world.[30]

Of course, the application of those *middos* is a science unto itself, which is only mastered by a small handful of qualified individuals in each generation. And the new additional *halachos* that read "in between the lines" have to fit in with the spirit of the rest of the Torah, which again can only be fully sensed by those few qualified individuals who have a proper sense of what the spirit of the law is!

Is God Still Talking to Us?

One *Shabbos* morning, students came to the *beis midrash* for *Shacharis* and there was a strange-looking fellow, obviously not a student, and obviously mentally ill, putting on *tefillin*. It didn't seem as though he

---

[30] See *Masseches Soferim* (16:5): If the entire Torah had been committed to writing, and had been (so to speak) "etched in stone," and there would not have been any rabbinic input, the rabbis of the later generations would not have had any way to keep the "living" Torah in touch with the changing world.

"Is God Still Talking to Us?" was originally published in 2006 on TorahWeb.org

simply had not realized that it was *Shabbos*, so we all stayed away from him. When Rav Dovid Lifshitz arrived, he walked over to the young man and spoke to him softly in Hebrew. He pointed out that it was *Shabbos* and *tefillin* are not worn. The young man responded that he knows that, but he had received a *nevua* (a prophecy) that he should wear *tefillin* today, despite the fact that it was *Shabbos*! Reb Dovid was not fazed by his reply. He simply continued the conversation and asked, "In what language was this *nevua*?" The young man replied, "In English." Whereupon Rav Dovid told him softly, "You must be mistaken. *Nevuos* are only given in Hebrew." Whereupon the young man thanked him for his clarification and proceeded to remove his *tefillin*.

We were stunned watching all of this! You have to master abnormal psychology to be able to convince a *meshugena* that he's wrong. The *pasuk* in *Sefer Melachim* I 5:11 says that King Shlomo was blessed with wisdom, and was "wiser than any other person." The Rabbis understand this to imply "אפילו מן השוטים" – that he was even wiser than the *meshugaim*!!

God gave His Torah and promised that He would supply us from time to time with prophets to guide us (*Devarim* 18:15). When מעמד הר סיני is described, the Torah says (*Devarim* 5:18) that *Hashem* spoke to the Jewish people in a loud booming voice ("*kol gadol*"), and He did not stop ("*velo yasaf*"). The Rabbis (*Shemos Rabba* 28) understand this to refer to the fact that God continues to communicate with us, both through the prophets as well as through the *talmidei chachamim*.

But not every person who sets himself up as a "*navi*" is to be listened to. Our tradition (see Rambam, *Hilchos Yesodei HaTorah* chap. 7) has prerequisites that must be met before one qualifies to be recognized as a *navi*. Likewise, our tradition has guidelines regarding the substance of the prophecy (ibid., chap. 8-10). If one tells us that he has received a prophecy to permanently do away with any one of the *mitzvos*, or to worship *avoda zara* even if only temporarily, we know that he is a false prophet.

Similarly, there are guidelines regarding a rabbi rendering a halachic view. There is room for *chiddush*, but no room for *shinnui*. One of the 13 principles of our faith is that the Torah laws cannot change. But at the same time, the *Midrash* tells us (see *Yalkut Shimoni* to *Sefer Shoftim* 5:8) that *HaKadosh Baruch Hu* cherishes *chiddushei Torah*, and it is for that reason that the *talmidei chachamim* engage in *milchamta shel Torah*, in order to come up with such *chiddushim*. It is a fine line that distinguishes between *chiddush* and *shinnui*.[31]

If a learned, God-fearing individual comes up with original insights by applying the מידות שהתורה נדרשת בהן which were transmitted by the Torah *shebe'al peh*, then we have the right to assume that God is is still communicating with us via the *pesak* of the rabbi. And the *pesak* of the rabbi is binding because we believe that "God will reveal His secrets to those who fear Him" (*Tehillim* 25:14; see *Sotah* 4b).

When the Torah (*Shemos* 20:1) describes the proclamation of the Ten Commandments, the expression used is that "God spoke **all** of these words (**kol hadevarim**)," and our tradition has it that the word *kol* is referring to the fact that everything intelligent that any future *talmid chacham* comes up with was implicitly included in the Torah that God gave us at *Har Sinai*.

When Rambam formulates what he considers to be the 13 principles of our faith (*Sanhedrin, Perek Chelek*) he writes that not only do we believe that at one time (מעמד הר סיני) God revealed Himself to us and gave us His Torah, but also that the Torah **as we observe it today** is *min haShamayim*. There are individuals who consider themselves Orthodox

---

[31] See Rav Soloveitchik's *The Halachic Mind*, footnote 98.

who believe that at one time the Jewish people did have a Divine Torah, but the *amoraim* misunderstood the *tannaim*, the *rishonim* misunderstood the Talmud, and the *acharonim* misunderstood the *rishonim*. "But don't get me wrong," they would say, "I'm Orthodox! And therefore I feel that the laws of the *Shulchan Aruch* are all binding, even though I think everything is in error." This is not the Orthodox position. If one is really convinced that a certain *pesak* is in error, he is not permitted to follow it.[32] To err is **human**, and a *Shulchan Aruch* which is full of mistakes is a **man-made** Torah as opposed to a Divine one. Rav Chaim of Volozhin was fond of signing off his *teshuvos*, "the God of truth gave us a Torah of truth, and our eyes are only focused on the truth."

We believe that God protects His Torah from errors. Any mistakes made over the years by *poskim* will ultimately be corrected. The *pesak* of the rabbis is binding because we have the right to assume that God has, behind the scenes, "revealed His secrets to those who fear Him."

The story is told of Rav Yechezkel Landau, author of the *Sheilos uTeshuvos Noda BeYehuda*, that on one occasion he was presented with a *"shayla"* in *hilchos treifos*. After thinking for a few moments, he insisted that the *shayla* was not real, that the organ of the animal must have been tampered with after the *shechita*. When the guilty *ba'al habayis* finally admitted to the charge, Rabbi Landau explained how he knew: for many years whenever he would *pasken* a *shayla*, he would have a very comfortable and confident feeling that he had received assistance from heaven to *pasken* correctly. On this occasion, even though he had formulated a clear-cut halachic opinion, he did not feel comfortable issuing his *pesak*. He felt that on this occasion he was not receiving any heavenly assistance, and he

---

[32] It goes without saying that when evaluating a *pesak*, one must factor in any discrepancy between his own knowledge and qualifications vs. those of the *posek* espousing the *pesak* in question, and what such a discrepancy may indicate regarding which person is the one who is in error.

wondered why. He quickly came to the conclusion that Divine assistance not to err in *pesak* is a miracle of sorts, and God is not in the practice of performing miracles unnecessarily. Obviously in this instance there was no need for any heavenly assistance; the *shayla* was a fake!

I recently read a fascinating article encouraging the Conservative movement to adopt as its new slogan the slogan of some Christian group: "God is still speaking." The writer states that she is a Conservative Jew because she believes this to be true, that God is still speaking. And she concludes her essay with the complaint, "why do so many Conservative leaders seem too often to be listening only to what God said to generations past?" (*Jewish Week,* May 12, 2006, pg. 27).

This has always been the position of the Orthodox. That's where all of the *chiddush* is. God is still speaking to us through the rabbis' further development of the *Torah shebe'al peh*. But just as we only follow the instructions of a prophet if who he is and what he has to say are within certain bounds; so too the rabbis are entitled, and indeed encouraged, to be "*mechaddeish*" if what they have to say is within the bounds of the *middos* of the Torah *shebe'al peh*.

The *Mishna* in *Avos* tells us that God created the entire world with ten pronouncements. The *Chafetz Chayyim* pointed out (*Sefer Chomas Hadas,* chap. 11) that the Rabbis of the Talmud felt that whatever was initially created directly by the word of God was stronger, healthier and better than the offspring of that initial creation. Tradition has it (see Rashi to *Bereishis* 1:21) that after *mashiach* comes, there will be a *seuda* for the *tzaddikim*, and the *livyasan* will be served. This refers to the original fish created by God's words. Although that fish will have been preserved for over 5000 years, it is assumed that it will be either tastier or healthier than any of its offspring, even though they are fresher.

Similarly, the Rabbis say (*Berachos* 34b) that at that meal for the *tzaddikim*, special wine will be served, made from the original grapes created (during the six days of creation) directly by the word of God. Wouldn't it make more sense to make some wine from freshly grown grapes? Obviously the Rabbis' tradition was that those original grapes, created directly by the word of God, were superior to any others.

The Talmud (*Avoda Zara* 8a) transmits a tradition that Adam *haRishon* brought as a sacrifice the original ox created by the word of God. That animal was obviously considered "the choice," to be preferred over any of its offspring.

With respect to Torah, however, this is not the case. We do not consider those laws of the Torah directly dictated by God to Moshe *Rabbeinu* as more important than the laws developed by the rabbis of the later generations. King David says in *Tehillim* 119:72, "...טוב לי תורת פיך," that the Torah from God's mouth is to be preferred over thousands of gold or silver pieces. Does the Torah "from God's mouth" refer only to the text of the *Chumash* dictated word for word and letter for letter by God? Rav Chaim of Volozhin pointed to the story related in *Gittin* 6b that two *amoraim* expressed differing views regarding the biblical story of the *pilegesh beGiva*. Soon after, Rav Avyasar met Eliyahu *haNavi* who told him that just then *HaKadosh Baruch Hu* was also learning that *parasha* in *Sefer Shoftim*, and He Himself said over the two suggestions of the two *amoraim*. Apparently, any honest, intelligent *chiddush* which a later *talmid chacham* comes up with will also become "תורת פיך" by virtue of the fact that *HaKadosh Baruch Hu* will say it over also.

The "Giving" of the Torah

In our *tefillos* we refer to Shavuos as זמן מתן תורתנו. *Hashem* gave us

---

"The "Giving" of the Torah" was originally published in 2011 on TorahWeb.org

the Torah as a gift (a *matana*). When one gives someone a gift, he no longer owns it and the recipient now becomes the "*ba'al habayis*." When *Hashem* "gave" us the Torah we became the *ba'alei batim*. The Talmud relates (*Temura* 16a) that after *Moshe Rabbeinu* passed away, several thousand *halachos* were forgotten. The people approached Yehoshua, as they had always approached Moshe *Rabbeinu* during the previous 40 years, and requested that he ask *Hashem* what the correct *halacha* was. Yehoshua replied, "לא בשמים היא", that the one and only *navi* to whom *Hashem* told *halachos* was Moshe *Rabbeinu*.

This idea is implied by the closing *pasuk* both in *Sefer Vayikra* and *Sefer Bamidbar*. The Talmud (*Megilla* 2b; see Maharsha) understands the language of these *pesukim* to imply that only Moshe was given prophecy regarding matters of *halacha*. All other *nevi'im* were only told matters of *hora'as sha'a* (issues of a temporary nature, as opposed to *halachos* which are binding throughout all generations).

This is the meaning of the seventh principle of faith (in Rambam's listing of the 13 *ikarei ha'emuna*).[33] The *Zohar* mentions that Moshe *Rabbeinu* represents Torah *shebichsav*, because he always received direct dictation from *Hashem* regarding all matters of *halacha*. This is why the *Chumash* is referred to as "*Toras Moshe*" at the end of *Sefer Malachi*, because everything was dictated to Moshe word for word and letter for letter.[34] Moshe is therefore called "ספרא רבה דישראל – the great scribe of the Jewish people." All other *nevi'im* and *talmidei chachamim* must figure out the *halacha* on their own. The Jewish people are the *ba'alei batim* over the Torah!

The Talmud (*Bava Metzia* 76a) relates that on one occasion there was a dispute between *HaKadosh Baruch Hu* and the angels regarding a certain matter of *halacha*. Because the Torah had been "given" to the Jewish

---

[33] See the end of the first chapter of Rav Yosef Dov Soloveitchik's *hespeid* for his uncle Rav Yitzchak Ze'ev Soloveitchik (*Divrei Hagus VeHa'aracha* pp. 65-68).

[34] This is why the rabbis derive *halachos* from the fact that words in the *Chumash* are written with an extra letter or missing a letter.

people, they (*Hashem* and the angels) felt that the question must be submitted to a rabbi who was an expert in the field for a final decision. Rabba sided with *HaKadosh Baruch Hu* (in the last halachic decision he made before his death). Rambam (end of *Hilchos Tzaraas*) has not accepted Rabba's view, and *paskens* against the *Ribbono Shel Olam*! Isn't that odd? The *Kesef Mishneh* explains that this is based on לא בשמים היא. The *Ribbono Shel Olam* Himself instructed us that revelations of His will outside the context of the *mesora* we were given on *Har Sinai* are not relevant in determining the *halacha ledoros*. He made us the *baalei batim* over the Torah, and halachic issues must be decided by human *talmidei chachamim*.

We are only the *baalei batim* over deciding Torah matters within the bounds of the מידות שהתורה נדרשת בהן. Even in the area of establishing the Jewish calendar (as well as *kiddush hachodesh* and *ibbur shana*), where we have a principle that "אתם אפילו מוטעין", that even if the *beis din* declared *rosh chodesh* in error, their *pesak* still stands, our control is only within certain bounds; no month can have fewer than 29 days or more than 30 days, and no year can have fewer than 12 or more than 13 months.

Talmidei chachamim should be aware of the great responsibility which was placed upon them when they were tasked with determining what the *halacha* should be. This awareness should result in their making halachic decisions with a proper degree of seriousness.

"Anochi"

The *Gemara* (*Shabbos* 105a) points out several places in the Torah where we find *roshei teivos*. Rabbi Yochanan says that one such place is the opening word of the *Aseres HaDibros*, "*Anochi*," which is an acronym for "אנא נפשי כתבית יהבית – I have given you My soul by writing down and giving you the

---

"Anochi" was originally published in 2015 on TorahWeb.org

Torah." Our tradition has it that the Torah is not merely a collection of *mitzvos*, but by means of a *mashal* is a description of *Hashem*'s essence. *Ma'amad Har Sinai* consisted of a *gilui Shechina* not only in the sense that there was a heavenly light shining at the time (see *Moreh Nevuchim* I:64), but also because *HaKadosh Baruch Hu* "revealed Himself" to us (*gilui Shechina*) by giving us the laws of His Torah, a description of *Elokus*, His soul.

Rashi (*Shemos* 21:13) quotes the *midrash* interpreting the phrase (*Shmuel* I 24:13) "משל הקדמוני" as referring to the Torah. The entire Torah is a *mashal* of *HaKadosh Baruch Hu*, who is "the Ancient One," since He was around before the world was brought into existence. This is the rationale behind the principle of faith, articulated by Rambam, that the laws of the Torah are immutable. The *Navi* (*Malachi* 3:6) tells us that although everything that was created is always changing, the essence of *Hashem* never changes. Therefore it follows that since the Torah is a description of the essence of *Hashem*, the *mitzvos* of the Torah can also never change. This is also the reason that the opening *pesukim* in *kerias Shema* tell us that the way to develop a love for *Hashem* is to learn His Torah. When we get to understand His soul better, we can develop a greater love for Him; to the extent that one gets to know Him, one can come to love Him.

Every morning when we recite the special *berachos* before learning Torah, we ask of *HaKadosh Baruch Hu* that by learning His Torah we should all get to know "His name," since the entire Torah is a description of Him, which is the same as "His name." The reason the *chachmei hamasora* included this concept into the text of *birchos haTorah* is the that entire institution of *birchos haTorah* is derived (*Berachos* 21a) from the *pasuk* "when I mention the name of *Hashem*, everyone give praise to our God" (*Devarim* 32:3), and the *chachamim* knew that "the name of *Hashem*" is a reference to the entire Torah (see introduction to *Sefer Ginas Egoz*).[35]

---

[35] For further discussion of this idea by Rav Schachter, see the following divrei Torah: "Torah and Nevuah" "Ego and Humility in Torah Study" "Interacting Directly With Hashem" and "In the Pursuit of Happiness" on TorahWeb.org.

*Rabbi Eliakim
Koenigsberg*

The Individual and the Community

In *Parashas Bamidbar*, the Jewish people are counted by "תולדתם למשפחתם לבית אבתם במספר שמות"; each *shevet*, each family, each individual. After the Torah enumerates each of the *shevatim*, it then gives the sum total of all of them. Why does the Torah have to be so lengthy and repeat the same formula for each *shevet* over and over again? And why does it have to give the sum total at the end?

Rashi writes at the beginning of *Parashas Shemos* that *Klal Yisrael* is compared to the stars, about which the *pasuk* says, "המוציא במספר צבאם לכלם בשם יקרא – He brings forth their hosts by number; He calls each of them by name" (*Yeshayahu* 40:26). There are billions of stars in the universe, but *Hashem* calls each one by its own name, because each one has a specific purpose. The same is true with *Klal Yisrael*. While *Hashem* counts the entire Jewish people as one large group, He also counts each individual, because He cares about each and every Jew. He values each one; He cherishes each one. No one is just a number. Every Jew has a special name because each one has a unique role to play in this world.

"Do not belittle any person... because there is no one who does not have his time" (*Avos* 4:3). The *Mishna* teaches that we should treat every person with respect, because everyone has something to contribute to the world; every person has his moment to shine (*Tiferes Yisrael*). But at the same time, it is important for each individual to realize that standing alone diminishes one's effectiveness to accomplish. This could be what Hillel meant when he said, "If I will not care for myself, then who will care for me; but by myself, what am I worth?" (*Avos* 1:14). While every individual certainly has value, when he is part of a *tzibbur* his value increases exponentially, because together with others, he can achieve so much more.

"**The Individual and the Community**" was originally published in 2016 on TorahWeb.org

In *Parashas Bamidbar*, the Torah counts the Jewish people *bemispar sheimos*. It counts each *shevet* one by one to show how much *Hashem* cares about the *sheim*, the special name, of each and every individual. But then it gives the sum total, the *mispar*, of all the *Bnei Yisrael*, to demonstrate that the whole is greater than the sum of its parts, because when all the individuals of *Klal Yisrael* join together, they can accomplish so much more as a community.

This perhaps is one reason why *Parashas Bamidbar* is always read before *Shavuos* – to highlight the idea that *talmud Torah* is for every individual, not just for a select few. But in order for each individual to accomplish the most in his Torah learning, he should not study alone. Rather, he should learn together with others (*Berachos* 63b).

We say at the end of the *Shemoneh Esrei*, "ותן חלקנו בתורתך". We ask that we be given our own special portion in Torah. But only by learning together with others will we maximize our accomplishments in Torah and achieve our full potential.

Rabbi Yaakov Neuburger

From Censure to Sinai:
A Fresh Look at *Shavuos*

Why are we doubling up so many *parshiyos*, and why between *Pesach* and *Shavuos*? The answer takes us back to the time of Ezra, who reestablished the Jewish community in Israel and prepared the way for the rebuilding of the *Beis HaMikdash*. Amongst much other legislation, Ezra and his *beis din* mandated that we read the *tocheicha* (*parasha* of rebuke) of *Bechukosai* before the celebration of *Shavuos*, and this year we had to play "catch-up" in order to maintain that rule (*Megilla* 31b). Interestingly, according to Ramban, this *tocheicha* describes the Diaspora between the two commonwealths, the Diaspora that Ezra was bringing to a close at that time.

Indeed, our time-honored custom to initiate the annual Torah reading cycle after *Sukkos* is probably a result of various similar legislations of Ezra. It was Ezra who established that we read the *tocheicha* of *Ki Savo*, focusing on our present Diaspora, before *Rosh HaShana*. Ezra's mandated timing of the two *tocheicha* readings, together with the *minhag* of reading *Va'eschanan* after *Tisha beAv*, work very well with beginning *Bereishis* after *Sukkos*.

Nevertheless we should appreciate that Ezra most likely established the reading of *Bechukosai* before *Shavuos* much like the way that we read *Zachor* before *Purim* and *Parah* before *Pesach*. The *Gemara* (*Megilla* 31b) explains that both *Rosh HaShana* and *Shavuos* are days of judgment, and Ezra determined that we should read a *tocheicha*, a lengthy rebuke, before a day of judgment. In doing so, the community prays that any evil decreed on the last day of judgment should terminate with the end of the year governed by that day, and that the current day of judgment should usher in months

---

"From Censure to Sinai:...." was originally published in 2012 on TorahWeb.org

replete with only blessings. It is not unlike the *simanim* that we eat on *Rosh HaShana* night, which symbolically enhance our prayers for a sweet year.

In order to establish that *Shavuos* is in fact a day of judgment, the *Gemara* refers us to the practice of bringing the double loaves of bread in the *Beis HaMikdash* (*Rosh Hashana* 16a). These two loaves were baked from the new wheat harvest and initiated its usage in the *Mikdash*. *Chazal* understood this service as a prayer for the success of our upcoming fruit season. After all, in *Gan Eden*, the wheat stood as tall as a tree and delivered ready-made fresh rolls, much as apples grow on apple trees. By taking the initial harvest and dedicating it to the service of *Hashem*, explains Rav Chaim Friedlander (*Sifsei Chayyim* vol. 1), we present ourselves as people who will use every *beracha* in the service of *Hashem*. In that merit and with that kind of attitude, we hope we will earn *Hashem*'s grace.

However, aside from decorating the *shul* with greenery, which according to some is to remind us of the impending judgment, very little focuses us on the *yom tov* as a *yom hadin*. There is no "*hineni*," no *Tefillas Tal* or *Geshem*, no *kittel* nor *Yamim Noraim nussach*. Perhaps this has led others to find a deeper connection between judgment, holiday, censure and Sinai.

Truthfully, I had not in the past paid much attention to a very brief Rashi (*Vayikra* 26:4) commenting on the blessings that precede the rebuke in this week's *parasha*. Rashi, as is his wont, addresses a subtle change of nuance in the *pesukim*. There we are promised that the trees will give their fruit, whereas when it comes to rain, *Hashem* says He will give the rains without using the clouds or any other medium. Rashi remarks that this inconsistency records that all trees, even non-fruit-bearing trees, will, if we merit, return to their state in *Gan Eden*. Indeed, a remarkable *midrash* on these *pesukim* spells this out as well.

Consequently, the trees in blessing and rebuke, and therefore in judgment as well, not only convey *Hashem*'s bestowal of commercial and agricultural success and the improvement of communal prosperity. Far more important, the non-fruit-bearing trees, and the wheat stalks, stand witness to our lack of merit and readiness for messianic times which will return the world to its original *Gan Eden* purpose and profile.

Accordingly, the judgment of *Shavuos* should launch the most pervasive and piercing exploration. Do we really yearn to see Eden-like foliage, rolls on wheat trees and fruits on willow branches? Perhaps the greenery in the *shul* was meant to inspire that thought. Should the world once again stand still waiting to hear נעשה ונשמע, would it indeed endure? When we celebrate the day that gave creation meaning and purpose, do our attitudes and practices still hold that same promise that they did some three thousand years ago?

Thus we read *Bechukosai* to conclude the year governed by last *Shavuos* as our prayer that the judgment of last year, which found us unworthy of those trees and its fruit, should indeed be last year's decree, and that this year, in the wee hours of *Shavuos* night when so many Jews are studying *Hashem*'s Torah, He will find us all longing for and worthy of the greatest blessing of all.

Rabbi Michael Rosensweig

Shavuos: Celebrating Human Responsibility and Involvement in the Giving and Receiving of the Torah

The Torah's treatment of *chag haShavuos* relative to its presentation of the other festivals is absolutely unique. *Shavuos* is the only one of the holidays that is not given a traditional name connected with a specific theme or salient performance associated with that holiday (such as *chag hasukkos, chag hamatzos*). In *Parashas Re'eh*, the Torah does designate the festival as *chag haShavuos* (see also the formulation in *Pinchas*), but does not explicate the significance of this title. Moreover, *Shavuos* is also the only holiday whose purpose is not explicated. The *mesora*, reflected in our *tefilla, birkas hamazon* and *kerias haTorah*, links it with the anniversary of the giving of the Torah, but it is particularly striking that this critical fact is not explicated in the Torah itself. Why would the Torah omit this central theme? Moreover, the *Gemara* (*Shabbos* 88a) records a debate regarding the exact date of *matan Torah*. According to the view of R. Yosi, the Torah was actually revealed on the seventh of *Sivan*, a day after *Shavuos*! (See *Tosafos Avoda Zara* 3a, *Magen Avraham Orach Chayyim* 496, and *Teshuvos Rivash* no. 96.) It is astonishing that the date of *gilui Shechina*, the greatest day and climax of human history, is shrouded in some obscurity and subject to debate.

Furthermore, the Torah conveys that *Shavuos* falls 50 days after the initiation of the counting of the *omer*, which takes place "*mimacharas haShabbos.*" This intriguing yet obscure reference sparked a heated debate between the *Tzeddukim* and the Rabbis. The *Tzeddukim* (literalists) argued that the count always commences on *motzaei Shabbos*, whereas the *mesora* (rabbinic tradition) asserts that this phrase refers to *motzaei yom tov*. Why did the Torah formulate the date of the holiday of *Shavuos* in a

---

"***Shavuos*: Celebrating Human...**" was originally published in 2011 on TorahWeb.org

manner that relies exclusively upon rabbinic tradition, practically defying the unvarnished literal text? Why is the very purpose of *Shavuos* made contingent upon the rabbinic *mesora*?

Perhaps the Torah's perspective on *Shavuos* underscores that the true focal point of revelation and the giving of the Torah transcends the event and experience itself, and even goes beyond the received content of the Torah. While *matan Torah* – the giving of the Torah – was, indeed, pivotal, it was *Klal Yisrael*'s acceptance of the yoke of observance and their anticipated role and involvement in Torah life that was truly unique. The Torah was given with an accompanying *mesora* of information and interpretation that ensured and accentuated responsible human participation. In addition, the concepts and principles of Torah law were entrusted to the *chachmei hamesora*. Their comprehension, analysis and judgment in accordance with the transmitted methodology enabled the *halacha* to extend its scope across all geographic and temporal boundaries. Thus, the very theme of *matan Torah* as the centerpiece of *Shavuos* is specifically transmitted by means of the oral tradition entrusted to human transmission, because it is precisely the human component that singularly characterizes Torah life that is uniquely celebrated on this day. In the same vein, the Torah grounds the timing of *Shavuos* in the obscure phrase "*mimacharas haShabbos*," which highlights the need for rabbinic interpretive tradition with all that it implies about the halachic system, to accentuate man's responsible and contributing role.

According to this perspective, the greatest moment of human history, Divine revelation, is celebrated not merely as a passive albeit awesome experience, but also as the foundational moment for the establishment of a covenant-partnership in which *Klal Yisrael* would play a crucial function. It is noteworthy that the *Yam Shel Shlomo* (introduction to *Bava Kamma*) emphasizes that each individual present at this historic and transcendent moment received the Torah according to his own understanding and personality. He argues that this initial personal reception of the Torah was the basis for the concept of *eilu ve'eilu divrei Elokim chayyim*, which validates a range of authentic understandings of the *mesora*.

The *Gemara* in *Pesachim* (68b) explains that while generally R. Eliezer rules that one can apply an exclusively spiritual focus (*kulo laHashem*) to *yom tov*, he acknowledges that *Shavuos* must include a personal and physical component, "as it is the day on which the Torah was given." This ruling and explanation seems counterintuitive, as one would have anticipated that the awesome Divine revelation at Sinai would actually more likely underscore the theme of "*kulo laHashem*." However, in light of our analysis, we may posit that *Klal Yisrael*'s role, exhibited and symbolized by the role of gatekeepers of the *mesora* and repository and practitioners of Torah *shebe'al peh*, specifically projects the centrality of human input and responsibility. The responsibility to transmit the *mesora* faithfully from generation to generation demands exceptional devotion and investment. Moreover, the Oral Torah includes not only information but particularly halachic principles and a methodology for their application. This tradition dictates that the Torah can be applied across the ages and in all circumstances by responsible halachists, whose contributions constitute a vital part of the process and content of Torah.

Earlier, we noted the debate surrounding the actual date of *matan Torah*. Some sources (*Tosafos*, *Avoda Zara* 3a) indicate that even according to R. Yosi, *Shavuos* is celebrated on the sixth of *Sivan* because *Hashem* was prepared initially to give the Torah on that day had not Moshe *Rabbeinu* prevailed upon *Hashem* to delay one more day so that *Klal Yisrael* might be more fully prepared to receive it. The very notion that even someone of the stature of Moshe could and would request a delay of the telos of creation, and that *Klal Yisrael*'s state of readiness would justify a postponement, seems astonishing at first glance, but is perfectly consistent with the perspective that *kabbalas haTorah*, alongside *matan Torah*, was an essential dimension in the *gilui haShechina* and transmission of the Torah at Sinai. Surely it is no coincidence that *Shavuos*'s *korban shtei halechem*, which is projected so prominently in *Parashas Emor*, requires no *kemitza*, the component of the *mincha* generally dedicated exclusively to *Hashem*. (The fact that this *korban* consists of *chametz* is symbolically significant and consistent with the *Shavuos* theme of "*lachem*." It also reflects and expresses the dramatic transition from *Pesach*, perhaps by means of the *sefira* process, which is also a decisive factor in bridging between *Pesach* and *Shavuos*. I hope to speak more extensively about these themes elsewhere.)

The *Gemara* in *Pesachim* (68b), cited previously, records that R. Yosef used to celebrate *Shavuos* with a lavish feast, declaring that if not for this day and the celebration of *matan* and *kabbalas haTorah*, he would not have been able to have made the singular contributions that defined the very uniqueness of his existence ("כמה יוסף איכא בשוקא"). By means of its intentional obscurity and ambiguity, the Torah's presentation accentuates the indispensable role of *mesora* and *Torah she-be'al peh*, and thereby dramatically captures the authentic character of the *Shavuos* celebration.

Rabbi Yonason Sacks

Anticipating *Kabbalas HaTorah*

We find ourselves in an intense period awaiting זמן מתן תורתנו. The days of the *omer* in general, and the שלשת ימי הגבלה in particular, challenge us to appreciate and internalize the profound significance of *kabbalas haTorah*. Ramban explains that the very purpose of *sefiras ha'omer* is to connect the experience of *yetzias Mitzrayim* with that of *ma'amad Har Sinai*. This linkage emphasizes the need to view our freedom from the bondage of *Mitzrayim* as a means toward heightened *avodas Hashem*.

How do we prepare ourselves for the *Shavuos* experience? Which aspects of our *avodas Hashem* require the most considerable emphasis?

Unquestionably, we must approach our *limmud haTorah* with a profound sense of passion, diligence and commitment. We must perceive Torah study as an act of קבלת פני השכינה, Divine revelation.

Rabbeinu Yonah, however, underscores *tikkun hamiddos*, perfection of character, as a necessary condition for *kabbalas haTorah*. Commenting on the teaching of Rabbi Elazar ben Azarya, "אם אין דרך ארץ אין תורה" (*Avos* 3:17), *Rabbeinu* Yonah explains, "תורה אינה שוכנת לעולם בגוף שאינו בעל מידות טובות"; Torah can only reside in a *ba'al middos tovos*, one who posses a refined or exemplary character.

Interestingly, the Avudraham cites a *minhag* limiting the recitation of *Pirkei Avos* to the weeks between *Pesach* and *Shavuos*, highlighting *tikkun hamiddos* as a prerequisite for *kabbalas haTorah*.

The *Avnei Neizer* explains that the students of R. Akiva who, לפי מדרגתם (at their level), failed to exhibit proper *kavod* for each other, died specifically during *yemei hasefira*, a time designated for *tikkun hamiddos*.

"Anticipating *Kabbalas HaTorah*" was originally published in 2002 on TorahWeb.org

Both *limud haTorah* and *tikkun hamiddos* require our constant attention and concern. Just as the Torah characterizes the weeks of *sefira* as "*temimos*" (whole; perfect), so too our commitment to *limmud haTorah* and *tikkun hamiddos* must be incessant and continual. May we merit a meaningful and profoundly significant *kabbalas haTorah*.

Rabbi Zvi Sobolofsky

Our Master and Our Beloved: A Dual Approach to *Avodas Hashem*

At the time of *yetzias Mitzrayim*, *Bnei Yisrael* entered into a dual relationship with *Hashem*. Simultaneously, *Bnei Yisrael* became both *avdei Hashem* and His *kallah*. "כי־לי בני־ישראל עבדים הם אשר־הוצאתי אותם מארץ מצרים" (*Vayikra* 25:55), and "זכרתי לך חסד נעוריך אהבת כלולתיך" (*Yirmeyahu* 2:2). Both of these aspects of our relationship with *Hashem* reached their fruition at *matan Torah*.

In the introductory words to *kabbalas haTorah*, the Jewish people are instructed to be an "*am segula*" (*Shemos* 19:5). The *Mechilta* understands this to mean "תהיו קנויים לי – you should be acquired to Me." The *Beis Halevi*, in his commentary on *Chumash*, elaborates upon this explanation. It is only an *eved*, who literally sells himself to another, who can possibly be obligated to fulfill every command of his master. It was only through becoming *avadim laHashem* that we became obligated to observe all of the *mitzvos*.

Yet *matan Torah* has another dimension. Rashi (*Shemos* 19:17) sees similarities to a wedding in the *Har Sinai* experience. Many customs we observe at a wedding are reminiscent of Sinai, such as lighting candles, symbolic of the flashes of lightning that accompanied *matan Torah*. What is the significance of this dual relationship, and how does it express itself practically in our *avodas Hashem*?

Ramban (*Shemos* 20:8) observes that the division of *mitzvos* into positive and negative commandments reflects two aspects of *avodas Hashem*. Positive *mitzvos* stem from *ahavas Hashem*, a desire to act in a way that will bring you closer to your Beloved. Observance of prohibitions is a reflection of one's *yiras Hashem*; one refrains out of fear and awe from violating the word of one's Master. The true *eved Hashem* will never violate a

---

"**Our Master and Our Beloved...**" was originally published in 2000 on TorahWeb.org

mitzvas lo sa'aseh, and a *yedid Hashem*, a beloved of *Hashem*, will constantly search for positive ways to draw closer to his Beloved.

Ramban sees these two parts of *avodas Hashem* in the dual obligations of *Shabbos*. *Chazal*, in *Masseches Berachos* 20b, interpret the phrase "זכור את יום השבת" as referring to the positive commandment to sanctify *Shabbos* with *kiddush*, and "שמור את יום השבת" as referring to the prohibition of *melacha*. "*Zachor*" is an example of a *mitzvas asei*, which stems from *ahavas Hashem*, whereas "*shamor*," a *lo sa'aseh*, has its roots in *yiras Hashem*.

Following the words of Ramban, we can reach a deeper understanding of what *Chazal* mean when they state, "זכור ושמור בדיבור אחד נאמרו – '*zachor*' and '*shamor*' were said with one utterance." Not only does this refer to these specific *mitzvos* of *Shabbos* which were recited simultaneously at *Har Sinai*, but it applies to both aspects of *avodas Hashem* that must always go hand in hand. One who perfects his *ahavas Hashem* can potentially reach a feeling of closeness and comfort with *Hashem* in which he forgets that he is ultimately infinitesimal in relation to his Creator. Yet, one who strives for perfection in his *yiras Hashem* may do so at the expense of being able to relate to *Hashem* with a sense of love and friendship. This is why we are instructed in *Pirkei Avos* (1:3) to serve *Hashem* out of love, yet simultaneously not to forget "יהי מורא שמים עליכם". Even at a time of love, one must be in awe of *Hashem*.

The perfection of these two aspects of *avodas Hashem* – *ahava* and *yira*, *eved* and *yedid*, is our goal on *Shavuos* and throughout the year. May we always reach this perfect blend of "זכור ושמור בדיבור אחד נאמרו".

You Can Be a *Kohein* and a King

"ואתם תהיו־לי ממלכת כהנים" – and you shall be for Me a kingdom of *kohanim*" (*Shemos* 19:6). As a prerequisite to receiving the Torah, the

---

"**You Can Be a *Kohein* and a King**" was originally published in 2007 on TorahWeb.org

Jewish people are commanded to become a kingdom of *kohanim*. This obligation is difficult to comprehend, since only a select group of individuals were chosen to be *kohanim*. Before the *cheit ha'eigel* this group was comprised of the first born; afterwards the *leviyim*, specifically the descendants of Aharon, took their place. How, then, could the **entire** Jewish people be called upon to be *kohanim*?

A similar problem exists with the word "*mamleches* – kingdom." This term refers to royalty, yet the realm of royalty is reserved for the tribe of Yehuda and specifically the descendants of Dovid *haMelech*. How can the **entire** Jewish people be called upon to be kings when most of us are excluded from this role?

Upon further examination, we see that the *kohein* and the *melech* have dual roles. While our immediate association with being a *kohein* is serving in the *Beis HaMikdash*, each *kohein* served in the *Beis HaMikdash* for only a few days a year. The system of *mishmaros* which divided the *kohanim* into different groups and enabled each *kohein* to have a chance to serve in the *Beis HaMikdash* also limited each individual *kohein* to a small amount of time per year to actually offer *korbanos*. What else was the *kohein* expected to do during the year? When the Torah describes the *talmidei chachamim* who sat on the highest court, the *Beis Din HaGadol*, it refers to them as *kohanim, leviyim veshofetim*. Even a *yisrael* can be part of the *Beis Din HaGadol*, yet many of the greatest Torah leaders were *kohanim* and *leviyim*. Furthermore, the *navi* Malachi describes the *kohein* in detail as the model teacher of Torah. Free from the responsibilities associated with owning land, the *kohanim* were expected to devote themselves to becoming *talmidei chachamim* and teachers of the entire Jewish people.

Just as a *kohein* had a dual leadership role, so too did the *melech*. While the *melech* was the political and military leader, this was only one dimension of his leadership. The *melech* was also commanded to carry a *sefer Torah* with him constantly, thereby showing that the ultimate authority is *Hashem* and His word. Additionally, not only did the *melech* personally study the Torah, he was charged with teaching the entire Jewish people its message. Every seven years during *hakheil*, when the Jewish people as a whole learned Torah together in the *Beis HaMikdash*, it was the *melech* who was given the privilege to read from the Torah publicly.

Rambam (*Hilchos Talmud Torah* 3:1) elaborates on the three crowns that were presented to the Jewish people, i.e., the crowns of *kehuna*, *malchus* and Torah. In contrast to the crowns of *kehuna* and *malchus* that were bestowed upon particular families, the crown of Torah was given to anyone who wants to acquire it through hard work and dedication to its study. However, the crown of Torah is not entirely distinct from the other two crowns. The crown of *kehuna* is made up not only of offering *korbanos*, but also of teaching Torah. Similarly, the military and political leadership of the Jewish people, as well as the communal teaching of Torah, are included in the crown of *malchus*. Each and every Jew can become a partial *kohein* and *melech*, since the dimension of Torah study and teaching that is such an integral part of *kehuna* and *malchus* does not depend on genealogy.

As we approach זמן מתן תורתנו, it is incumbent upon all of us to rededicate ourselves to our role of being a *mamleches kohanim*. Whether we are *kohanim* and *melachim*, i.e., formal teachers of Torah, or have followed any other calling in life, we are each required to respond to the call of *mamleches kohanim*. Let us become, each in our own way, a proud member of the *mamleches kohanim*. By reaffirming our commitment to the Torah ideals of *kehuna* and *malchus*, may we merit to see the *kohanim* and the *malchus beis Dovid* teaching us the Torah in the *Beis HaMikdash*, במהרה בימינו.

Guarding the Ultimate Treasure

A Torah-observant Jew is often referred to as a שומר תורה ומצוות. The requirement to be *shomeir mitzvos* is repeated several times throughout the Torah. What is the significance of being *shomeir* – literally, guarding – the *mitzvos* and why does this define the essence of a Torah way of life?

We are taught in *Parashas Bamidbar* about the *mitzva* of *shemiras HaMikdash*, i.e., the guarding of the *Mishkan* and later the *Beis HaMikdash* that was performed by the *kohanim* and *leviyim*. According to many *mefarshim* in *Masseches Tamid*, this "guarding" was not to actually protect the *Beis HaMikdash*, but rather to indicate the significance of what we are watching over. Similarly, *shemiras hamitzvos* is not merely performing *mitzvos*, but rather a declaration of the supreme importance of *mitzvos* in our lives.

What does *shemiras hamitzvos* entail above and beyond the fulfillment of *mitzvos*? *Chazal* articulate several times the dual obligation of "לשמור ולעשות – to watch over and to perform" the *mitzvos*, wherein *lishmor* refers to learning and *la'asos* addresses actual fulfillment. Learning Torah is the ultimate expression of *shemira*. If one truly views the *mitzvos* as the will of *Hashem*, one will spend all of his time and effort to understand them. As such, the constant dedication to *talmud Torah* is the greatest acknowledgement of the significance of the *mitzvos*, and thus the ultimate expression of *shemiras hamitzvos*.

Chazal relate that when one who learns Torah enters the next world, he is greeted with the words, "אשרי מי שבא לכאן ותלמודו בידו – happy is the one who comes here with learning in his hand." This seems to be a strange way to describe one who learns; what is meant by the one whose learning is "in his hand"? The most precious of one's assets are not

---

"Guarding the Ultimate Treasure" was originally published in 2012 on TorahWeb.org

left for someone else to watch, but rather kept in one's own possession. Rashi comments that when Yaakov sent multiple gifts to Esav, he also sent him precious jewels. Although not mentioned explicitly in the Torah, these jewels are alluded to by the *pasuk* that describes gifts sent from "the hand of" Yaakov (*Bereishis* 32:14), since what was in Yaakov's own hand must have been the most important. Perhaps this is the "learning in one's hand" that *Chazal* are referring to. It is not mere learning that warrants the special welcome in the world to come, but rather it is the acknowledgement of the significance of Torah and *mitzvos* that is demonstrated by a lifetime of *talmud Torah* that accompanies a person to the next world and merits such a welcome.

As we approach the *yom tov* of *Shavuos*, we rededicate ourselves to שמירת התורה ומצוות. It is though the vehicle of *talmud Torah* that we demonstrate the significance of Torah in our lives. May we merit on this *Shavuos* not only to receive the Torah, but also to hold it in our hands as befits the precious gift that *Hashem* has bestowed upon us.

Days and Weeks: Two Worlds, Yet One Goal

As *sefiras ha'omer* reaches its culmination, we are actually concluding two different counts. *Chazal* (*Menachos* 66a) teach us that there are two parts to this *mitzva*, i.e., the counting of days and the counting of weeks. These two dimensions of *sefiras ha'omer* conclude with the *yom tov* of *Shavuos*, which celebrates the completion of both days and weeks. Although we are all familiar with the one-day celebration of *Shavuos* (with a second day outside of *Eretz Yisrael*), during the time of the *Beis HaMikdash* there was an entire week of celebration. Specifically, if a person couldn't bring the *korbanos* of *Shavuos* on the first day, there was a week of *tashlumin* to make up these *korbanos*.

"Days and Weeks: Two Worlds,..." was originally published in 2013 on TorahWeb.org

The *Or Sameach* suggests that there may be halachic ramifications of the dual count. The counting of days, which culminates in the one-day celebration of *Shavuos*, does not depend on the *Beis HaMikdash*, as this one day celebration occurs in all places at all times. Therefore, the counting of days is a *mitzva deOraysa* even today. The counting of weeks, on the other hand, which concludes with the week-long celebration in the *Beis HaMikdash*, does not apply *mideOraysa* today, in the absence of the *Beis HaMikdash*. This is the rationale for the view of *Rabbeinu* Yerucham who maintains that, in fact, the counting of days today is *mideOraysa*, whereas the counting of weeks is *mideRabbanan* as a *zeicher leMikdash*.

These dual aspects of counting go beyond the actual *mitzva* of *sefiras ha'omer* and subsequent celebration on *yom tov*. There is a fundamental distinction between the unit of time of a day and that of a week. Days correspond to the physical reality of the earth rotating on its axis. Other units of time, such as months and years, are also rooted in the world of astronomy; a month measures a lunar cycle and a year measures the earth's revolving around the sun. A week, however, corresponds to nothing in the physical universe. The unit of a week only has meaning because *Hashem* created the world in six days and sanctified the seventh. The counting of days relates to this world, whereas the counting of weeks belongs to the world of *kedusha*. Counting of days can exist even without a *Beis HaMikdash*, whereas the counting of weeks is in the realm of the *Beis HaMikdash*. *Shavuos* is the culmination of both counts, because the essence of זמן מתן תורתנו is our ability to count both days and weeks.

Chazal relate to us how the angels tried to dissuade *Hashem* from giving the Torah to the Jewish People. It was only the response of Moshe that we, as human beings, need the *mitzvos* of the Torah, which are not relevant for pure, spiritual beings such as angels, which ended the argument in favor of giving us the Torah. On *Shavuos* we celebrate our ability to infuse *kedusha* into a physical world, our ability to combine the counting of weeks to complement our counting of days.

As we approach the *yom tov* of *Shavuos*, we realize that our ability to truly transform our physical world into a world of *kedusha* is inhibited by our lack of a *Beis HaMikdash*. *Chazal* understood that even without an actual *Beis HaMikdash*, we must continue to count weeks, albeit as a *zeicher laMikdash*. It is our constant yearning to once again have a *Beis HaMikdash* that keeps us focused on the fact that our physical world is not yet complete. As we anticipate the counting of weeks and the celebrating of the entire week of *Shavuos* in the *Beis HaMikdash*, we look forward to the day when *kedusha* will infuse our physical world. When *Hashem* returns that opportunity to us, זמן מתן תורתנו will have finally achieved its goal. May we merit that day very soon.

Shavuos: Do Not Forget, for Ourselves and Our Children

The receiving of the Torah was the most significant event in the history of the Jewish people. Not only does the *yom tov* of *Shavuos* revolve around the experience of *Har Sinai*, but we are also commanded to never forget the events that occurred on that first *Shavuos*. We are given a two-fold commandment: "Do not forget the things that your eyes have seen... and transmit them to your children and grandchildren" (*Devarim* 4:9). What precisely must we be careful not to forget? What exactly are we to impart to the next generations?

We are taught (*Pirkei Avos* 3:10) that one must be exceedingly careful not to forget what one has learned, and one who forgets even one word of what he has learned is in violation of the prohibition mentioned above. Although one who tries to retain the information studied and

---

"*Shavuos*: **Do Not Forget,...**" was originally published in 2014 on TorahWeb.org

doesn't succeed does not violate this prohibition, the essence of this *halacha* emphasizes the significance of remembering as much Torah knowledge as possible. The corollary of this prohibition is the positive commandment to transmit all of our knowledge to our children.

There is a dispute between *Rabbeinu* Yonah, Rambam, and Ramban as to the precise nature of this dual commandment. *Rabbeinu* Yonah, in his commentary to *Pirkei Avos*, explains why the Torah insists that we not forget what we have learned. One who forgets will inevitably commit errors in his *mitzva* observance. According to *Rabbeinu* Yonah, the Torah is highlighting the role of *talmud Torah* as the prerequisite for the proper observance of the *mitzvos*. We are required to do everything in our ability to maintain proper observance for ourselves and our children, and this begins with a thorough knowledge of the Torah.

Rambam (*Hilchos Talmud Torah* 1:10) emphasizes a different aspect of *talmud Torah* concerning the prohibition of forgetting. Rambam cites the prohibition against forgetting one's learning as the source that one must learn until the end of one's life. Rav Moshe Feinstein explains that Rambam is addressing the dimension of *talmud Torah* as an end in itself. How much must one learn to fulfill this *mitzva* properly? One must learn the entire Torah. One who forgets any Torah must continue to learn because otherwise this *mitzva* is not fulfilled in its entirety. Thus, Rambam saw in this *pasuk* the source for an independent, never-ending obligation to study Torah; not study just as a way to fulfill other *mitzvos*. Only if we dedicate ourselves to maintaining a complete mastery of Torah as a goal in and of itself can we impart this knowledge properly to our children.

Ramban in *Sefer HaMitzvos* (negative commandments omitted by Rambam, #2) interprets this dual obligation as focusing on the general experience of *Har Sinai*, rather than addressing forgetting a specific part of the Torah as *Rabbeinu* Yonah and Rambam did. Ramban explains why the nature of the *Har Sinai* experience must constantly be remembered. It is only this experience which enables the Torah to remain eternal in our eyes. If we would have only received the Torah from Moshe without seeing *Hashem*'s presence revealed on *Har Sinai*, we could potentially be led to believe by a subsequent *navi* that a new Torah had been given. We who saw with our own eyes that *Hashem* gave us this Torah are certain that this Torah will remain eternal. We must constantly strengthen our own faith in this principle and transmit it to our children.

As we celebrate that monumental day at *Har Sinai*, we have to once again commit ourselves to all aspects of *kabbalas haTorah*. We must constantly strive to reach greater heights in *talmud Torah*, enabling ourselves and our children to properly observe the *mitzvos*. *Talmud Torah* must also be an independent goal; mastering as much Torah as we can must be an absolute priority for ourselves and our children. Finally, an absolute commitment to the eternal truth of the Torah must be maintained. This cornerstone of Jewish belief must be guarded and transmitted properly to the next generation.

Rabbi Dr. Abraham J. Twerski

Shavuos: Dawn of Intellectual Emotion

We did our thing. We were up all *Shavuos* night, and were inspired by the dramatic account of *matan Torah*. And now? Business as usual, right?

After the awesome revelation at Sinai, *Hashem* said, "Return to your tents" (*Devarim* 5:27), and commentaries say that the message was, "Here at Sinai you reached the lofty level of spirituality, נעשה ונשמע. Take this spirituality back to your tents, and conduct your daily lives with the attitude of נעשה ונשמע." We must take the spiritual gain of *Shavuos* with us as we return to our daily routine.

The gift of Torah was *daas*. "If there is no *daas*, how can one distinguish right from wrong?" (Jerusalem Talmud, *Berachos* 5:2). "If you have *daas*, you lack nothing" (*Nedarim* 41a). The Chasidic writings say that in the enslavement of Egypt, the Israelites were bereft of *daas*. As slaves, they had no opportunity to exercise *daas*, so it atrophied. During the seven weeks between the exodus and Sinai, they began to reclaim *daas*, although this was not fully attained until 40 years later, as Moses said, "But *Hashem* did not give you a heart *ladaas* (to know) ...until this day" (*Devarim* 29:3). The failings that they had in the desert were due to their lack of *daas*.

I used to take offense at the scientific classification of man as *Homo sapiens*, which in simple English means "a baboon with intellect." It is clear to me that intellect is not the primary feature that gives man his uniqueness and separates him from other creatures. Firstly, it is evident that animals do have intellect. If you observe a lion stalking its prey, one can see that the lion calculates just the right moment to make its attack. Secondly, if intellect is the primary characteristic that defines man, then the person with the highest intellect should be the most ideal human being, and this

---

"***Shavuos*: Dawn of Intellectual...**" was originally published in 2010 on TorahWeb.org

is simply not true. Prior to World War II, the country most advanced in intellect was Germany.

In *Happiness and the Human Spirit*, I elaborated on the concept that it is the *spirit* rather than intellect that gives us our uniqueness as human beings.

But I have gained new respect for intellect, and am perfectly comfortable with being a *Homo sapiens*. It is only a matter of putting *sapiens*, the intellect, to proper use.

Yes, animals, too, have intellect, but except for domesticated pets that can pick up human traits, animals use their intellect solely to satisfy their own needs. Animals are driven to act by their bodily desires, and they use their intellect to satisfy them. The animal intellect is a tool that serves the desire.

In the *Tanya*, the *Alter Rebbe* posits that the human being has *two* spiritual components, one that is identified with the physical body (*nefesh habehamis*) and one that is identified with the *neshama* (*nefesh elokis*). Both of these are comprised of intellectual traits and of affective or emotional traits. The difference between the two is that in the *nefesh habehamis*, as in all animals, the motivation is provided by the affects, and the intellect is then used to satisfy the affective drive; i.e., the intellect is a *tool* of the affect.

In the *nefesh elokis*, the *Alter Rebbe* says, the reverse occurs: *The intellect gives rise to the affect.* This is reminiscent of the story of the doctor who told the patient, "You can eat whatever you like, and here is what you are going to like."

This is a revolutionary idea. Conventional wisdom is that we like something because we like it. Our emotions are spontaneous. You cannot tell someone that he must develop a particular emotion, and that he must like something.

The *Alter Rebbe*'s position, however, is proven by the *mitzva* in the Torah, "You shall love *Hashem*" (*Devarim* 6:5). One can be commanded to do something, such as to put on *tefillin* or to sit in a *sukka*, or to refrain from doing something, such as working on *Shabbos*. Actions can be legislated, but how can one be ordered to love something? Yet, we are commanded to love *Hashem* (*ahava*) and to be in awe of *Hashem* (*yira*), both of which are emotions that are not subject to volition. But the Torah does not ask the impossible of us.

Rambam addresses this question, and says that the way to develop *ahavas Hashem* is to contemplate His wondrous creations (*Hilchos Yesodei HaTorah* 2:2). The commentary explains that Rambam is redefining *ahava* to mean not only love, but also *adoration*, and appreciation of *Hashem*'s wondrous creations can indeed produce adoration.

The *Alter Rebbe* introduces a novel concept: *intellectual emotion*. I.e., if a person does not feel love for *Hashem*, but understands intellectually that *Hashem should be loved*, that, too, is fulfillment of the *mitzva* to love *Hashem*.

Mesillas Yesharim addresses this issue by citing a principle found in *Sefer HaChinuch*, that behavior can determine emotion. I.e., even if one is unable to feel love for *Hashem*, if one acts *as if* one did feel love, these actions will generate love.

Whichever approach one takes, the *Alter Rebbe*'s point is validated. *Intellect can produce emotions*. This use of intellect is uniquely human, and allows me to accept the appellation *Homo sapiens*.

This is more than a philosophical discussion. We are witnessing an unprecedented incidence of failure of marriages. As Chana Levitan explains in *I Only Want to Get Married Once*, Western civilization's concept of "love" is more rightfully called "infatuation," an affect originating in the *nefesh habehamis* which gradually wanes, resulting in couples "falling *out of* love." It is possible, however, to develop a true love à la *nefesh elokis*, a love generated by the intellect. Respect for another person and appreciation of that person's character traits and virtues can produce an *ahava* which does not wilt with the passage of time.

If this concept seems strange, it is because we have been impacted by the idea of "love" that prevails in our environment, which threatens the stability of marriage. If we implement the *sapiens* properly, to be master of the affects rather than its tool, we can preserve the wholesomeness of marriage. This is the Torah concept of *da'as*, which was given to us at Sinai and which we commemorate on *Shavuos*. We must take this spiritual gain of *Shavuos* as we return to our daily routine.

Shavuos: A Recall Phenomenon

In commanding the *mitzva* of *sefiras ha'omer*, the Torah says that we should begin counting "from the morrow of *Shabbos*" (*Vayikra* 23:15). The Talmud says that this means on the morrow of the first day of Passover. Inasmuch as *yom tov* is a rest day, it is referred to as *Shabbos*. However, the Sadducees took this verse literally, that *sefiras ha'omer* must begin on Sunday, and *Shavuos* must always be on Sunday.

The *Bnei Yisaschar* asks: What is the point of the Torah referring to the first day of Passover as "*Shabbos*," thereby giving the Sadducees the option of misinterpreting it? Why did the Torah not simply say "on the morrow of Passover?"

The *Bnei Yisaschar* explains the difference between *Shabbos* and

---

"*Shavuos*: A Recall Phenomenon" was originally published in 2011 on TorahWeb.org

the festivals. The festivals occur on a particular day of the month – e.g., Passover on the 15th of *Nisan*. Inasmuch as the calendar is determined by the *Sanhedrin* on the appearance of the new moon, the *kedusha* of the festivals is essentially dependent on an act of the *Sanhedrin*. Not so *Shabbos*, which occurs on the seventh day of the week, independent of the *Sanhedrin*. This is why we say "ברוך אתה ה' מקדש השבת," that *Hashem* sanctifies the *Shabbos*, whereas on the festivals we say "ברוך אתה ה' מקדש **ישראל** והזמנים." *Hashem* sanctified Israel (i.e., the *Sanhedrin*), who, in turn, sanctified the festivals.

Passover was unique among the festivals, because the Jews of the exodus were not deserving of the revelation of *Hashem*. The angels said to *Hashem*, "In what way are the Israelites better than the Egyptians? They are both idolatrous." Yet *Hashem* revealed Himself to them. As we say in the *Haggada*, "'with great awe' refers to the revelation of the *Shechina*." Thus, Passover was as unique as *Shabbos*, receiving a *kedusha* from *Hashem*. To indicate this, the Torah refers to Passover as "*Shabbos*."

Shavuos, too, was an extraordinary Divine revelation. When we say that *Shavuos* is זמן מתן תורתנו, it is not only in the historic sense. We can experience *matan Torah* today as our ancestors did then.

In medicine there is a "recall phenomenon." An infant is immunized with several injections, causing the body to build up a huge quantity of antibodies to the virus. Over a period of time, the antibodies disappear from the bloodstream, so that years later, their presence is virtually undetectable. If, many years later, the person is given a "booster" injection, the body promptly produces a massive amount of antibodies, just as with the initial immunization. The body "recalls" the earlier experience and reproduces it.

So it is with the intense spirituality of *matan Torah*. Even if we are not at a lofty level of spirituality, with proper observance of *Shavuos*, we can have a "recall phenomenon," re-experiencing the extraordinary spirituality of our ancestors' declaration of נעשה ונשמע.

Rav Shlomo Wolbe in *Alei Shur* says that we should use our powers of imagery to see ourselves at the foot of Sinai, seeing the mountain ablaze and trembling, hearing the thunder and *shofar*, seeing Moses standing atop the mountain, and hearing the voice of *Hashem* saying, "I am the Lord, your God." In this way, we can have a "recall phenomenon." זמן מתן תורתנו can refer to a current experience rather than only to a historic one.

Rabbi Mayer Twersky

As One Person with One Heart

"'And a man will stumble over his brother' (*Vayikra* 26:37), [which is interpreted to mean] man will stumble because of his brother's iniquity. This teaches that all Jews are responsible for one another (כל ישראל ערבין זה בזה)" (*Shevuos* 39a).

The principle of *areivus* teaches that all Jews are bound together in a covenant of mutual responsibility and liability. The fundamental conceptual underpinnings of *areivus* emerge from consideration of the following *halacha*. "Ahava the son of R. Zeira taught: with regard to all the blessings, the rule is that even though one has fulfilled (*yatza*) his own obligation to recite a particular blessing, he can cause others to fulfill (*motzi*) their obligation to recite that blessing [with the exception of blessings of enjoyment]" (*Rosh HaShana* 29a).

This *halacha* of "*yatza motzi*" *prima facie* contradicts the rule of the *Mishna* that, "whoever is not obligated in a particular matter cannot cause the public to discharge their obligation [vis-a-vis that matter]" (ibid.). Rashi and other *rishonim* ad loc. reconcile this apparent contradiction by explaining that the *Mishna*'s rule applies to one who was never obligated in the *mitzva*. One who was obligated in the *mitzva*, however, even after having performed the *mitzva*, **remains** obligated by virtue of any other Jew's unfulfilled obligation and need for assistance. The basis for this continuing obligation is the principle of *areivus*.

Let us briefly analyze this explanation. In order to cause others to fulfill their obligation vis-a-vis a particular *mitzva*, one must be obligated in the same *mitzva*. Thus it emerges that *areivus* is not an independent *mitzva* or free-standing concept such as loving one's fellow Jew; rather it is an integral internal component of each and every *mitzva*. One's

---

"As One Person with One Heart" was originally published in 1999 on TorahWeb.org

personal obligation vis-a-vis any particular *mitzva* dictates not only that he individually perform the *mitzva*, but also that he assist any other Jew in doing the same.

Let us briefly digress and consider the following teaching of Rav Soloveitchik *zt"l*. The Rav often explained that Judaism conceives of the Jewish nation (as well as any microcosmic Jewish community) not simply as a large aggregate or massive partnership of individuals, but rather as a distinct metaphysical entity (*vide* the Rav's essay "The Community," in *Tradition* vol. 17, no. 2, pp. 9-10, fn. 4. See also *Meshech Chochma* on the *haftara* of *Parashas Devarim*).

Upon further reflection, in light of the Rav's teaching, it emerges that the concept of *areivus* reflects a fundamental Torah principle. Prior to the giving of the Torah, *Hashem* promised the Jewish people that if they accept the Torah, "You shall be My special treasure among nations… you will be a kingdom of priests and a holy nation to Me," (*Shemos* 19:5-6). Torah was not given to six hundred thousand plus individuals. Rather, the Torah was given to the Jewish people as a distinct metaphysical entity. Every Jew is derivatively endowed with sanctity (*kedushas Yisrael*) and is obligated in *mitzvos* by virtue of his or her belonging to the Jewish nation. *Mitzvos* were given to the Jewish people as a whole, and thus the derivative obligation of every individual Jew is to facilitate fulfillment of the *mitzvos* by all members of the Jewish people – himself as well as others. The principle of *areivus* which underlies the *halacha* of *yatza motzi* encapsulates this fundamental notion.

This concept of the Jewish people as a dictinct metaphysical entity illumines the *Gemara's* phraseology regarding *areivus*. The *Gemara's* phrase ערבין זה בזה is conventionally understood in terms of the primary meaning of the root ע-ר-ב, to guarantee. Hence the translation, all Jews are guarantors, or responsible, for one another. Nonetheless, it seems quite plausible that the phrase should be understood in light of the root's secondary meaning, to mix or blend. And thus, the *Gemara*'s apothegm should be understood thus, "all Jews are bound up with each other," expressing not merely mutual responsibility and liability, but existential unity and identity. The use of the "*ba-*" in כל ישראל ערבין זה בזה" suggests this alternate understanding, because in Hebrew idiom when the root ע-ר-ב connotes guaranteeing, it is followed by the propositional letter "ל," and when it connotes mixing, it is followed by the propositional letter "ב" (*vide Chiddushei haRitva* ad loc., who apparently advances both interpretations).

Recognizing the metphysical identity of the Jewish people allows us to fully appreciate the following teaching encoded in the Torah, decoded by our Sages. The Torah describes the Jewish people's journey to Mt. Sinai to receive the Torah: "**They** had departed from Rephidim and had arrived in the Sinai Desert, camping (*vayachanu*) in the wilderness. **Israel** camped (*vayichan*) opposite the mountain" (*Shemos* 19:2). Our Sages (*Mechilta* ad loc.), prompted by the Torah's apparent linguistic inconsistency in shifting from the plural (*vayachanu*) to the singular (*vayichan*), comment that when the Jewish people arrived at Mt. Sinai, they achieved a remarkable degree of unity, hitherto unattained. They were as "one person with one heart" (ibid.); hence the shift from the plural to the singular form of speech. In light of the aforementioned remarks, it is abundantly clear that this remarkable achievement did not coincidentally precede the giving of the Torah. Rather it was a *sine qua non* for the giving of the Torah to the Jewish people who, unified, emerged as a distinct metaphysical entity. As long as divisions and divisiveness separated Jews, they remained individuals, unworthy of the Torah. The Jewish nation crystallized and became worthy of the Torah when this remarkable state of unity was achieved.

And finally, appreciating the indispensability of Jewish unity to *matan Torah* provides insight into a famous Talmudic passage. The

Gemara in *Yevamos* 62b records the tragic history of the period spanning *Pesach* and *Shavuos*, during which time R. Akiva's twenty four thousand disciples perished "because they did not accord each other proper respect" (as measured by the highest of standards to which they, disciples of R. Akiva, were held). Surely, the timing of the Divine punishment was not happenstance, but rather was determined in accordance with the sin. Every year between *Pesach* and *Shavuos* we prepare ourselves to re-create the giving of the Torah. Reattaining the remarkable unity which was a *sine qua non* for *matan Torah* is thus of the highest priority. At a time of heightened sensitivity to and striving for unity, R. Akiva's disciples' interpersonal deficiency was especially egregious and accordingly punished.

The Dangers of Drinking; Consolidating Spiritual Gains

Chazal comment that the *parasha* of *nazir* (the nazirite) is juxtaposed to that of *sota* (the adulteress) to teach us that "one who witnesses the corruption and downfall of the *sota* should accept upon himself an oath to abstain from wine."

Chazal are commenting on a typological case where intoxication was a major contributing factor to the sin of adultery. This causal nexus between intoxication and loss of appropriate inhibition is all too prominently manifest in contemporary American society, most infamously on college campuses. But adultery in particular, and promiscuity in general, are only two of the manifold dangers of intoxication. *Ona'as devarim* (hurtful speech) commonly issues forth from lips loosened by the effects of intoxication. Nor should we forget for even a moment the sacrilege perpetrated by those who are visibly intoxicated on *Shabbos* during *Musaf* after participating in their *kiddush* club. *Shabbos* is a day consecrated "*laHashem Elokecha*";

"The Dangers of Drinking..." was originally published in 2007 on TorahWeb.org

tefilla (prayer) involves standing before *Hashem* and speaking to Him. What a compounded *chillul Hashem* to be intoxicated while *davening* on *Shabbos*!

The Sochatchover Rebbe, with great insight and sensitivity, recognizes in the aforementioned comment of *Chazal* vital guidance for a life of continuous ascent in *avodas Hashem* (service of *Hashem*). Why is it necessary, asks the Rebbe, to accept an oath? One who witnessed the gruesome death of the adulteress will forever be deterred from drinking by this powerful memory. The answer, he explained, is that the force of even the most vivid and powerful experience gradually wanes and dissipates. As the memory becomes more distant, its effect on the person diminishes until it ultimately disappears entirely.

One can, however, prevent this process. While in the firm grip of the powerful experience, one makes a *kabbala* (resolution). A clearly defined, practical *kabbala* introduces permanent change into a person's life in a very concrete fashion. The memory of the *sota* will steadily weaken and its influence will dissipate, unless he reacts by accepting an oath.

At various points and times in our lives we are blessed with moments of inspiration and exceptional clarity. The possible sources of inspiration are many. Perhaps it was a *devar Torah* we heard, or the experience of *Shabbos* or *yom tov*. At such moments, we gain clarity about life and its priorities. The inspiration and pursuant clarity, however, will be short-lived unless we **immediately** translate them into action.

Case in point: *be'ezras Hashem* the *yom tov* of *Shavuos* will be such a source of inspiration. In order to consolidate the spiritual gains of *yom tov*, however, we must make *kabbalos*. What additional learning *sedarim* are we going to accept? When precisely are we going to learn? What – and at what pace – are we going to learn? How are we going to enhance the quality of the time that we already devote to *talmud Torah*? The inspiration and clarity afforded by the *yom tov* of *Shavuos* can permanently impact our lives if we ask and successfully answer these questions.

Eat, Drink and Be Merry... For Today We Accept the Torah

Mitzvas simchas yom tov triggers a dispute between Rabbi Yehoshua and Rabbi Eliezer. According to Rabbi Yehoshua, the Torah mandates חציו לה' וחציו לכם, i.e., half the day must be devoted to *davening* and learning, and half to eating and drinking. According to Rabbi Eliezer, on the other hand, the Torah does not insist on any such balance. One may, if he wishes, divide the day as prescribed by Rabbi Yehoshua. But, if he so desires, one may also devote the entire day either *laHashem* (*davening* and learning) or *lachem* (eating and drinking).

Famously, the *Gemara* adds a caveat: "בעצרת כולי עלמא מודו דבעינן נמי לכם. מאי טעמא? יום שנתנה בו תורה לישראל – on *Shavuos* even Rabbi Eliezer insists that part of the day be devoted to eating and drinking. Why? Because the Jewish people received the Torah on *Shavuos*."

The question is obvious: eat, drink and be merry... for today we accept the Torah?!

The answer is to be found in the Torah's approach to the physical. "בראתי יצר הרע ובראתי לו תורה תבלין". *HaKadosh Baruch Hu* says to the Jewish people, "I created the evil inclination, and I created the Torah as seasoning/spices for it."

The *yeitzer hara* – the inclination for the physical – is not something that needs to be suppressed. *Tavlin* do not suppress; they lend

---

"Eat, Drink and Be Merry..." was originally published in 2013 on TorahWeb.org

flavor. The analogue: our physical inclinations are to be disciplined and thereby redeemed. The discipline and consequent redemption of the physical is an integral part of Torah. To reflect this crucial part of Torah, we do indeed eat, drink and (with the appropriate *koved rosh*) make merry on *Shavuos*.

But the significance of eating and drinking on *Shavuos* reaches yet deeper. Rambam penned a remarkable responsum to an inquiry as to the permissibility of listening to Arab music and lyrics. In essence, his response: for various reasons, most decidedly *asur*. Rambam concludes on the following note: our mandate is to be a *goy kadosh*. This means to devote and direct all our energies to the source of *kedusha* – *HaKadosh Baruch Hu*. In particular, Rambam fails to see how listening to Arabic music will advance that sacred agenda. In general, we should strive that everything we do be calculated and geared to *avodas Hashem*. Rambam develops this idea in the third *perek* of *Hilchos De'os*, as well as identifying it with the maxim of *Chazal*, "וכל מעשיך יהיו לשם שמים – all your deeds should be for the sake of Heaven," and with the teaching of Shlomo *haMelech*, "בכל דרכיך דעהו – know Him in all your ways" (*Mishlei* 3:6). These are all-encompassing mandates; even activities such as eating and drinking should be calibrated and geared towards *avodas Hashem*. Eat, drink and be healthy so after breakfast you may go to the *beis midrash* and concentrate upon your learning.

This pivotal idea is also reflected in the mandate of eating and drinking on *Shavuos*.

Ratza HaKadosh Baruch Hu LeZakkos Es Yisrael

Challenge and response is a category employed in the study of history. This category of thought recognizes that people, individually and/

"Ratza HaKadosh Baruch Hu…" was originally published in 2014 on TorahWeb.org

or collectively, rise to meet challenges. In so doing, ofttimes they achieve what otherwise they would not have achieved.

In truth, the *Midrash* already expresses this idea as one understanding of *nisyonos* (trials or tests). HaKadosh Baruch Hu does not need to administer tests to discover results. People need challenging tests to achieve results.

This idea provides one perspective on the incomparable blessing of Torah.

"רצה הקב"ה לזכות את ישראל" – the Holy One, Blessed Be He, wanted to bestow merit upon the Jewish people"; "לפיכך הרבה להם תורה ומצוות – therefore He bestowed a vast Torah with a plethora of *mitzvos*" (*Makkos* 23b).

The more Torah and *mitzvos*, the greater the challenge and the higher we are induced to rise. And, at times, when we struggle in our *avodas Hashem*, we should remember that the greater the initial challenge, the greater the subsequent achievement.

May we all be *zocheh* to קבלת התורה באהבה.

Rabbi Mordechai Willig

Bamidbar and *Shavuos*

Parashas Bamidbar is always read just before *Shavuos*. The *Midrash* provides several connections between the very first *pasuk* in *Bamidbar*, "And *Hashem* spoke to Moshe in the Sinai desert, in the *Ohel Moed* ..." and *kabbalas haTorah*:

Hashem spoke to Moshe in the desert to teach us that one who does not transform himself into a "desert," something *hefkeir*, cannot acquire wisdom and Torah. The connection between humility and Torah acquisition is found in a number of Talmudic passages. The *Gemara* (*Eruvin* 54a) states that one who makes himself like a desert, which all can step on, is given Torah as a gift. Rashi explains that such a quality indicates a lack of arrogance. Another similar passage is found in the Talmudic prayer (*Berachos* 17a) with which we conclude the *Amida*: "May my soul be like dust [which everyone can step on] ...open my heart to Your Torah." A final example is a passage (*Pesachim* 66b) that states that humility is a prerequisite for true Torah knowledge, and haughtiness can cause wisdom to be lost.

Hashem confined His revelation to Moshe, speaking to him from within the tent (*Ohel Moed*), because modesty is beautiful. The proof text, "and walk humbly **with** your God" (*Micha* 6:8), shows that *Hashem*, too, walks humbly and modestly. The honor of Torah itself, referred to as the *bas melech*, the child of Moshe the king, is inward –"*penima*" (*Tehillim* 45:14).

The beauty of modesty (*tzenius*) is cited by Rashi (*Shemos* 34:3) in the context of *kabbalas HaTorah* itself. The first *luchos*, which were given publicly, with great noise and fanfare, were overcome by the evil eye and destroyed. The permanence of the second *luchos*, which were given privately to Moshe, demonstrates that nothing is more beautiful than modesty.

"***Bamidbar* and *Shavuos***" was originally published in 2000 on TorahWeb.org

As we read *Bamidbar* and prepare for *Shavuos* and our own personal *kabbalas haTorah*, we should look at our own great Torah scholars and leaders as role models. It is no coincidence that our greatest sage, Moshe *Rabbeinu*, was also the humblest man who ever lived.

Even if we realize our smallness compared to Torah giants of then and now, we often fail to be *hefkeir lakol*, to treat those less accomplished than ourselves with proper respect. This failure to emulate Moshe *Rabbeinu* and *gedolei Yisrael*, who cared for and respected the common man, prevents us from acquiring Torah to the best of our ability and capacity.

We must learn from *Hashem* Himself and walk modestly with Him. As He modestly hides His greatness, so too, we must avoid flaunting our accomplishments. Indeed, modesty in our actions is a reflection of humility in our hearts.

These timeless lessons take on a greater sense of urgency in our world of publicity-seekers and conspicuous consumption. These ills, which have affected the Jewish world at large, have also permeated the Torah world. If we think and act with the lessons of *Midrash Bamidbar*, we will be blessed with a greater measure of *kabbalas haTorah*.

Modesty: A Timeless Principle

I

"*Hashem* spoke to Moshe in the ... *Ohel Moed*" (*Bamidbar* 1:1), the private tent of meeting. The *Midrash* (*Bamidbar Rabba* 1:3) elaborates on *Bamidbar*'s opening *pasuk* as follows:

Hashem had spoken to Moshe earlier from the burning bush,

"Modesty: A Timeless Principle" was originally published in 2010 on TorahWeb.org

in *Mitzrayim*,… and on Mt. Sinai. Once the *Ohel Moed* stood, however, *Hashem* said: *Tzenius* is beautiful, as it says (*Micha* 6:8), "to walk humbly before ('*im*') your God," and He spoke to Moshe in the *Ohel Moed*. And so said Dovid (*Tehillim* 45:14): "All honor to the *bas melech* (princess) within." *Bas melech* refers to Moshe… *Hashem* said, such is My honor, that I will speak from within the *Ohel Moed*."

Although the *Midrash* quotes the *pasuk* in *Micha* to explain *Hashem*'s behavior, the *pasuk* seemingly refers to the *tzenius* of man before *Hashem*, not that of *Hashem* Himself. The *Midrash*'s use of the *pasuk* indicates, as the *peirush* Maharzu explains, that "*im*" does not mean "before," but rather "with." Man must be *tzanua* with *Hashem*, Who modeled *tzenius* by speaking from the *Ohel Moed*.

The *peirush* Maharzu offers two explanations of the reference to Moshe as *bas melech*. First, Moshe may be the king (see Ibn Ezra and Ramban, *Devarim* 33:5), and Torah is the private princess. (The Gemara in *Moed Katan* 16a-b, based on the *mashal* in *Shir Hashirim* 7:2, compares the Torah to the *yerech*, a part of the body that is covered.) Alternatively, *bas melech* may refer to Moshe, since he was raised by *bas Pharaoh*, daughter of the king of Egypt (*Tanchuma*). Moshe, the greatest human being in history, is thus praised for his *tzenius*, which is undoubtedly related to his incomparable humility (*Bamidbar* 12:3).

The phrase "*tzenius* is beautiful" is found once again in the context of *matan Torah*. Before giving Moshe the second *luchos*, *Hashem* told him, "No man shall ascend with you [up the mountain]" (*Shemos* 34:3), on which Rashi comments, "The first *luchos*, because they were given with fanfare and great sound and in a throng, were affected by the evil eye. There is nothing more beautiful than modesty."

Why, indeed, were the first *luchos* given with such great publicity?

Because the revelation at Sinai is the cornerstone of our belief in *Hashem* and the Divinity of the Torah (Rambam, *Hilchos Yesodei Hatorah* 8:1). *Hashem*, Who models *tzenius* to the point of being invisible, deemed it necessary to be uncharacteristically demonstrative so that we shall believe in the Divinity of the Torah forever (*Shemos* 19:9).

On *Shavuos*, the anniversary of *matan Torah*, we encounter *tzenius* again in the story of Rus. When Boaz saw Rus, he asked, "To whom does this young woman belong?" (*Rus* 2:5). As *Rus Rabba* 4:6 elaborates, "Since he saw her beautiful deeds, he asked about her. All the women bent down and gathered grain [thereby revealing the legs and highlighting the shape of the body (*Eitz Yosef*)], but she (Rus) sat down and gathered [lowering her entire body in a modest way (*Eitz Yosef*)]. All the women flirted with the farmers, but she behaved modestly (*matzna'as atzma*)." The exemplary modesty of Rus, in both her dress and her behavior, was noticed by Boaz. As a result he married her, and she merited to be the mother of royalty, the ancestress of Dovid, and ultimately, the *Mashiach*.

The *Midrash* relates that the legitimacy of the marriage of Boaz and Rus was questioned. Some said that all Moabite converts, including Rus, are prohibited (*Devarim* 23:4). Others argued that this restriction is limited to male converts. What is behind this dispute?

The *Midrash* (see also *Yevamos* 76b) refers to the Torah's reason a Jew may not marry a Moabite, "Because of the fact that they did not greet you with bread and water in the road when you were leaving Egypt" (*Devarim* 23:5). Ramban explains that since Avraham saved Lot, the ancestor of the Moabites, their debt of gratitude to Avraham's descendants should have motivated them to greet *Am Yisrael*. Their display of ingratitude resulted in the marriage prohibition. Even though we would never expect the Moabite women to greet the Jewish men, one opinion suggests that they are prohibited since they should have greeted the women of *Am Yisrael*.

Remarkably, the *Midrash*, which begins by extolling Rus' modesty, concludes that her permissibility (and that of all Moabite women) is based on precisely the same notion of modesty: based on the aforementioned reference to a princess dwelling within, the way of a woman is not to go out towards wayfarers, even women, to bring them bread and water.

Hashem requires modesty from all people. The additional modesty expected of women applies to non-Jews, such as Moabites, as well (see, however, Maharshal, *Yevamos* 77a). Indeed, *Hashem*'s first command to mankind implies that a woman should not be a gadabout (Rashi, *Bereishis* 1:28).

II

Notwithstanding the immutability of the Torah's principle of modesty and its particular application to women, the precise details are subject to communal standards which often change and/or vary from place to place. This is true regarding some parts of a woman's body which must be covered (*Shulchan Aruch, Orach Chayyim* 75:1). Nonetheless, there are other parts which must be covered regardless of communal standards.

The *Mishna Berura* draws the line at the elbow and the knee (ibid., 75:2). Some interpret "*shok*" (*Berachos* 24a) as the calf (since the thigh is called *yerech*), and include it in objective *erva* (see *Chazon Ish, Orach Chayyim* 16:8). Yet others imply that since the requirement to cover the arms and legs is *das Yehudis* (*Kesubos* 72a), i.e., a custom of Jewish women (Rashi), it may be subject to change (see *Kaf HaChayyim* 75:2, *Iggeros Moshe Even Ha'ezer* 1:69). *Sha'ar Hatziyyun* 75:5 disagrees.

However, a woman's torso is certainly *erva* (see Rambam *Hilchos Kerias Shema* 3:16), and must be covered. Unfortunately, many otherwise observant women follow fashions, such as very low necklines, which expose the flesh inappropriately. Women who wear tight-fitting clothes which explicitly delineate a woman's figure are also in violation, as the *Midrash*, contrasting Rus and the other women, implies (see *Kuntres Dinei Malbush Nashim*, pp. 12, 13).

The distinction between variable details and timeless principles is not limited to dress. It applies, in a more complex and nuanced way, to the definition of *tzenius* in the Torah society. For example, public speaking by a woman in front of mixed audiences is commonplace in some circles and unheard of in others. For many parts of Torah society, it depends upon the place, the occasion and other factors. Similarly, interaction between men and women, another subject of the *midrash* about Rus, is also dependent upon local custom (*Beis Shmuel* 62:11; see *Otzar Haposkim* there). This includes separate seating, entrances, *mechitzos*, etc. Here, too, context is clearly critical.

It must be noted that the opposite of *tzenius* is *peritzus* (*Kesubos* 3b), a term linked to one who breaks a fence (*Koheles* 10:8), and different communities legitimately build their fences in different places. As such, a garment, speech, or event can be labeled as *peritzus* in one place, but be acceptable in another.

However, even though the details can change, the Torah principles are eternal. General society rejects the Torah's inherent emphasis on modesty and its distinction between men and women. In particular, egalitarianism is antithetical to the Torah's principles of modesty and gender distinction (see *Iggeros Moshe Orach Chayyim* 4:49). Even in changing times, the Torah has established absolute gender-specific parameters regarding a woman's public role which can not be included in the category of communally-dependent details. Even if sincerely motivated, efforts to impose external values on the halachic system, instead of interpreting and applying timeless halachic values, are unacceptable.

Parashas Bamidbar and *Shavuos* coincide with the summer season, when the lack of *tzenius* in dress is most flagrant. The principles of modest behavior, for men and even more so for women, do not depend on the time or the season. They are Divine principles derived from *Hashem*'s choice of the *Ohel Moed*, the inwardness of a princess, Moshe, the Torah, and the modesty of Rus. Even as details vary, we must practice and accept the eternal fundamentals of Torah – נעשה ונשמע.

Rabbi Benjamin Yudin

A Healthy Tension before *Matan Torah*

Parashas Bamidbar is read annually before the *yom tov* of *Shavuos*. In the *Shulchan Aruch* (*Orach Chayyim* 428:4) we find "מנו עצרו" which means "count and celebrate *Shavuos*." The Torah teaches that the mandate to count *Bnei Yisrael* is couched in the phrase "שאו את ראש," which means literally "lift the head" or "elevate" the nation of Israel. How is counting an elevation? Ramban in his commentary (*Bamidbar* 4:13) explains that counting each individual is acknowledging that each person has self-worth, importance and dignity. You are not only important because you are part of the nation of Israel, but you have your own purpose and mission as well.

It is interesting to note that each person's EKG is different, and no two people have the same fingerprints. Our Rabbis couch this idea as "כשם שפרצופיהם שונים כך דעותיהם שונות." By this they mean that each person is unique not only physically, but in intelligence and character as well. Because each person possesses a unique temperament, his spiritual challenges and his *yeitzer hara* are also relevant only to him. Therefore, each person's service of God is different from everyone else's.

While the book of *Bamidbar* begins with the important message of the worth of each man individually, each person is counted as part of *Bnei Yisrael*. This dual nature might well be compared to a symphony orchestra. The ultimate beautiful result is the integration and blending of each instrument. However, unless each musician fine-tunes his or her instrument, and practices to perfection, the sum which is even greater than all its individual parts will be lacking. "מנו עצרו" might therefore require that we develop our own individuality to be able to join the collective *kabbalas haTorah* of *Shavuos*.

Moreover, this directive of "מנו עצרו" really thrusts a major

---

"A Healthy Tension before..." was originally published in 1999 on TorahWeb.org

philosophic difficulty on thinking Jews. On the one hand, we have stressed our own individual *avodas Hashem*. On the other hand, the greatness of *kabbalas haTorah* is "כאיש אחד בלב אחד – as one person with one heart," joining with the rest of the Jewish nation. How is one to budget his time and energies between his own needs for growth and those of others? Maharsha in his commentary to *Sanhedrin* 99b suggests that the *pasuk* in *Iyov* 5:7, "אדם לעמל יולד" ("people are born to work") expresses this tension. לעמל is an acronym for "ללמד על מנת ללמד – study and master in order to share and teach to others." What scale should we use to determine how to balance our personal studying, which as we know never ends, and our communal responsibility, which likewise seems never-ending?

Rav Shimon Shkop *zt"l*, in his introduction to *Sha'arei Yosher*, writes that just as in the physical/material realm we are commanded "עשר תעשר" (*Devarim* 14:22), to tithe our possessions on behalf of the Levites and the poor (depending on the year), and are promised that doing so will bring us blessing, so too regarding the realm of the soul, we are to give a tenth of our time to helping others. Giving to others is the best way to insure one's wealth. Moreover, the more we give, the more we are promised God will bless us.

Similarly, the *Meshech Chochma* in his commentary on "ויחל נח איש האדמה" (*Bereishis* 9:20), which can be understood as "Noach debased himself as a man of the earth," cites the *Midrash*, which contrasts the Torah's depiction of Noach, first as " a righteous man" and subsequently as a "man of the earth," with its description of Moshe *Rabbeinu*, who is initially referred to as "an Egyptian man" but who ultimately becomes a "man of God." He explains that there are two different ways to serve God. One is to isolate oneself from the community and focus completely on oneself. The other way is to be involved with the needs of the community. Logic dictates, reasons Rav Meir Simcha *haKohein* of Dvinsk, that one who does the former will excel and develop himself and his true potential, while one who does the latter, involving himself with the needs of others, will not be able to attain that level of greatness and maturity. The reality, points out the *Midrash*, is just the reverse. Through our helping others, we ultimately help ourselves the most. May we all be *zocheh* to reach out and spiritually touch not only those around us, but ultimately ourselves, ensuring our successful personal and communal *kabbalas haTorah*.

Torah: Spiritual CPR

The *Gemara* (*Shabbos* 88b) teaches in the name of R. Yehoshua ben Levi, "with every single statement that emanated from the mouth of the Holy One at Sinai the souls of the Jewish people departed from their bodies, as it is stated, 'My soul departed as He spoke' (*Shir HaShirim* 5:6). How did they receive the subsequent statements? *Hashem* brought down the dew with which He will resurrect the dead in the future and He resurrected them," as found in *Tehillim* (68:10).

I believe that there are two profound lessons contained in this metaphysical teaching. The first is that Torah living engenders a different quality of life. To receive the Torah (aside from the physical preparations found in *Shemos* chapter 19), the Jewish people had to undergo a spiritual transformation; they could not be the same people who arrived at *Har Sinai*. The *Zohar* teaches that *Hashem*, His nation Israel, and His Torah are one. Thus, experiencing the prophecy of His Torah was a transformative infusion of Godliness. This is also indicated by the Talmud's (*Shabbos* 105a) understanding of the opening word of the Decalogue, "*Anochi*," to be (in addition to its literal meaning) an acronym for "אנא נפשי כתבית יהבית," meaning that *Hashem* not only transmitted commandments to the Jewish nation, but gave part of His soul to them. As part of the song "*Dayyeinu*," we praise *Hashem* not only for the content and teachings of the Torah, but

---

"**Torah: Spiritual CPR**" was originally published in 2008 on TorahWeb.org

also for bringing us to *Har Sinai* per se and inducing this transformation.

The Talmud (*Shabbos* 146a) further emphasizes this spiritual metamorphosis by stating that at Sinai "פסקה זוהמתן – they were purified," enabling them to receive their Sinaitic souls. The *Kuzari* expresses this idea by stating there are five strata of beings: the inanimate, plant life, animals, man and Israel. The difference between each stratum is dramatic, including the difference between Israel, imbued with this Sinaitic soul, and the rest of society. Being on this higher stratum enables us to absorb Torah into our lives.

R. Eliyahu Lopian *zt"l*, in his introduction to *Sefer Shemos*, writes that the charge leveled by our enemies over the centuries that the Jew is too rich and successful is provoked by a *midda* that *Hashem* implanted in our nature: "One who loves money will never be satisfied with money" (*Koheles* 5:9). The *Midrash* comments, "If one has one hundred [units of money], he wants two hundred." This is understood by *Chazal* in a spiritual sense, that the Jewish *neshama* is drawn to the infinite. If this trait is not channeled positively towards spirituality, the Jew will apply it to this-worldly affairs.

The second lesson that emanates from the resurrection at Sinai is the exciting concept of "מרבה תורה מרבה חיים – an increase in Torah increases life" (*Avos* 2:8). Why, one may ask, did the Jews' elevated souls depart after each commandment, necessitating a further act of resuscitation? Perhaps to teach future generations that although they attained one level of Torah and spirituality, they are still "lifeless" compared to the next level, and require Divine assistance to climb higher. "Saw you at Sinai" is not only a clever phrase to introduce/reconnect two singles, but the fact that all Jewish souls were present at Sinai means we each experienced this repeated revival. This experience not only enables us to constantly improve our quality of life, but also to become a fundamentally different person through increasing our Torah learning and observance of *mitzvos*.

This concept emerges from a fascinating detail regarding the accidental murderer. The Torah teaches, "He shall flee to one of these cities [of refuge] and he shall live" (*Devarim* 4:42). The Talmud (*Makkos* 10a) rules that if a student establishes residence in a city of refuge, his teacher must visit him regularly to maintain the *rebbe-talmid* relationship, as the Torah mandates "and he shall live," i.e., we must provide him with arrangements to be able to live. The Rambam (*Hilchos Rotzeach* 7:1) codifies this law, stating that life without the study of Torah is akin to death. Given that the permanent residents of the cities of refuge were the Levites, whose role is to "teach Your ordinances to Yaakov and Your Torah to Yisrael" (*Devarim* 33:10), and thus there certainly was Torah and a Torah environment in the city of refuge, why do we specifically require that **his** teacher travel to the city of refuge to teach him Torah? Because without **his** teacher, the one who can inspire him and raise him as no one else can, he will not reach the same level of spirituality, and the absence of that achievement is called "lifelessness" by the Torah.

This is further substantiated by a fascinating dialogue between R. Tarfon and R. Akiva (*Kiddushin* 66b). After a lengthy debate over a particular intriguing *halacha*, R. Tarfon conceded to the opinion of R. Akiva. When he took leave of him he said, "Akiva! Whoever separates himself from you it is as if he separated from life itself!"

The exciting teaching of the resurrection of the Jewish nation at *Har Sinai* gives new meaning to the prayer of "*Ahavas Olam*" (recited every night before reciting *Shema Yisrael*). There it states, "כי הם חיינו – for they [Torah and *mitzvos*] are our life." This is to say that not only does Torah validate the *Kuzari*'s designation of Israel as a class unto itself, but within the Jewish nation Torah gives each individual a daily opportunity to renew and upgrade his or her lease on life.

Na'aseh VeNishma: Faith and Intellect

Our nationhood and redemption started with *emuna*, progressed with *emuna* and is perpetuated by *emuna*. When Moshe acquiesced and accepted the mantle of leadership to be the spokesman of *Hashem* to His enslaved nation, the Torah informs us that the people believed Moshe that he was the messenger of their emancipation (*Shemos* 4:31). The *Midrash* (*Shemos Rabba* 5:13) comments on this verse that it was not the signs and wonders that Moshe performed that won them over, rather it was the faith that the one who brought the message of "פקד יפקד – *Hashem* will redeem you" (*Bereishis* 50:24), is the true representative of *Hashem*.

Regarding the Jews at *Yam Suf* we are told, "and they had faith in *Hashem* and in Moshe, His servant" (*Shemos* 14:31). Finally, at Sinai "*Hashem* said to Moshe, 'Behold! I come to you in the thickness of the cloud, so that the people will hear as I speak to you, and they will believe in you forever'" (*Shemos* 19:9). Thus, the revelation at Sinai was predicated on faith and maintains that faith.

The Talmud (*Shabbos* 88a-b) relates that Rava was questioned, how could the Jewish nation at Sinai not question *Hashem* as to the content of His Torah prior to accepting it? Unlike all other nations who asked, "What is written in it?"; "what are its laws?"; "let us see if we can comply with it" (*Sifrei* 343), the Jewish nation responded "נעשה ונשמע – we will do and we will obey" (*Shemos* 24:7). Rava answered by citing the verse from *Mishlei* 11:3, "תמת ישרים תנחם – the perfect faith of the upright shall lead them." Rashi understands this to mean we trusted *Hashem* out of love, and relied on Him that He would not burden us with something we could not do. *Kabbalas haTorah* was based on the pure faith of our ancestors, that not only could we observe and follow His Torah, but that this is the best possible life for us.

"*Na'aseh VeNishma*: Faith..." was originally published in 2013 on TorahWeb.org

The Talmud (*Nidda* 70b) asks: what should a person do to become rich? Rabbi Yehoshua answers that (1) he should invest time in his business, (2) he should conduct his business affairs with integrity and (3) he should pray to *Hashem*, the source of all wealth. The above is understandable. As the *Kli Yakar* (*Vayikra* 25:36) explains, the prohibition of charging interest to a Jew is based upon the reality that for all business transactions one needs Divine assistance. Will they be successful, will they and their merchandise find favor in the eyes of others? Willy-nilly, the merchant looks heavenward, prays for success in his endeavors. Not so the one who lends on interest; he has taken care of matters himself. He is ensured of his success and profit by stipulating in advance the interest he will take. Such an individual has removed *Hashem* from the equation. The Torah therefore prohibits lending with interest, to bolster and maintain the faith of the businessman.

What is fascinating however, is the earlier question posed in the above *Gemara*. What should a person do to become a scholar? Rabbi Yehosua answered that he should spend more time studying in yeshiva, spend less time in business, and pray to *Hashem* for wisdom, as He is the source of all wisdom. Regarding wealth, it is understandable that one is to pray, as this reinforces the faith and recognition that ultimately it all comes from On High. But what role does prayer play in obtaining Torah knowledge?

Every morning we are privileged to recite two blessings prior to the recitation of the *Shema*. The first speaks of *Hashem* as the Creator, and of His daily renewal of nature. In the second blessing we thank Him for the gift of Torah. In fact, if one is late in coming to synagogue and did not yet recite *birchos haTorah*, one can satisfy their obligation with this second *beracha* of "אהבה רבה" (*Shulchan Aruch Orach Chayyim* 46). Note, in it we not only ask *Hashem* for Divine assistance "to instill in our hearts the desire to understand and to discern, to listen, to learn and to teach, to observe and to perform and to fulfill all the teachings of Your Torah with love." We also ask *Hashem*: "in the merit of our ancestors who trusted in You and to whom You taught the laws of life, be gracious also to us and teach us." As the original *kabbalas haTorah* was predicated on *emuna*, so too our personal and communal *kabbalas haTorah* is only meaningful if it is coupled with faith. Specifically, we have faith that the Torah speaks to our generation and provides meaning and purpose for life, as it did for the generation at Sinai and to all subsequent generations. We pray to Him daily that we remain steadfast in our faith.

Perhaps this is why we almost always read *Parashas Bamidbar* on the *Shabbos* prior to *Shavuos*. While there are no specific *mitzvos* found in this *parasha*, the setting of the desert is conducive to the acceptance of the Torah. As our Rabbis inform us, "The Torah was only given to those who ate and were nourished by the *mon*, the daily ration of manna that descended from heaven" (*Mechilta*). *Hashem*, who could have provided them with their gift of *mon* annually, chose to do so daily in order to bolster their *emuna*. We, their proud descendants, are the beneficiaries of their basic training in *emuna*, enabling us to take *Hashem*'s Torah and "transform wastelands into Eden" (*Yeshayahu* 51:3).

Also available from TorahWeb

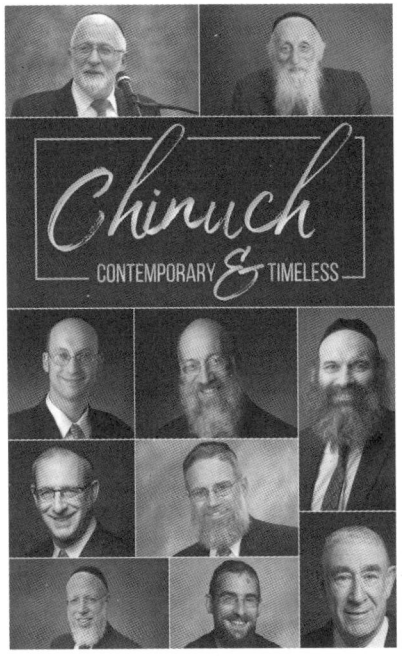

Distributed by Menucha Publishers

Available on Amazon.com

Rav Hershel Schachter's notes from
Rav Yosef Dov Soloveitchik zt"l's *gemara* shiurim

ו' חלקים יצאו לאור:

- מס' גיטין
- מס' קידושין, פרקים א' - ב'
- מס' שבת
- מס' פסחים, ר"ה, יומא, ומגילה
- הלכות נדה

Distributed by Rabbi Yaakov Levitz